The torch of love
is lit in the kitchen.

FRENCH PROVERB

To ______________________

From ______________________

ALSO BY
BARBARA MILO OHRBACH

The Scented Room

The Scented Room
Gardening Notebook

Antiques at Home

Simply Flowers

A Token of Friendship

Memories of Childhood

A Bouquet of Flowers

A Cheerful Heart

The Spirit of America

Merry Christmas

Happy Birthday

All Things Are Possible—
Pass the Word

Food for the Soul

Delicious Thoughts to Nourish Mind and Heart

By BARBARA MILO OHRBACH

CLARKSON POTTER/PUBLISHERS NEW YORK

Published by Clarkson N. Potter, Inc., 201 East 50th Street,
New York, New York 10022.
Member of the Crown Publishing Group.

Random House, Inc., New York, Toronto,
London, Sydney, Auckland

http://www.randomhouse.com/

CLARKSON N. POTTER, POTTER and colophon
are trademarks of Clarkson N. Potter, Inc.

Printed in the United States of America
Design by Dania Martinez Davey

Library of Congress Cataloging-in-Publication Data
is available upon request

ISBN 0-517-88770-3
10 9 8 7 6 5 4 3 2 1
First Edition

A heartfelt thanks to everyone who helped work on this book: Beth Allen, Gayle Benderoff, Dania Martinez Davey, Joan Denman, Deborah Geltman, Chip Gibson, Annetta Hanna, Mel Ohrbach, Andrea C. Peabbles, Rodica Prato, Pat Sadowsky, Lauren Shakely, Michelle Sidrane, and Jane Treuhaft.

Introduction

Cooking is an act of love.

Alain Chapel

The pleasures of food and dining have nourished our souls as much as our bodies since the beginnings of civilization. As the Bible proclaims, "A man hath no better thing under the sun than to eat, and to drink, and to be merry." And Virginia Woolf more recently noted, "One cannot think well, love well, sleep well, if one has not dined well." Hospitality, warmth, and love are all sitting around the table with us when we share a good meal.

Each year more cookbooks are written, and countless new restaurants open. Clearly, we are more sophisticated about food than ever before. Yet it seems that we are spending less time really *enjoying* our food. We tend to rush through breakfast, and grab lunch on the go. Then home after work, we rustle up some fast food so that the kids can get to Little League or play practice on time. Cicero said, "One should eat to live, not live to eat." Perhaps we have taken that advice a bit too far.

One of the joys of European travel is *still* being able to spend two hours savoring a relaxing meal in the middle of the day. I think Julia Child has it right when she says, "I've discovered that people who are not interested in food always seem rather dry and unloving and don't have a real gusto for life."

Experiencing the pleasures of the table is one of the *real* pleasures of life. That we are dependent on food for our survival goes without saying, but what I find intriguing is how much dining spiritually enriches that survival. The writer Lin Yutang observed that "the Chinese do not draw any distinction between food and medicine." And anyone who has cured a cold by sipping Grandma's homemade chicken soup would agree.

There have been many spirited words written about cooking and dining, and this book is a celebration of some of the most mouthwatering and heartwarming of them. They range from the biblical "Give us this day our daily bread" to Diana Vreeland's more pungent "People who eat white bread have no dreams." There are quotes from great cooks like James Beard: "I don't like gourmet cooking or 'this' cooking or 'that' cooking. I like *good* cooking"; musings from historical figures like Queen Victoria: "Things taste better in small houses"; and thoughts from authors like Joyce Carol Oates: "If food is poetry, is not poetry also food?" The quotes are accompanied by engaging illustrations that come from my own collection of antique cookbooks and food ephemera. As M.F.K. Fisher wrote, "There is a communion of more than our bodies when bread is broken and wine is drunk. And that is my answer, when people ask me: Why do you write about hunger, and not wars or love?"

So invite some good friends over for a snack or a feast—it really doesn't matter which. What does matter is that you are breaking bread together, sharing food, drink, common thoughts, good conversation—and lots of laughter. *Bon appétit!*

—Barbara Milo Ohrbach

Hunger is
the first course
of a good dinner.

FRENCH PROVERB

Never eat more
than you can lift.

MISS PIGGY

Great cooking is the source of true happiness.

ESCOFFIER

The smell of coffee cooking was a reason for growing up, because children were never allowed to have it and nothing haunted the nostrils all the way out to the barn as did the aroma of boiling coffee.

EDNA LEWIS

Rather go to bed supperless than
run in debt for a breakfast.

POOR RICHARD'S ALMANAC

Only dull people are brilliant at breakfast.

OSCAR WILDE

All happiness depends on a leisurely breakfast.

JOHN GUNTHER

A simple enough pleasure, surely, to have breakfast
alone with one's husband, but how seldom married
people in the midst of life achieve it.

ANNE MORROW LINDBERGH

Hope is a good breakfast . . .

FRANCIS BACON

I am one who eats breakfast  gazing at morning glories.

BASHO

Which came first—the chicken or the egg?

ANONYMOUS

There is always a best way of doing everything,
if it be to boil an egg.

RALPH WALDO EMERSON

Don't put all your eggs in one basket.

ITALIAN PROVERB

Put all your eggs in one basket,
and—watch the basket.

MARK TWAIN

An egg today is better than a hen tomorrow.

POOR RICHARD'S ALMANAC

Can you unscramble eggs?

J. PIERPONT MORGAN

*A*s everybody
knows, there is only
one infallible recipe
for the perfect
omelette: your own.

ELIZABETH DAVID

One cannot think well,

love well, sleep well, if one has not dined well.

VIRGINIA WOOLF

A watched pot never boils.

ANONYMOUS

The pot calling the kettle black.

ANONYMOUS

In the childhood memories of every good cook,
there's a large kitchen, a warm stove,
a simmering pot and a mom.

BARBARA COSTIKYAN

Out of the frying pan into the fire.

ANONYMOUS

I saw him even now going the way of all flesh,
that is to say towards the kitchen.

JOHN WEBSTER

If you can't stand the heat, get out of the kitchen.

HARRY TRUMAN

On days when warmth
is the most important
need of the human heart,
the kitchen is the
place you can find it;
it dries the wet sock,
it cools the hot little brain.

E. B. WHITE

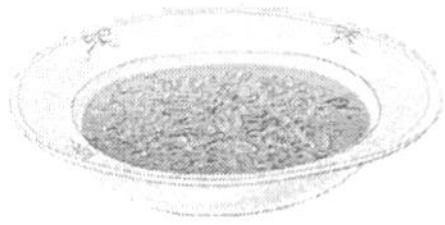

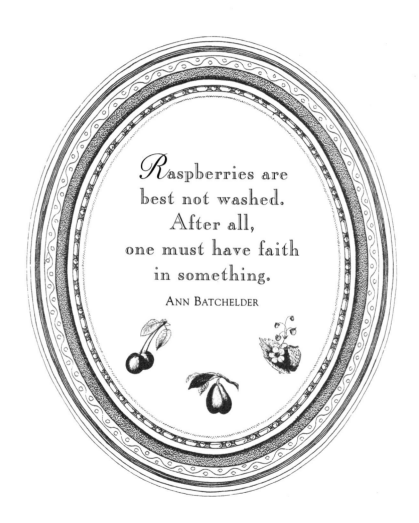

*R*aspberries are
best not washed.
After all,
one must have faith
in something.

ANN BATCHELDER

Talking of Pleasure, this moment
I was writing with one hand and with the other
holding to my Mouth a Nectarine—good God
how fine. It went down soft, pulpy, slushy, oozy—
all its delicious embodiment melted down my throat
like a large Beautiful strawberry.

John Keats

Life is just a bowl of cherries.

Anonymous

An apple a day keeps the doctor away.

English proverb

Men and melons are hard to know.

Poor Richard's almanac

He is the very pineapple of politeness.

Richard Sheridan

When one has tasted watermelons, one knows what angels eat. MARK TWAIN

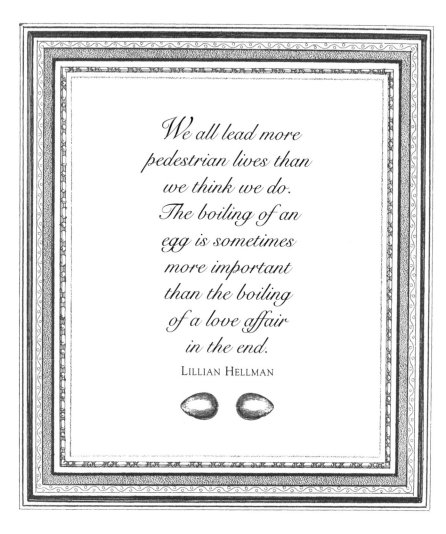

We all lead more pedestrian lives than we think we do. The boiling of an egg is sometimes more important than the boiling of a love affair in the end.

LILLIAN HELLMAN

When men reach their sixties
and retire, they go to pieces.
Women just go right on cooking.

GAIL SHEEHY

Cooking is like love. It should be entered into
with abandon or not at all.

HARRIET VAN HORNE

The fricassee with dumplings is made
by a Mrs. Miller whose husband has
left her four times on account
of her disposition and returned
four times on account
of her cooking and is still there.

REX STOUT

Kissing don't last: cookery do!

GEORGE MEREDITH

Bread is the warmest, kindest of words.
Write it always with a capital letter,
like your own name.

Russian café sign

The history of the world is the record of a man
in quest of his daily bread and butter.

H. W. van Loon

Man shall not live by bread alone.

Luke 4:14

Half a loaf is better than none.

English proverb

Give us this day our daily bread.

Matthew 6:2

Bread is like dresses, hats and shoes—
in other words, essential!

Emily Post

To cook well
one must love and
respect food.

CRAIG CLAIBORNE

People who eat white

bread have no dreams.

DIANA VREELAND

A good cook is like a sorceress
who dispenses happiness.

ELSA SCHIAPARELLI

A man seldom thinks with more earnestness
of anything than he does of his dinner.

SAMUEL JOHNSON

Above all, friends should possess the rare gift of sitting.

M. F. K. FISHER

The art of dining well is no slight art,
the pleasure not a slight pleasure.

MONTAIGNE

Laughter is brightest where food is best.

IRISH PROVERB

A good eater must be a good man;
for a good eater must have
a good digestion, and a good digestion
depends upon a good conscience.

BENJAMIN DISRAELI

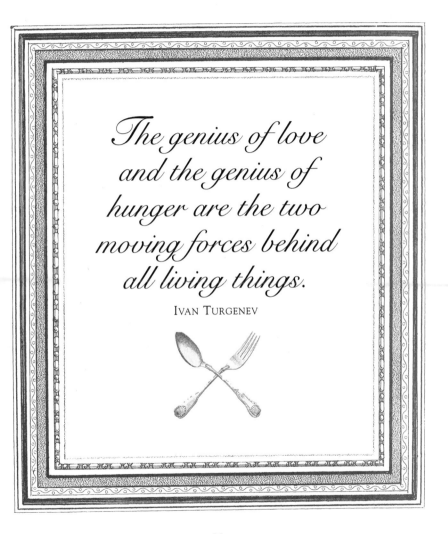

The genius of love and the genius of hunger are the two moving forces behind all living things.

IVAN TURGENEV

There is no sight on earth more appealing than the sight of a woman making dinner for someone she loves.

THOMAS WOLFE

Things taste better in small houses.

QUEEN VICTORIA

Whenever I get married,
I start buying *Gourmet* magazine.

NORA EPHRON

The way to a man's heart is through his stomach.

MRS. SARAH PAYSON PARTON

Marriage, as I have often remarked,
is not merely sharing one's fettuccine
but sharing the burden of finding
the fettuccine restaurant in the first place.

CALVIN TRILLIN

Everything you see I owe to spaghetti.

SOPHIA LOREN

No man can be wise on an empty stomach.

GEORGE ELIOT

My idea of heaven is a great big baked potato and someone to share it with.

Oprah Winfrey

Under certain circumstances there are few hours more agreeable than the hour dedicated to the ceremony known as afternoon tea.

HENRY JAMES

If you are cold, tea will warm you—
If you are heated, it will cool you—
If you are depressed, it will cheer you—
If you are excited, it will calm you.

W. E. GLADSTONE

Tea! thou soft, thou sober, sage,
and venerable liquid, thou female
tongue-running, smile-soothing,
heart-opening, wink-tippling cordial,
to whose glorious insipidity I owe the
happiest moments of my life,
let me fall prostrate.

COLLEY CIBBER

Love and scandal are the best sweeteners of tea.

HENRY FIELDING

Manhattan is a narrow island off the coast of New Jersey devoted to the pursuit of lunch.

RAYMOND SOKOLOV

I never eat in a restaurant that's over a hundred feet off the ground and won't stand still.

CALVIN TRILLIN

A restaurant is a fantasy—a kind of living fantasy in which diners are the most important members of the cast.

WARNER LEROY

The best way to lose weight is to close your mouth—something very difficult for a politician.

ED KOCH

A tablecloth restaurant is still one of the great rewards of civilization.

HARRY GOLDEN

I was 32 when
I started cooking;
up until then,
I just ate.

JULIA CHILD

Only
the pure
of heart
can make
good soup.

BEETHOVEN

To make a good soup, the pot must only simmer, or "smile."

FRENCH PROVEB

No, I don't take soup.
You can't build a meal on a lake.

ELSIE DE WOLFE

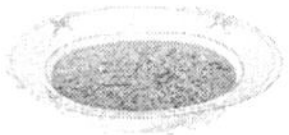

Too many cooks spoil the broth.

ENGLISH PROVERB

Good manners: The noise you
don't make when you're eating soup.

BENNETT CERF

Onion soup sustains.
The process of making it is somewhat like the process of learning to love. It requires commitment, extraordinary effort, time, and will make you cry.

RONNI LUNDY

Beautiful soup
so rich and green,
waiting in a hot tureen;
who for such dainties
would not stoop?
Soup of the evening,
beautiful soup!

LEWIS CARROLL

"When I couldn't
write I cooked,"
she said,
"when I couldn't
cook I wrote."

M. F. K. Fisher

It's good food and
not fine words that
keeps me alive.

Molière

If food is poetry, is not poetry also food?

Joyce Carol Oates

Poultry is for the cook
what canvas is for the painter.

Anthelme Brillat-Savarin

Good cooking is an art which is easily acquired.

Fannie Farmer

Dining is and always was
a great artistic opportunity.

Frank Lloyd Wright

After dinner sit a while;
After supper walk a mile.

Anonymous

There are many miracles in the world to be celebrated and, for me, garlic is the most deserving.

Leo Buscaglia

If the purpose of flavor
is to arouse a special
kind of emotion, that flavor
must emerge from genuine
feelings about the materials
you are handling.
What you are, you cook.

MARCELLA HAZAN

Appetite is the best sauce.

FRENCH PROVERB

Salt is white and pure—
there is something holy in salt.

NATHANIEL HAWTHORNE

Pepper is small in quantity and great in virtue.

PLATO

England has three sauces and 360 religions; whereas
France has three religions and 360 sauces.

TALLEYRAND

Spice a dish with love and it pleases every palate.

PLAUTUS

My salad days; When I was green in judgment.

WILLIAM SHAKESPEARE

You can put everything, and the more things the better, into salad, as into a conversation; but everything depends upon the skill of mixing.

CHARLES DUDLEY WARNER

There's someone at every party who eats all the celery.

FRANK HUBBARD

Salt the salad quite a lot, then generous oil put in the pot, and vinegar, but just a jot.

ITALIAN PROVERB

The Romans had a saying when they wanted something done quickly. "Do it," they said, "in less time than it takes to cook asparagus."

ALEXANDRE DUMAS

Once you taste
a tomato in
the summer,
you won't eat
a tomato in
the winter.

ALICE WATERS

A meal without wine is like a day without sunshine.

Anthelme Brillat-Savarin

To take wine into our mouths is to savor
a droplet of the river of human history.

CLIFTON FADIMAN

Eat, drink, and be merry.

ISAIAH 22:13

In vino veritas.

ALCAEUS

What is the definition of a good wine?
It should start and end with a smile.

WILLIAM SOKOLIN

Wine is bottled poetry.

ROBERT LOUIS STEVENSON

The soft extractive note of an aged cork being withdrawn
has the true sound of a man opening his heart.

WILLIAM SAMUEL BENWELL

Wine is sunlight, held together by water.

GALILEO

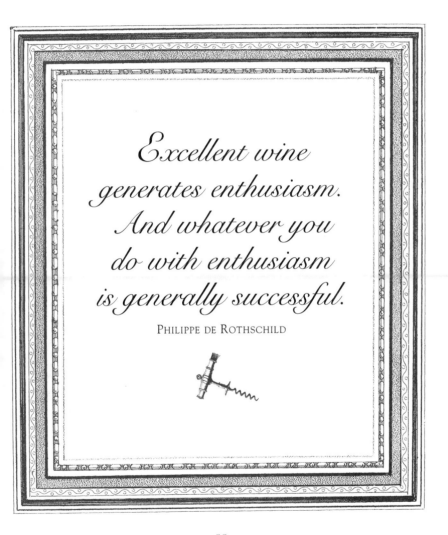

Excellent wine generates enthusiasm. And whatever you do with enthusiasm is generally successful.

PHILIPPE DE ROTHSCHILD

I can resist everything but temptation.

OSCAR WILDE

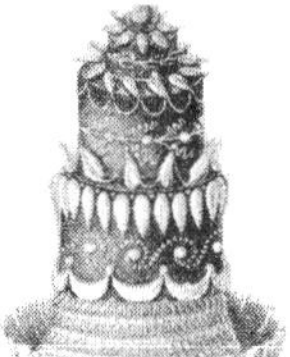

You can't eat your cake and have it too.

ENGLISH PROVERB

Good apple pies are a considerable
part of our domestic happiness.

JANE AUSTEN

You can't make a soufflé rise twice.

ALICE ROOSEVELT LONGWORTH

The proof of the pudding is in the eating.

MIGUEL DE CERVANTES

We dare not trust our wit for making our house
pleasant to our friend, so we buy ice cream.

RALPH WALDO EMERSON

Enjoy your ice-cream while
it's on your plate, that's my philosophy.

THORNTON WILDER

Come quickly,

I am tasting the stars!

DOM PÉRIGNON

I don't like
gourmet cooking
or "this" cooking
or "that" cooking.
I like good cooking.

JAMES BEARD

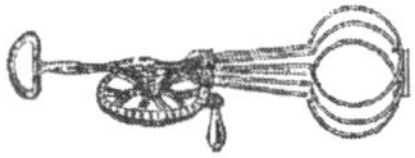

A meat-and-potato man

PROVERB

I never see any home cooking.
All I get is fancy stuff.

PRINCE PHILIP

Better a good dinner than a fine coat.

FRENCH PROVERB

The reason fat people are happy is that
the nerves are well protected.

LUCIANO PAVAROTTI

There is no love sincerer than the love of food.

GEORGE BERNARD SHAW

All's well that ends with a good meal.

ARNOLD LOBEL

Food is the first enjoyment of life.

LIN YUTANG

The cook must still regard the present time:
T'omit what's just in season is a crime.

WILLIAM KING

Bon appétit is a blessing.

MALCOLM FORBES

Dining is the privilege of civilisation. . . .

ISABELLA BEETON

Serenely full, the epicure would say,
Fate cannot harm me,—I have dined today.

SYDNEY SMITH

In cooking, as in all the arts,
simplicity is the sign of perfection.

MAURICE-EDMOND SAILLAND

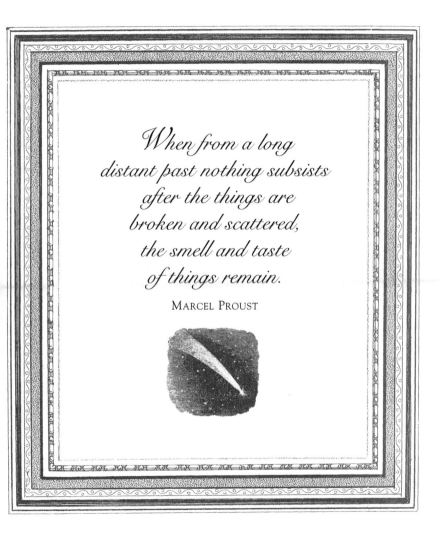

When from a long
distant past nothing subsists
after the things are
broken and scattered,
the smell and taste
of things remain.

MARCEL PROUST

The discovery
of a new dish does
more for the
happiness of man
than the discovery
of a star.

ANTHELME BRILLAT-SAVARIN

THE KIDS' BOOK OF GAMES

Text and illustrations by
Rudi McToots
Design by Dreadnaught

FOR CARS, TRAINS & PLANES

Bantam Books
Toronto · New York · London

WHAT'S THE HO-HO-HOLD-UP?
TOYS
MEEP! MEEP!
U-3
STARBUGGY

The Kids' Book of Games
for Cars, Trains & Planes

A Bantam Book / May 1980

Created, designed, and
prepared for publication at
Dreadnaught
24 Sussex Avenue
Toronto Canada.

ISBN 0-553-01230-4

Published simultaneously in the
United States and Canada

Bantam Books are published by Bantam Books, Inc. Its trademark, consisting of the words 'Bantam Books' and the portrayal of a bantam, is Registered in US Patent and Trademark Office and in other countries. Marca Registrada. Bantam Books, Inc., 666 Fifth Avenue, New York, New York 10019.

PRINTED IN THE UNITED STATES OF AMERICA

This book is for
nomads, travelers, gypsies, vagabonds, explorers, ramblers, hobos, hitch-hikers
and freewheelers everywhere.

Travel before the invention of the wheel.

RPM

CONTENTS

Mindgames

HARD AND SOFT

Count Me In!

FUN WITH NUMBERS

HOME
IS WHERE
YOU ARE

Bored Games

CHECKERS AND BEYOND

CONTENTS

ACKNOWLEDGMENTS

Thanks to these travelers, who said:

There is no place to go, and so we travel! You and I, and what for, just to imagine that we could go somewhere else.
EDWARD DAHLBERG

I travel light; as light ...
CHRISTOPHER FRY

The traveler with empty pockets will sing in the thief's face.
JUVENAL

For my part, I travel not to go anywhere, but to go. I travel for travel's sake. The great affair is to move.
ROBERT LOUIS STEVENSON

To travel hopefully is a better thing than to arrive.
ROBERT LOUIS STEVENSON

And a special thanks to Invisible Books, Ian Wiseman, Yuri Rubinsky, Al Moritz, Jim, Paula, Ken & Bonnie, MM, and the Kid Testing Team.

WOW! OUTER SPACE! JUST LIKE I PICTURED IT!
R.P.M.

INTRODUCTION

Why is a blueberry pie like a shoe? Because you can put your foot in it – if you want.

And why is traveling like imagining? Because you can do it anytime, anywhere – if you want. You can travel to the planets in an armchair, or you can travel over the Alps on the back of an elephant while waiting for the toaster to pop. To the casual observer you may seem to be sitting quietly daydreaming on a rainy day, but in your mind you might be mapping the ocean bottom in a submarine, paddling a canoe down a steaming tropical river in search of lost cities of gold, or pounding across the prairie on horseback with a band of Indian warriors. Some of the best traveling can be done even while you're sick in bed!

The 162 games and pastimes in this book are for travelers everywhere, whether they're in the backseat of a car or a canoe, in a bus or on a bicycle, or flying the magic carpet of their imagination. Most of the games have been entertaining tourists and travelers for hundreds or thousands of years. String figures are old as the hills, and the board game Senat was being played by the Egyptians before the pyramids were built. When our grandparents were children, they very likely played Geography or Beep, and they might have learned them from *their* grandparents. Dice are older than written history, which goes back a long way, and playing cards have been around almost as long.

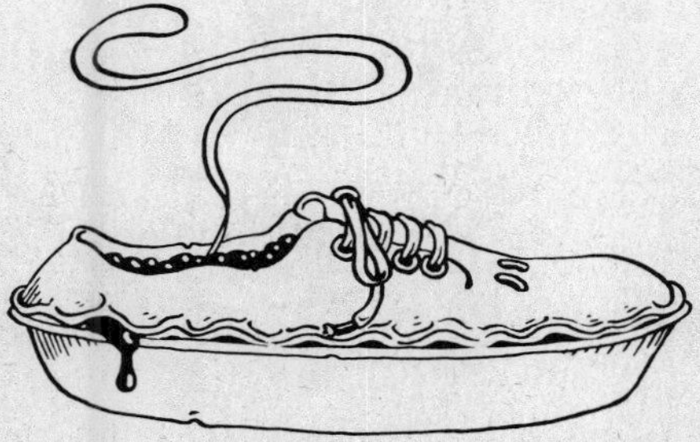

As well as the old favorites, there are some new games, and a few things that aren't even classified as games, such as the string figures and braiding, origami (paper folding), magic tricks, and storytelling. In other words, there are enough things here to help solve that age-old problem: entertaining and amusing the bored traveler.

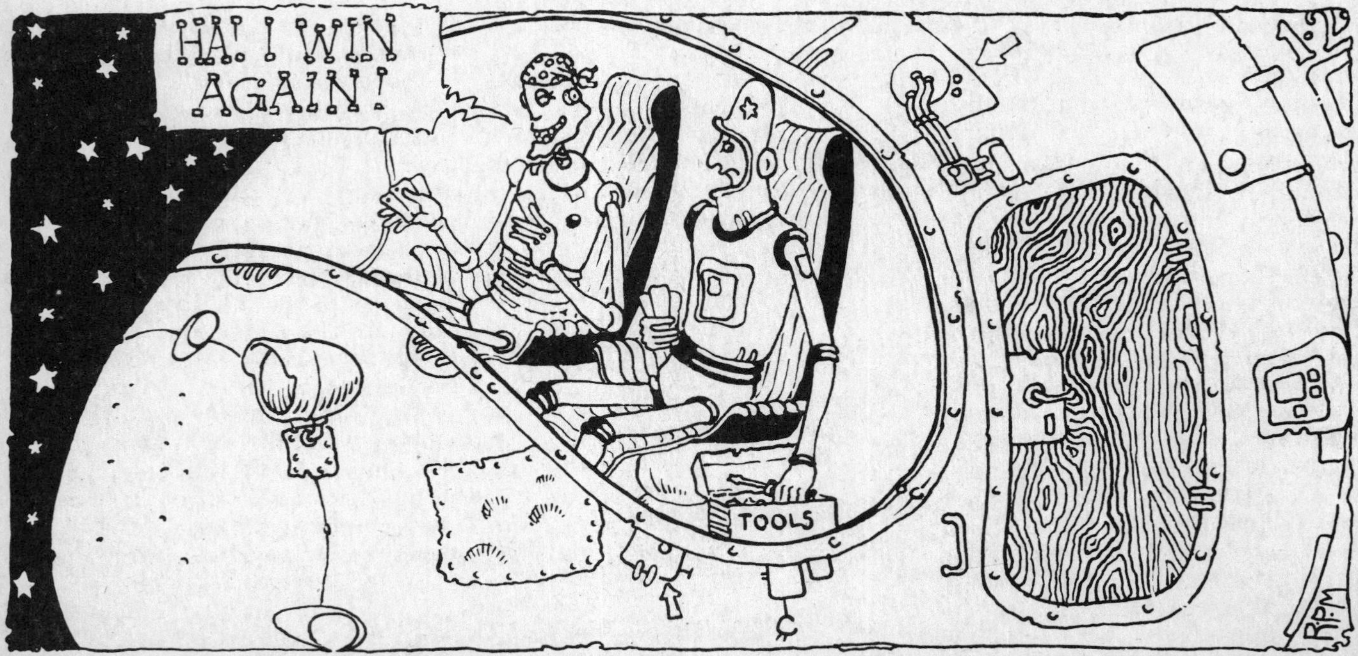
HA! I WIN AGAIN!
TOOLS
1:2
R.P.M

TRAVELING LIGHT

..3..2..1..0..Blast off!

Traveling at the speed of light (186,000 miles per second) in his trusty starwagon, it would take the average space gypsy well over four years to reach Proxima Centauri, the star nearest to our own solar system. So he would want to pack more than just a 'light' lunch!

Space gypsies have to travel light because their starwagons are very small. And since there are no roadside stops in space, they have to bring everything they are going to need along with them. So when they amuse themselves during the long night of space, they want to do it with the least amount of fuss and materials. A pad of paper and a pen, some string and coins, and maybe a deck of cards and a dictionary for tough wordgames: these are all that the enterprising space wanderer needs to keep boredom away.

Like the space gypsies, you should try to bring some of these things along with you in your own starwagon, since you may not get a chance to find them en route.

Another thing you may need is a hard, flat surface to write or draw on. A big book in your lap works well, or you could put a suitcase on the seat beside you to act as a table.

PAPER
pen
PENCIL
String
COINS
CARDS
DIK-SHUN-AIR-Y.

Because of the great speeds at which starwagons hurtle through the void, space gypsies must always be very careful of what they do and how they do it. They all learn while very young that they can't run around, shouldn't bump or distract the robot pilot, and should never yell, throw things or use sharp objects. This informal safety code is known to these void nomads as space etiquette, but it also applies to earthbound vehicles.

When your homeworld is just a speck of light fading fast in the distance, and the robot pilot is at work, humming softly to itself, and you've nothing to look forward to but a long uneventful ride through mile after mile of emptiness ... lean back, loosen your magnetic space boots and let the fun begin!

Tickets Please...
RPM

CARPET BAG

Land ho! Off the starboard bow!

If you were a ship's navigating officer in the days of the great wooden ships, part of your duties would include making daily entries in the ship's logbook, the official diary of the ship. In it would be recorded all the important daily events, as well as the ship's speed and direction, and any changes in course.

Well, you may or may not be the navigating officer on this trip, but you may still want to keep a logbook. You can make one out of a few sheets of paper folded in half and stapled or sewn along the fold, or you can use a new notebook. On the first page write down all the important information about the trip and yourself, such as the names of the ship, captain and crew members, date and time of departure, home port, destination, date and time of arrival, that kind of thing.

You can use your logbook for drawing pictures and for playing any games that need writing or drawing, like Tic Tac Toe, Sprouts, Connections or Hangman. And, as in the old ship's log, you can keep track of all the important events and interesting sights you've seen on your trip, such as whales off the port bow, men overboard, funny signs or town names, etc.

Another important fixture on any wooden ship was the ship's cat. It was the cat's job to keep down the number of mice and rats on board, or at least to make sure they had tickets! In many cases the cat was included as a silent partner in games the sailors played. You may have heard the expression 'The cat's got it' when neither player wins a game of Tic Tac Toe. If you give a point to the cat every time neither player wins any kind of game, you'll find tabby to be a stiff competitor! This is another thing you can use your logbook for, that is, keeping track of scores. It will be much more exciting if you keep a running score throughout the journey, from all games played, and tally up the scores at the end of the trip. Then, of course, you record the winner and runners-up in the logbook!

The logbook is also a good place to make a map of your journey. You could include all the points of interest on it, and even the miles if you want.

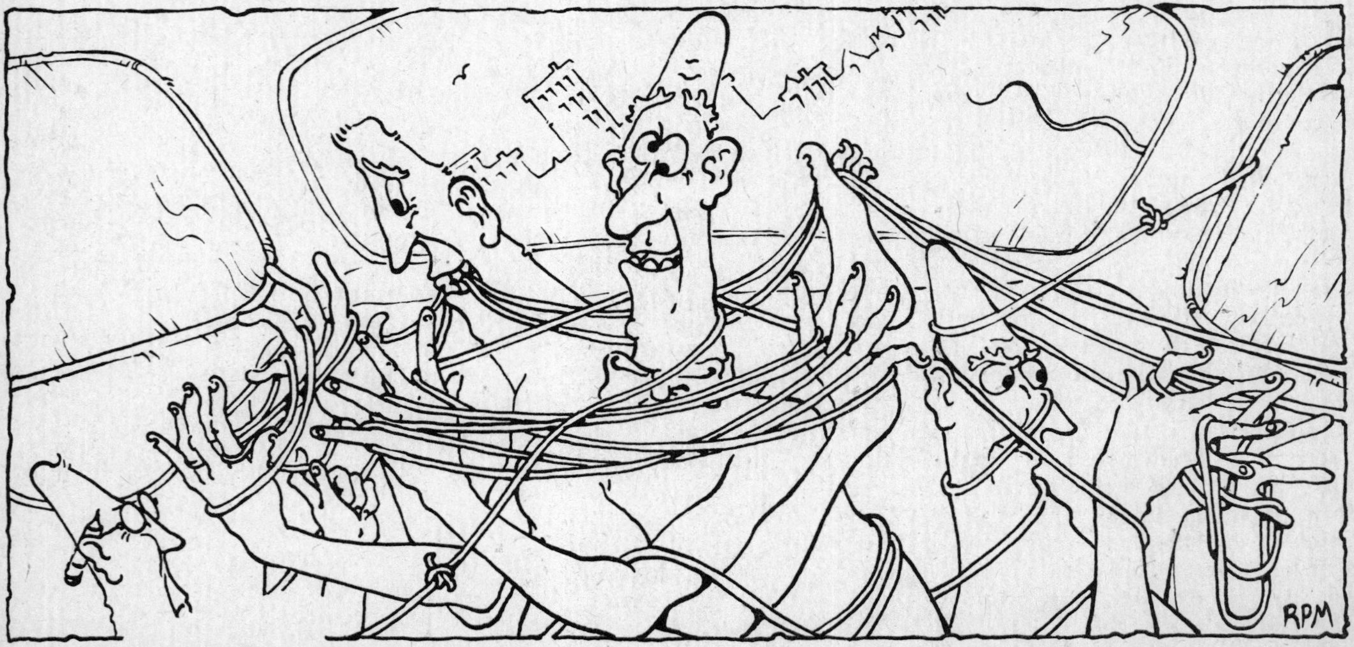
RPM

WHY KNOT?

Why knot? Well, think about it for a second ... Where would we be today without string and all its relatives? Imagine a cowboy without his lasso, or a sailboat without its rigging, or a weaver without thread, or a granny without her knitting! Fishermen would be lineless and netless, spiders would be webless, guitar and violin players would be stringless, birthday presents would be ribbonless, and Tarzan would be vineless! A world without string would be a pretty dismal place, you must admit.

Cordage and knots have been around for a long time. Fascination with them goes back to the days when a caveperson was crouched in a cave looking for uses for his new thumbs. He picked up a long strip of animal skin, and the first knot was born, along with the phrase 'all thumbs.' Since that time, string and rope have been used to make anything from snares, weapons, and cloth, to buildings and bridges. They have also been used to create art; in religious and magic ceremonies; as a secret 'handshake' of an Amerindian secret society; for mathematical calculations and counting; for making poems and telling stories; and for keeping track of the movements of the stars and planets. (As if they couldn't keep track of their own movements!) In short, the reef knot should be included along with the right angle as one of the cornerstones of our civilization.

Explorers found that they could communicate by means of string figures with natives all over the world, from isolated Pacific isles and the jungles of South America and Africa, to the plains of Asia and the icy lands of the north. In fact, no modern expedition sets out without taking along an expert on string figures. Anthropologists are baffled by the fact that string figures are the same among native peoples around the globe. I don't know if you've ever seen a baffled anthropologist, but it's not a pretty sight, believe me.

Now that you know a little more about the exciting family history of the humble substance called cordage, maybe you'll treat it with the respect it deserves. After all, you couldn't lace your sneakers without it!

One more thing: although all the activities in this chapter are a lot of fun, none of them classifies as competition-style games.

2
CUTTING STRING WITHOUT SCISSORS

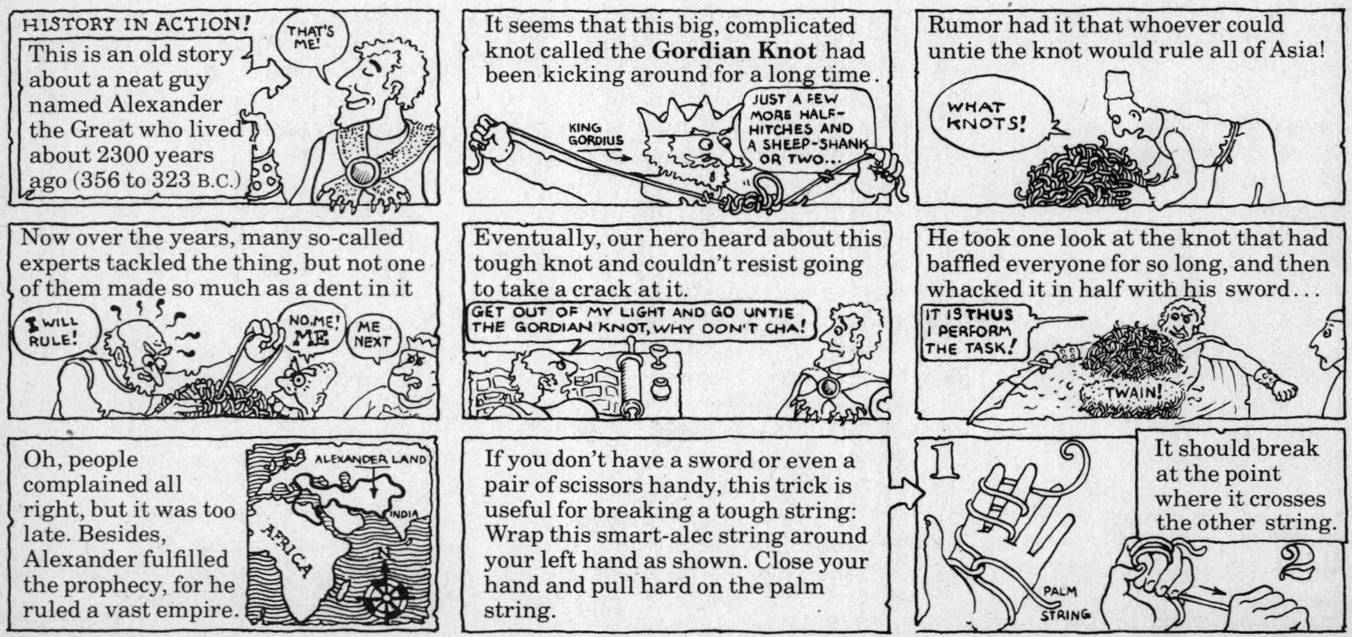
HISTORY IN ACTION!
This is an old story about a neat guy named Alexander the Great who lived about 2300 years ago (356 to 323 B.C.)
THAT'S ME!
It seems that this big, complicated knot called the **Gordian Knot** had been kicking around for a long time.
KING GORDIUS
JUST A FEW MORE HALF-HITCHES AND A SHEEP-SHANK OR TWO...
Rumor had it that whoever could untie the knot would rule all of Asia!
WHAT KNOTS!
Now over the years, many so-called experts tackled the thing, but not one of them made so much as a dent in it
I WILL RULE!
NO, ME! ME
ME NEXT
Eventually, our hero heard about this tough knot and couldn't resist going to take a crack at it.
GET OUT OF MY LIGHT AND GO UNTIE THE GORDIAN KNOT, WHY DON'T CHA!
He took one look at the knot that had baffled everyone for so long, and then whacked it in half with his sword...
IT IS THUS I PERFORM THE TASK!
TWAIN!
Oh, people complained all right, but it was too late. Besides, Alexander fulfilled the prophecy, for he ruled a vast empire.
ALEXANDER LAND
INDIA
AFRICA
N
If you don't have a sword or even a pair of scissors handy, this trick is useful for breaking a tough string: Wrap this smart-alec string around your left hand as shown. Close your hand and pull hard on the palm string.
1
PALM STRING
It should break at the point where it crosses the other string.
2

3
SOME STRING FIGURES

String figures are common to folks all over the globe. Eskimos, Indians, natives of the South Seas, Africans, Asians and Orientals can all show you string pictures of things from their daily lives. Often there is a story or chant that goes with the figure, and people from different cultures can even 'talk' with string! So you can see that string figures are not mere kid's stuff! In fact, Eskimo kids are forbidden to make string figures because of a superstition that they will be fumble-fingered fishermen when they are older.

Before you leap into action, study the first set of drawings. These show how to make 'opening A' which most string figures start with.

The fingers are described as 'thumb' (which is obvious); 'index,' which is next to the thumb; 'middle,' which is the long one next to the index; 'ring,' which is next in line; and 'little' – which is that small pinky at the end.

Any strings that cross the palm are, of course, called 'palm' strings.

The normal position of the hands is with the palms toward each other, and the fingers pointing up (as in opening A) and it is usual to return to this position after each movement of the strings.

Of each loop that goes around your fingers, there is a string closer to you, called the 'near' string, and one farther away, called the 'far' string.

When making the figures, a finger may be passed *over* or *under* a string, and you must be careful to get this right, and make sure that the loops don't get twisted!

Opening A

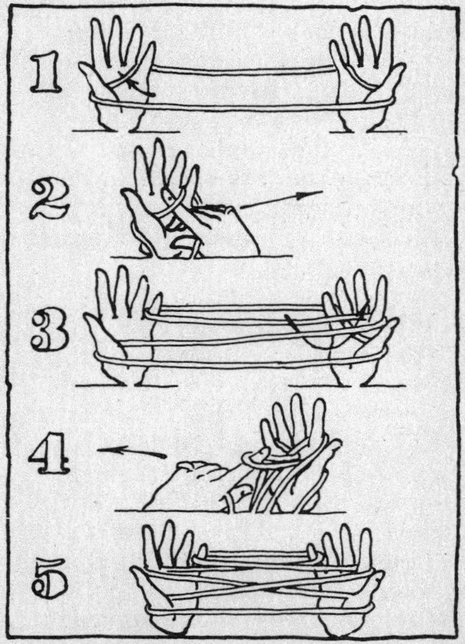
1
2
3
4
5

It's very difficult to describe string figures on paper. The instructions may look complicated, but in fact the figures are easy to do, so don't give up. Having someone else read the steps aloud may make it easier. All the tangles and curses of your first attempts will be worth it when you finally see the string picture magically appear between your hands.

The Two Headhunters

1 Start with opening A.

2 Bend the little fingers toward you, over all the strings except the near thumb string, and down into the thumb loop. Pick up the near thumb string with the backs of the little fingers and lift it clear of the thumbs, returning the little fingers to their original position. You should now have one loop on each index finger, and two loops on each little finger.

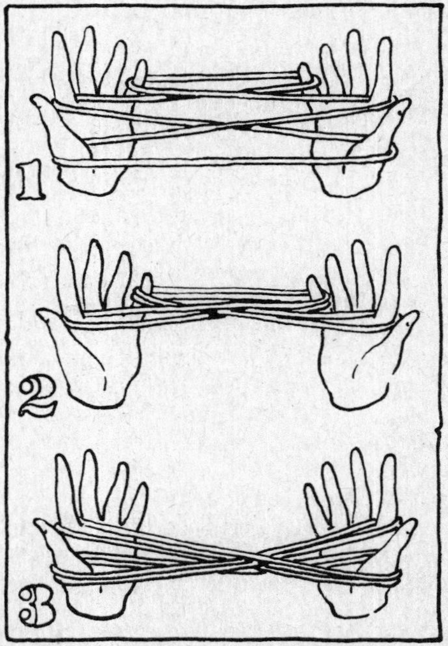
1
2
3

3 Move the thumbs away from you and *under* the index loop. Pick up from below, with the thumbs, the two near little finger strings and return the thumbs to their original position, releasing the little finger loops from the little fingers.

4 Bend the little fingers toward you over the index loop, and take up from below (on the backs of the little fingers) the two far thumb strings. Return the little fingers to position, but make sure to leave the thumb loops on this time!

5 You should see a small triangle formed of double strings in the center of the figure near the thumbs. Insert the tips of the index fingers into this triangle from below. Pulling out the sides of the triangle on

the backs of the index fingers, separate the hands.

6 Keep a firm hold on all the strings. Reach across with the right hand, and with the right thumb and index finger lift the lower single loop on the left index finger up over the other two index loops and off the tip of the finger, letting it fall between your hands. Now reach across with the left hand and do the same thing with the lower single loop on the right index finger. Then release the loops from the thumbs.

7 Now, by twisting the index fingers away from you (this is called navahoing) you should be able to twist the string around two or three times, the more the better. If you can't do this, don't worry. Just remove the loops from the index fingers (one finger at a time!) and twist them (the loops, not the

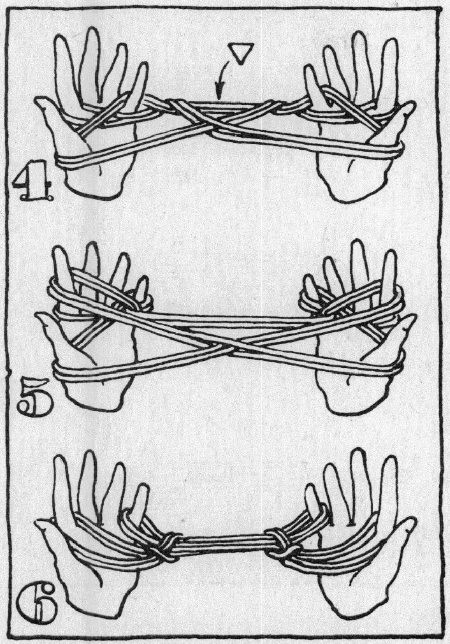
4
5
6

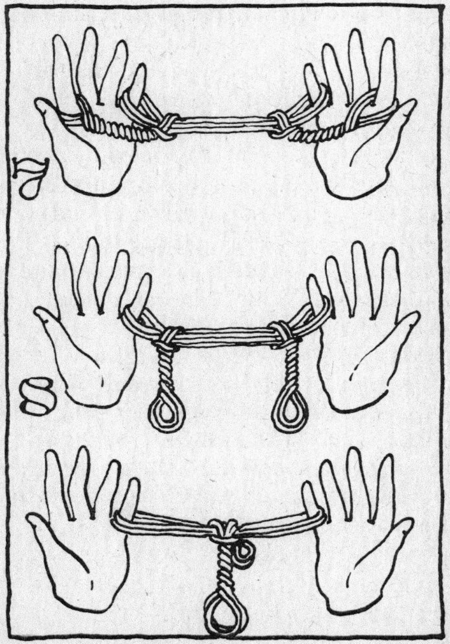
7
8

fingers) around three or four times.
8 Remove the twisted loops from the index fingers if they are not off already, and let the loops hang down. If you are using very stiff string, the loops might be convinced to stand up, making them more life-like, for these loops are the head-hunters. If you pull on the left little finger strings, the two savage hunters will charge at each other, each intent on taking the other's head home for a paperweight. When they meet, they bash at each other until one of two things happens: either they both kill each other and disappear, or one kills the other and walks off with the head. You have to see it to believe it!

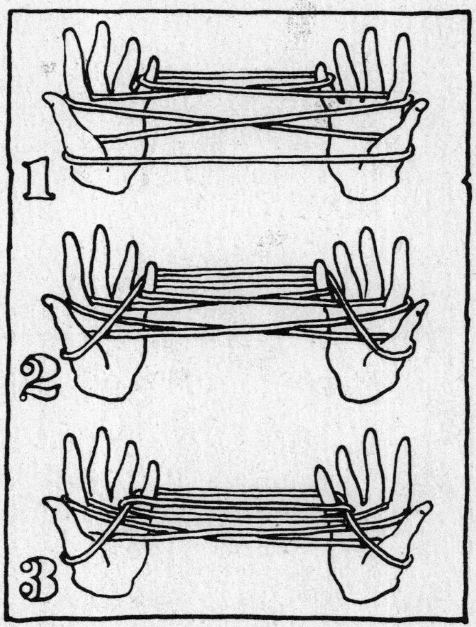

A String Boy Climbs a String Palm Tree

This is one of the easiest string figures and yet one of the most dramatic and exciting.

1 It starts with good old opening A.
2 Next bring the little fingers toward you, over the index finger loops and the far thumb string, and put them into the thumb loop from above, just like you did for the last string figure. Pick up the near thumb string on the backs of the little fingers and return the fingers to their original position, this time leaving the string on the thumbs.
3 With the thumb and index finger of each hand, lift the *original* far string off the little fingers, passing it over the loops just picked up, which remain in place. You must be

careful while doing this that you don't lose the strings on the other fingers.

4 Bend the index fingers down into their loops. When you do this you should push the string that crosses the index finger loops against the palm with the tip of the index fingers.

5 With your foot or a book, firmly hold down the far little finger string.

6 Release all the finger and thumb strings *except* those held by the index fingers against the palms. Shake the strings so that the loops are thoroughly untangled from each other. The figure should now look like the second last picture.

7 Pull up slightly on the left loop, then the right loop, and so on, and the boy will shinny up the tree. As he gets higher, he gets smaller and smaller until all that remains is a palm tree with a bunch of coconuts in the center.

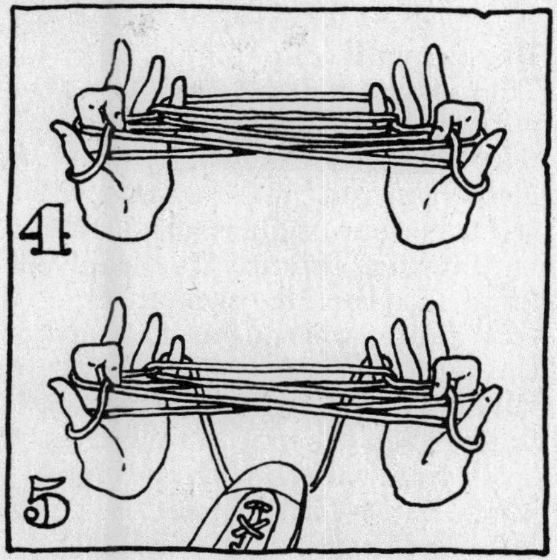
4
5

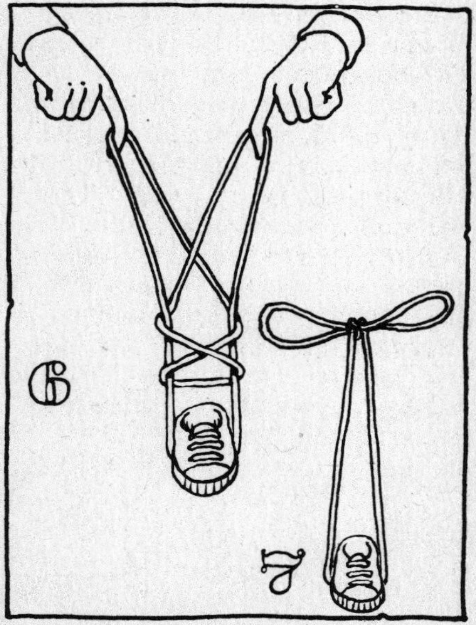
6
7

4

SPINNING A YARN

Twisted tales told with string

any number of players

If you've tried some of the preceding string figures, this will seem a welcome return to simplicity. It involves using a piece of string to form line pictures that illustrate a story you are telling. If there are two people playing, one could tell the story while another makes the pictures, or you could take turns. You could also form the pictures first, and try to make up a story from them. Here are a few of the endless number of things you could form with your storytelling string:

5

ONE MORE STRING FIGURE

This next string figure isn't any easier to describe than the first ones, but it *is* easier to do and does not start with opening A. You can use the same loop to do it.

Breakfast Escapes!
There is an exciting story that goes with this one, but you'll have to learn the trick first. Study the drawings, and the directions will seem as clear as glass. (The transparent kind, that is.) Hold your left hand with the fingers pointing straight up and the palm toward the right.

1 Hang the loop of string on one finger, then grasp it three inches down from the top with the right hand. Put the little finger of your left hand through the small loop and give the string a half-turn counterclockwise with the right hand.

2 Put the ring finger through the loop formed between the twist in the string and the right hand. Give the string a half-turn, this time clockwise.

3 Then put the middle finger through the small loop and give the string a half-turn counterclockwise.

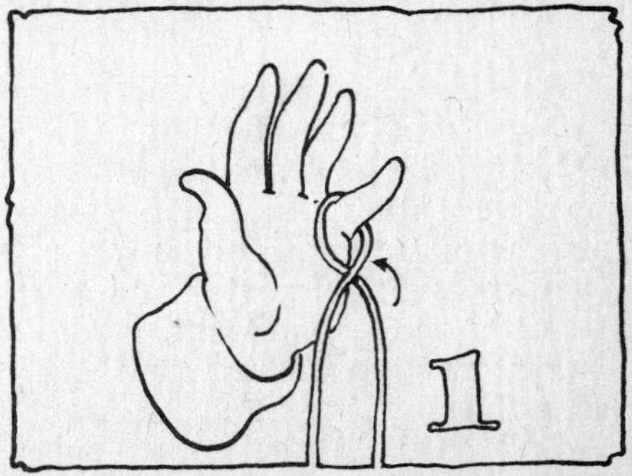
1

4 Next put the index finger through the loop in the same way and give the string a *full turn* clockwise, in between the index and thumb.
5 Put the thumb in the loop and give the string another half-turn counterclockwise.
6 Bring the loop back over the thumb and give the string a half-turn clockwise between the thumb and index finger. Put the index finger in the loop.
7 Give the string a half-turn counterclockwise and insert the middle finger in the loop. Continue giving half-turns in the opposite direction (clockwise, then counter) and insert the ring and little fingers. Your left hand should now be thoroughly tied up as in the last drawing. If you've done everything right, when you

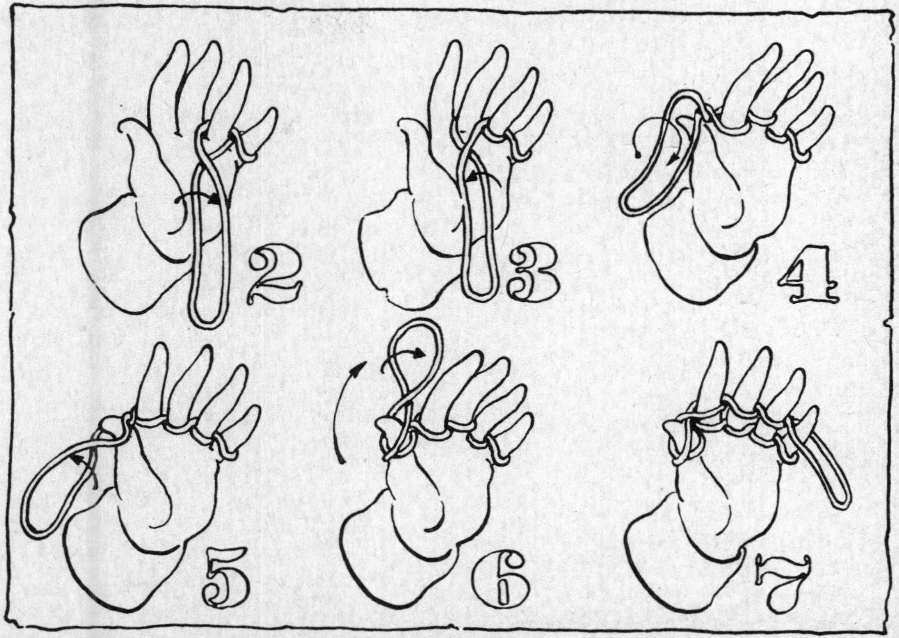
2
3
4
5
6
7

pull your thumb out of its loops and pull on the string with the right hand, all the loops twisted around the other fingers will seem to melt through the fingers and the string will fall off your hand. After you've practiced this a bit in private and can do the twisty-turny part fairly easily without muffing it, begin telling this story to your traveling companions: Five explorers (you say) set out exploring as explorers often will do. They wandered into the dense jungle on the isle of Glup-Gup and were promptly captured by a band of wild cannibals. Now, since the Glup-Gupians had just polished off several plump missionaries, they decided to save the explorers until the morning, and then have them hot, with milk and sugar, for breakfast. So they tied them up with one long loop of rope like this ... (at this point in the story you wind the string around your fingers as described above). And then they tied the rope to a post ... (now give the string to someone to hold tight, or loop it over your foot, or something solid like that). The cannibals were by now quite tuckered out, so they all crawled into bed and went to sleep. It just so happened that one of the explorers had been a Boy Scout in his youth, and with his knowledge of knots he managed to wriggle free of his bonds during the night, as the cannibals snored

soundly in their beds ... (pull your thumb out of its loops). He freed the rest of the explorers and they ran off to their boat ... (pull the left hand quickly and the string will fall off)!

In the morning the hungry cannibals found to their great disappointment that breakfast had run off in the night, leaving the end of the rope still tied to the post!

This also makes a great magic trick, especially if you tell your audience that you are going to cut your fingers off with string, and give the long end to someone, telling him to pull hard on the count of three. As he pulls, bend your thumb forward and the string quickly slips off and seems to cut through your fingers like a knife through butter! Make sure you practice the tying part thoroughly before you try this, or your fingers might *really* fall off!

6
A USEFUL STRING THING

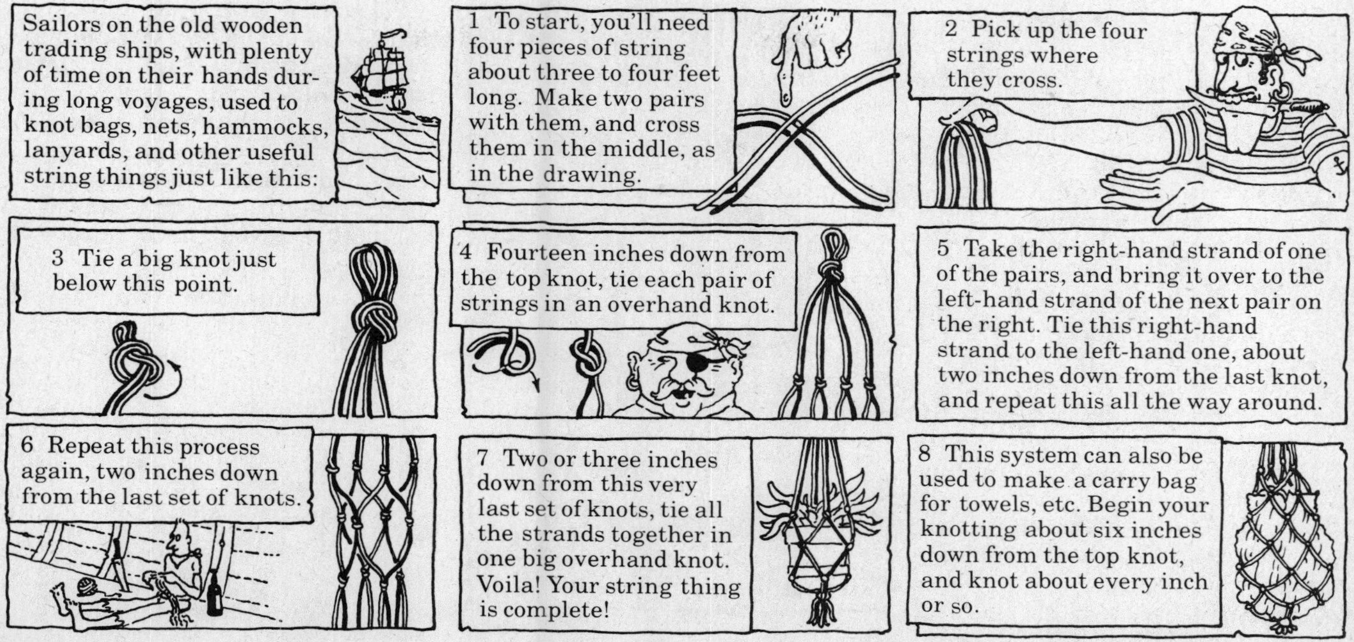
Sailors on the old wooden trading ships, with plenty of time on their hands during long voyages, used to knot bags, nets, hammocks, lanyards, and other useful string things just like this:
1 To start, you'll need four pieces of string about three to four feet long. Make two pairs with them, and cross them in the middle, as in the drawing.
2 Pick up the four strings where they cross.
3 Tie a big knot just below this point.
4 Fourteen inches down from the top knot, tie each pair of strings in an overhand knot.
5 Take the right-hand strand of one of the pairs, and bring it over to the left-hand strand of the next pair on the right. Tie this right-hand strand to the left-hand one, about two inches down from the last knot, and repeat this all the way around.
6 Repeat this process again, two inches down from the last set of knots.
7 Two or three inches down from this very last set of knots, tie all the strands together in one big overhand knot. Voila! Your string thing is complete!
8 This system can also be used to make a carry bag for towels, etc. Begin your knotting about six inches down from the top knot, and knot about every inch or so.

7
PLAITING

Almost everyone knows how to do ordinary plaiting or braiding, but this slight variation, called English sennit, is not as well known. It uses the usual three strands, but in a slightly different way.

1 The right-hand strand is carried over the center strand and *under* the left-hand strand.

2 The new left-hand strand (formerly the right-hand strand) is then carried over the center strand and under the new right-hand strand.

3 This operation is carried on, producing a flat braid.

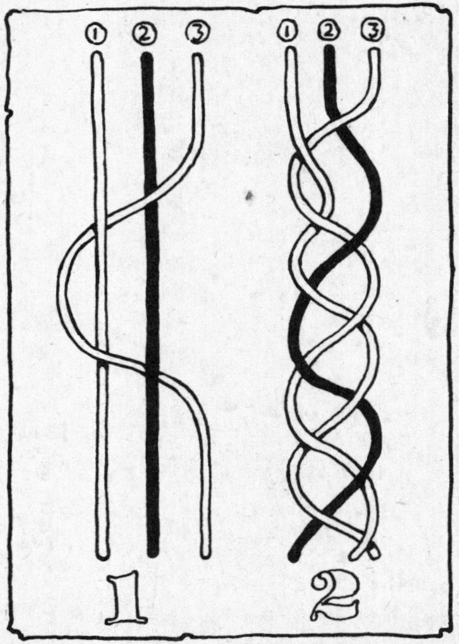
1
2
3
1
2
3
1
2

For a wider braid, more than three strands can be used, the outside strand being passed over *all* the center strands and under the outside strand on the opposite side.

This braid, like all the others described in this chapter, can be used for anything from bracelets and necklaces to belts and headbands.

8

THREE STRAND SOLID BRAID

This type of braiding works best with flat cord, or flat plastic or leather strips like the kind used in leather work, but almost any kind of string, yarn, twine or shoelace will do. It is especially nice with strands of different colors.

1 Start by tying your three strands in a knot at one end to hold them together. If you are right-handed, the strands are held in the left hand between the thumb and index finger, and the braid is built up from the bottom to the top.

2 Bring strand 1 from the front over to the right and put it between strands 2 and 3, but leave a small loop which you hold with your thumb as in the picture.

3 Bring strand 2 to the left over strand 1.

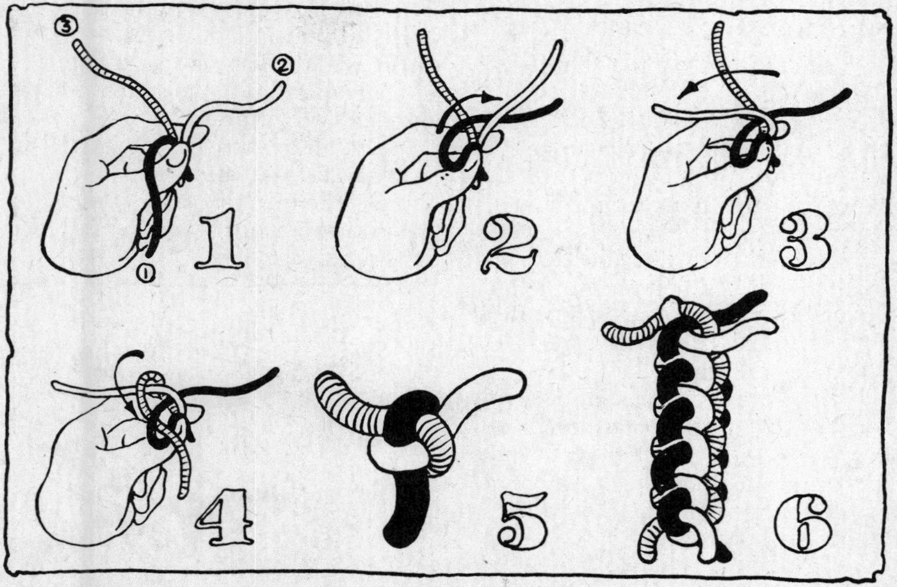
3
2
1
1
2
3
4
5
6

4 Bring strand 3 to the front over strand 2, and push it through the loop you left in strand 1. Tighten the strands.
5 You should now have a triangular knot like the one in picture 5.
6 Continue the operation the same way, this time using strand 3 to start off instead of strand 1, as it is the one at the front now. The strands will keep revolving, so on the next round you will start off with strand 2, then with strand 1 again, and so on.
7 When the braid is as long as you want it, cut off the loose ends, leaving about half an inch or so. Bend these ends down, and with a pen point, push them into the braid under the last row.

9
FOUR STRAND SQUARE BRAID

This one is usually done with flat cord or binding, but again, anything will do. It produces a four-sided braid that looks really good if done in two different colors.
1 Start off by crossing the strips or strands at their middles.
2 Pass the front strand, strand 1 over strand 2, but leave a small loop in strand 1.

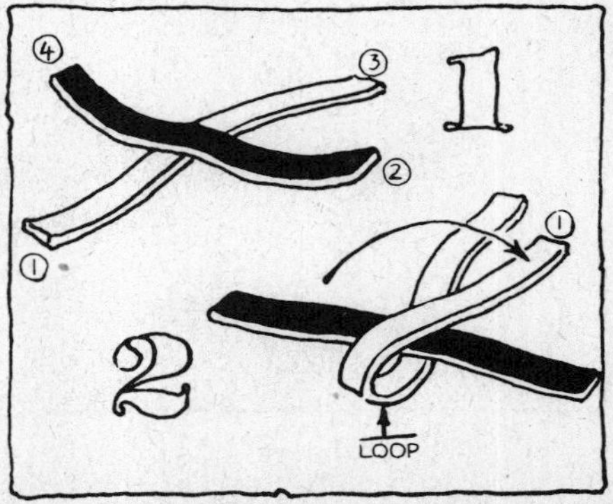
4
3
1
2
1
1
2
LOOP

3 Pass strand 2 over strand 1 so that it lies between strand 3 and strand 4.
4 Bring the back strand, strand 3, over strand 2 so that it lies between strand 4 and the little loop you left in strand 1.

2
3
4
3

5 Now bring strand 4 over strand 3 and push it into the loop in strand 1. Pull all the strands tight.

6 You should get a square knot that looks like picture 6.

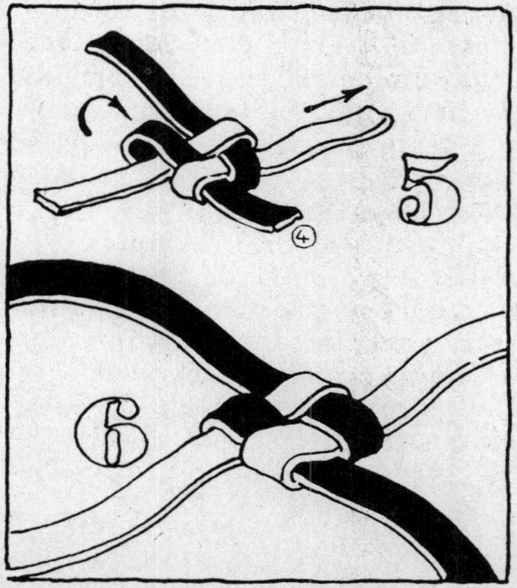
5
4
6

7 Pass the front strand, strand 3, over the top of the square to the back, and bring the back strand, strand 1, over the top of the square toward the front.

8 Bring strand 2 from the left and pass it over strand 3 and under strand 1. Bring strand 4 from the right and pass it over strand 1 and under strand 3.

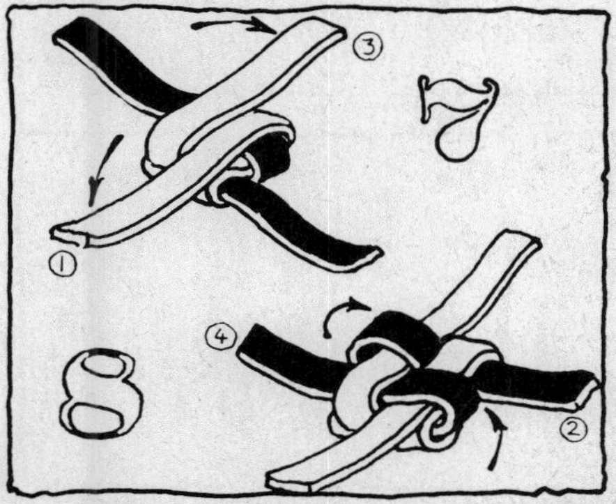
3
7
1
4
8
2

9 Look at picture 9. Does your braiding look like this? If so, continue in the same manner until it is as long as you want. Tuck in the ends as described in the last braid, or use them to tie your square braid to the zipper of your coat, to your key chain, or whatever.

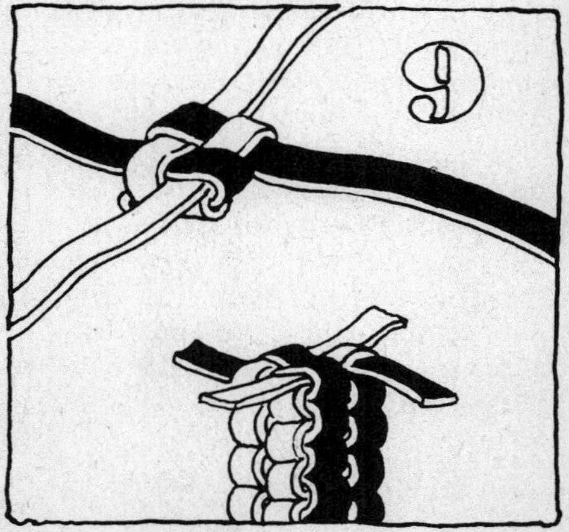
9

10
FOUR STRAND ROUND BRAID

This is another easy one.
1 Start with two strands of any type of cord, looped over a rod to produce four strands. The strands on the left (strands 1 and 2) should always remain on the left, and the right-hand strands on the right.
2 Pass strand 1 under strand 2 and around strand 3 so that it now lies in strand 2's former position, that is, between the far left strand and strand 3. See the drawing.
3 Now pass strand 4 under strand 3 and around strand 1 so that it lies in the former position of strand 3.
4 Keep repeating this, passing the far right and left strands alternately under the strand beside them and around the third strand (a shorter way of saying steps 1 to 3).

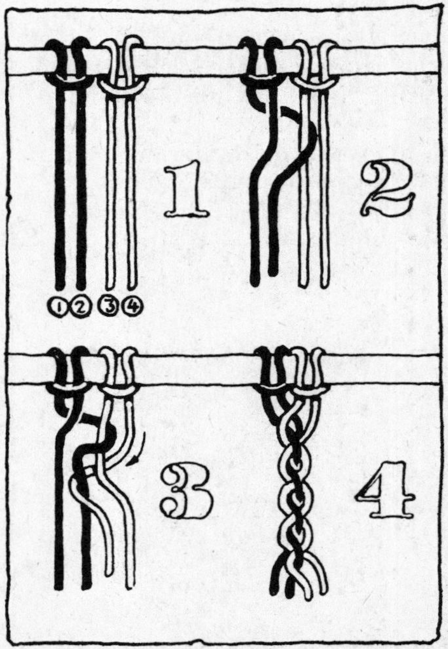
1
2
3
4
1 2 3 4

Your finished braid should look like the last picture.

When this type of braid is produced with thick strands, it is excellent for making into coasters or mats, and since it is so easy to do, you could even produce enough to make into something *really* big, like a scatter rug! You'll have to wait till you get to your destination or back home to do this, though, because it involves sewing.

Simply wrap the braid into a round or oval spiral on a flat surface where it won't be disturbed, and, starting at the center, sew the adjoining braids together with some strong thread. Voila! Carpet extraordinaire!

11
FIVE STRAND SENNIT

This particular braid is a little harder to do until you get the knack of it, but the finished braid is very beautiful, especially if you use colored strands. So if you're in the mood for something a little more challenging, this is the one to try, and you will agree that the end result is worth it. It produces a wide flat braid that can be used for book marks, belts, hat bands, carrying straps or bracelets. If you're feeling *really* industrious, you could even sew a few lengths of braid together to make a handbag, a glasses case or pencil case, or almost anything right up to a blanket for an elephant!

1 Start by bringing the far left strand, strand 1, over strand 2 so that it lies between strand 2 and strand 3.

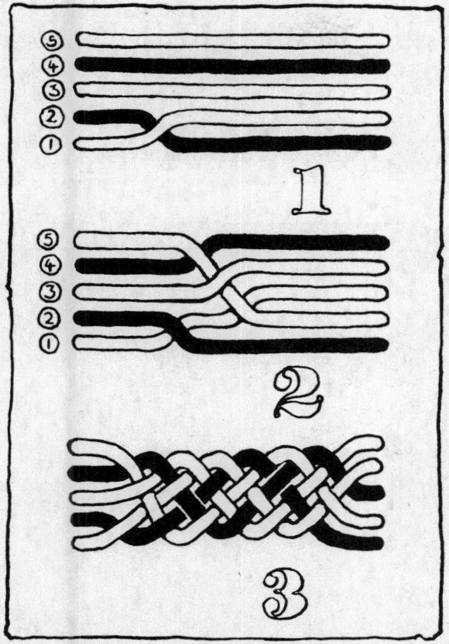
5
4
3
2
1
1
5
4
3
2
1
2
3

2 Next pass the far right strand, strand 5, over strand 4, under strand 3 and over strand 1. Strand 5 should now lie between strand 1 and strand 2.

3 Continue repeating the steps above, bringing the far left strand (now strand 2) over the strand to its right, then the far right strand (now strand 4) over, under and over the three strands to its left. The final braid should look like the last picture. The ends can be tucked back into the braid, left loose, sewn together or tied into a knot. If the band is being formed into a loop, simply tie each strand to its opposite strand at the other end of the braid.

12
CHAIN BRAID

This type is an easy one to do, but it is hard to make into an even braid. It is done, amazingly enough, with only one strand, and is actually the basic knot used in most knitting and crochet. Once you've tied one end of your cord around something solid, such as a book or your big toe, you are ready to start. (Just make sure you don't have to get up and move around in the next few minutes!) This is much easier to describe using pictures instead of words, so study the ones below very carefully until you catch on, then try it yourself.

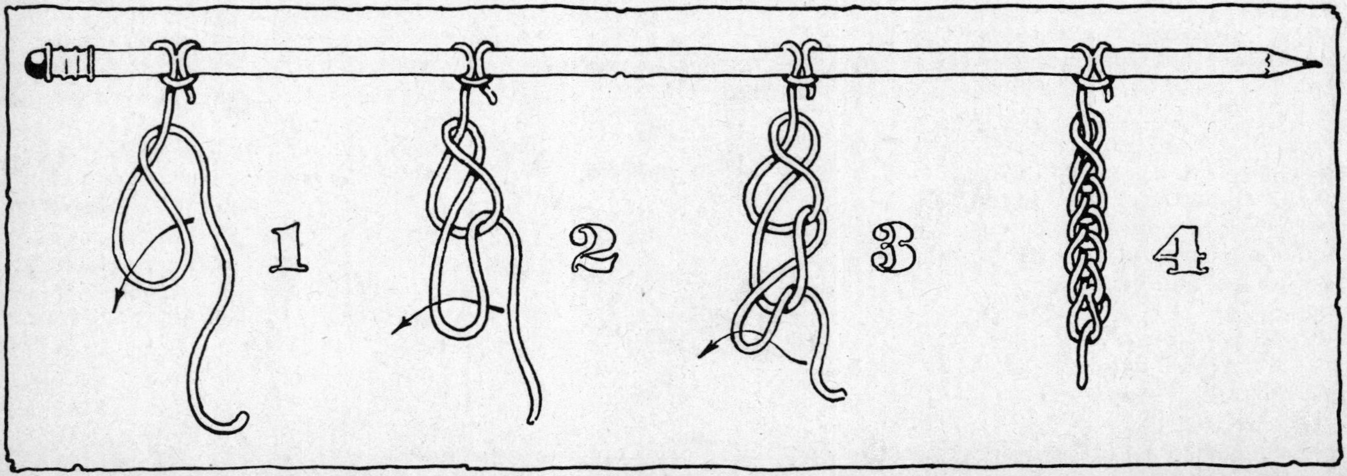
1
2
3
4

The Big Book Of Family Games – Jerome Meyer, Hawthorn Books, 1967

Games for a Team of One
180 Games for One Player – J B Pick, Phoenix House, 1954
How to Do Nothing With Nobody All Alone By Yourself – R P Smith, World's Work, 1958

Miscellaneous Magic
The Puffin Book of Magic – Norman Hunter, Puffin Books, 1975 (orig. edition 1968)
Sneaky Feats and *More Sneaky Feats* – both books by Tom Ferrell and Lee Eisenberg, Sheed and Ward, 1975, 1976
Close Up Magic – Harry Baron, Sphere Books, 1972

Look Out!
How to Amuse Yourself on a Journey – Judy Allen, Studio Vista, 1974

Other Books of Note
Odd Facts – Will Eisner, Tempo Books, 1975
Arnold Roth's Crazy Book of Science – Arnold Roth, Grosset and Dunlap, 1976

HI

RUDI McTOOTS

Rudi McToots was born on an obscure air force base in the wilds of eastern Canada. His family traveled widely in North America, and he has lived in southwestern Ontario, the Badlands of Alberta, the Saskatchewan prairie, and the Annapolis Valley of Nova Scotia. He left home at a tender age and rode the rails to the big city of Toronto. There he has worked as a soda jerk, handmade papermaker, printer, illustrator, photographer and writer. His earliest memories are of drawing and traveling, though he has had no formal training in either. Nor does he have a driver's license, and so remains the perpetual passenger. *The Kids' Book of Games for Cars, Trains & Planes* is the first of his many books.

Sneaky Feats and *More Sneaky Feats* – both books by Tom Ferrell and Lee Eisenberg, Sheed and Ward, 1975, 1976

Mindgames

The World Book of Children's Games – Arnold Arnold, Fawcett Crest, 1972

Psychological Exercises and Essays – A R Orage, Samuel Weiser, 1974 (orig. edition 1930)

The Big Book of Family Games – Jerome Meyer, Hawthorn Books, 1967

Mathemagic – Royal Vale Heath, Dover Publications, 1953 (orig. edition 1933)

Mathematical Magic Show – Martin Gardner, Vintage Books, 1978

Mathematical Carnival – Martin Gardner, Vintage Books, 1977

Bored Games

The World Book of Children's Games – Arnold Arnold, Fawcett Crest, 1972

Board and Table Games From Many Civilizations – R C Bell, Oxford University Press, 1960

Games Ancient and Oriental and How to Play Them – Edward Falkener, Dover Publications, 1961 (orig. edition 1892)

Make it with Paper and Things – Lella Gandini, Methuen Children's Books, 1975

Trash Can Toys and Games – Leonard Todd, The Viking Press, 1974

Fun with Pencil and Paper – Joseph Leeming, J B Lippincott, 1955

Dealing With A Card

Hoyle's Rules of Games – A H Morehead and G Mott-Smith, Signet, 1968

Official Rules of Card Games – A H Morehead, Fawcett Crest, 1968

Collecting Playing Cards – Sylvia Mann, Arco Publications, 1966

Radio Mania

Children's Singing Games – Alice Gomme, Dover Publications

Verse and Worse – Arnold Silcock, Faber, 1958

Juba This and Juba That – Virginia A Tashvian, Little, Brown 1969

Games for One Team

Juba This and Juba That – Virginia A Tashvian, Little, Brown, 1969

IF YOU LIKED THIS BOOK ...

If you have a special interest in some of the subjects covered in the games and activities in this book, or if you want to find out about more fun along the same lines, have a look over this list of good books. Many of them can be found in bookstores, or your bookseller will order them from the publisher for you. Your local library probably has a good many of them in stock as well. Read on ...

Why Knot?

Let's Knot, A Macrame Book – Donna M Lightbody, Lothrop, Lee and Shepard, 1972

Knots, Useful and Ornamental – George Russel Shaw, Collier Books, 1972 (orig. edition 1924)

String Figures and How to Make Them – Caroline Furness Jayne, Dover Publications, 1961 (orig. edition 1906)

Easy-to-do Entertainments and Diversions with Cards, String, Coins, Paper and Matches and *Diversions and Pastimes with Cards, String, Coins, Paper and Matches* – both books by R M Abraham, Dover Publications, 1961 (orig. editions 1933)

Fun with String – Joseph Leeming, Dover Publications, 1974 (orig. edition 1940)

Rip and Wrinkle

Easy-to-do Entertainments and Diversions with Cards, String, Coins, Paper and Matches and *Diversions and Pastimes with Cards, String, Coins, Paper and Matches* – both books by R M Abraham, Dover Publications, 1961 (orig. editions 1933)

Paper Folding and Modeling – A van Breda, Puffin Books, 1976 (orig. edition 1964)

The World Book of Children's Games – Arnold Arnold, Fawcett Crest, 1972

Flying Paper Airplane Models – Frank Ross, Jr., Lothrop, Lee and Shepard, 1975

Fun with Pencil and Paper – Joseph Leeming, J B Lippincott, 1955

For Fingers

The World Book of Children's Games – Arnold Arnold, Fawcett Crest, 1972

Hand Shadows to be Thrown Upon the Wall – Henry Bursill, Dover Publications, 1967 (orig. edition 1859)

More Hand Shadows – Henry Bursill, Dover Publications, 1968 (orig. edition 1860)

BRING 'EM BACK ALIVE!

Ten tips for longer living

When your vehicle is in motion:
1 Leave the driving to the driver. (Hands off the controls!)
2 Leave the driver to the driving. (Hands off the driver!)
3 Wear a seatbelt.
4 Lock the door.
5 Leave the key in the ignition when the vehicle is moving, or the car will enter a space-time warp of *n* dimensions from which it will *never return!*
6 Never throw anything out the window, especially yourself.
7 If the windows are open, keep all arms, legs and other limbs inside.
8 Never open the door to see what's under the car. There is *nothing* under the car.
9 Stay put – don't bounce around. If you get stiff, ask the driver to stop so you can let off some steam.

HARRY! WE'RE HERE!!
NO PARKING
K-9

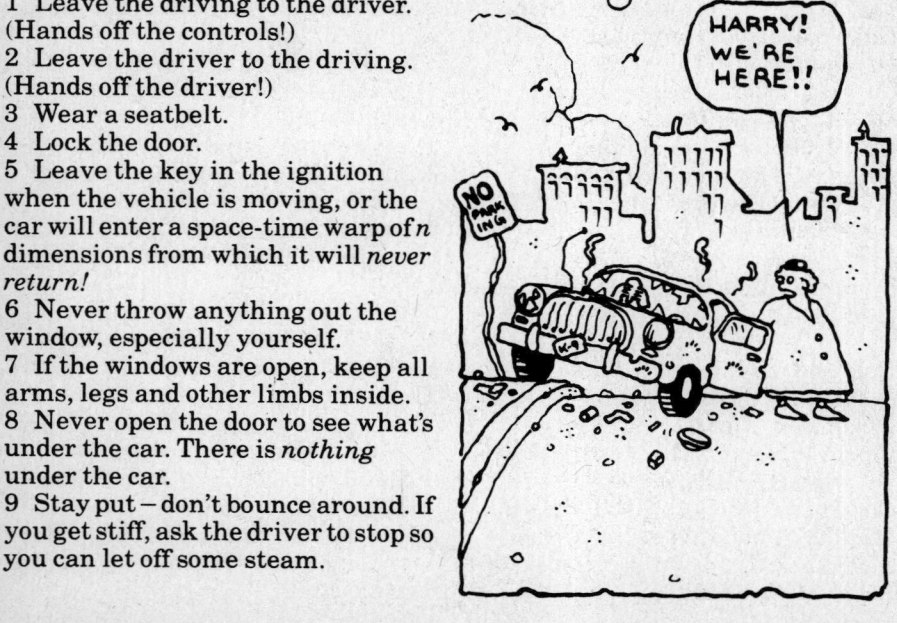

10 Avoid using sharp objects, such a scissors, pins, et cetera.
11 Never make toast in the shower. Hey! How did that last one get in there!? Oh well, you get the general idea. When traveling in a rapidly moving vehicle, remember that everything in the vehicle is also moving rapidly, and if the vehicle stops suddenly for any reason, whatever isn't nailed or seat-belted down will continue to travel at the same speed. A harmless looking pop bottle becomes a deadly weapon when it is moving at 50 miles per hour and you aren't. So be careful and use a heapin' helpin' of common sense; and *stay alive*.

THESE HIGH-SPEED COLLISIONS AIN'T ALL THEY'RE CRACKED UP TO BE...
RPM

like 'a' and 'the' are left out to make the telegram shorter. When you are making your telegraph message, it is all right to do the same thing.

For example, let's say that the first ten letters you spot are WWCDBYHTMN. One of the telegrams you make from these letters might go like this:

When Will Charlie Drop By Your House To Make Nitroglycerine?
or
We Won't Come Down Because You Have Too Many Nephews.

Remember that your telegram must make *some* kind of sense!

162
WE'RE GOING HOME...
two or more players

This game can be played in combination with one of the board games like Snakes and Ladders or H_2O, or you can make up your own game board. It should be the same kind of board as the H_2O board, a 'path' with many squares, complete with obstacles like marshes, washed out bridges, dead-end streets, toll bridges, and border crossings to slow you down. Number the squares on your game board so that you can remember where you are without using counters.

Players each pick some kind of object that they are bound to see a lot of, but make it something that is not *too* frequently seen. (Things like fenceposts or telephone poles are out of the question.) Choose something like a certain color car, or cows, or red barns, or pickup trucks, or whatever. Something that you see a lot of, but nothing you see all the time.

Let's say you choose to look for red vans. Each time you see one, you can move forward one square on the board. If you see a few in a row, you can move as many squares as there are red vans.

If you land on one of the obstacles, you must follow the directions – miss a turn, go back so many spaces, or whatever.

The first player home gets to warm up the TV...

160
WATCH OUT FOR COOTIES
two or more players

This is another game that uses license plates, only this time it's the first number that's important.

If you've ever played the game of Cooties, you'll recognize parts of it in this game.

Each player has a pencil and a piece of paper on which he draws his cootie. The object of the game is to be the first player to finish building a complete cootie. The drawing below shows how the cootie is put together. Each part of the ugly bug has a number, and to build it you have to spot the numbers in order on the first number of a license

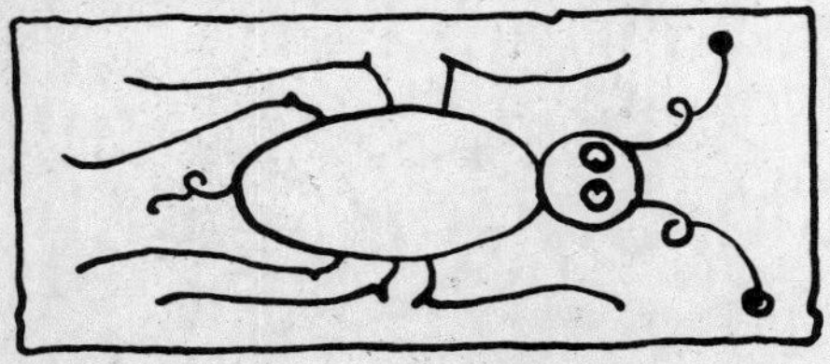

plate. For instance, you can't start drawing until you see a license plate with the number 1 at the beginning. Then you can draw the body. Next you must look for a number 2 to draw the head, then for *two* number 3s on two different license plates to draw the eyes, then two 4s for the antennae, one 5 for the tail, and then (hardest of all), *six* 6s for the legs.

Remember that you can use only the *first* number on any license plate, and if you spot a plate with a number you need, no one else can use that license, but must wait for another one to come along. Remember that you must spot the numbers in order.

The first player to finish drawing his own huggable cootie is the winner!

161
TELEGRAM
two or more players

Keep your eyes on those license plates! If they are the kind with letters on them, you're in luck!

Write down the first ten letters you see on license plates. All the players then have to take them in order as the first letter for a word. If you have ever seen a telegram, you will know that sometimes two or three sentences get jammed together without any periods to keep them apart. Sometimes, words

TELEGRAM

158
INITIALS
two or more players

Do you see a lot of license plates with three letters on them? Some countries, states and provinces have this kind of plate, and if you happen to be traveling through these areas, you are bound to see a lot of them. Sometimes the three letters form words, such as BOP, SAY, AIM, WAM or HAT. But what about the letters that don't form words, such as WBN, TDU, OPR or DVB? Maybe these letters are the initials for organizations, clubs, phrases or companies. For example, TDU might stand for Toy Ducks Unite! and UDL might be the initials of the United Doughnut League. How many of these zany companies and phrases can you make up from those three magic letters?

159
LETTER SPOT
two or more players

I hope you know your alphabet, because otherwise you'll have a hard time winning the game of Letter Spot. Players start out looking for any kind of object that starts with the letter A, then for an object that starts with the letter B, and so on, trying to find the whole alphabet, *in order*. If you see a zebra while you are still trying to find something starting with Q, you cannot use the zebra as one of your letters. Each item must be found in the right order.

Also, each player must find a different object for each letter. For example, the first player might use 'bus' for the letter B. The second player cannot use the bus, but must look for something else, such as a bridge.

If you like, you can make a rule that you can use letters from road signs and billboards to make the game move faster.

This is the kind of game that takes a long time, so it is best on long, tedious car or train rides of 100 miles or more.

Needless to say, the first player to finish the whole alphabet, or the player with the most letters at the end of the trip, is the winner!

player to find all three kinds of 'gold' is the winner. If you are choosing your own gold, make sure you don't pick out things that are too easy or too hard to find! If you like, you could write the names of different kinds of 'gold' on slips of paper and choose three out of a hat.

Here are some of the many things that make good 'gold':

crosswalks
ambulances
white or black cars
special kinds of trucks
horses
drive-ins
bicycles
billboards
cattle crossing signs
postmen

THE SEARCH GOES ON

two or more players

Did you ever notice how many stray letters there are along the road? Not the mailing kind, but the alphabet kind. There are letters on billboards, on road signs and license plates, on storefronts and the sides of barns, on trucks and vans, and almost everwhere in between. So with all these stray letters running around, it shouldn't be too hard to play a quick game of The Search Goes On.

In this game, each player thinks up any word or phrase that contains eight letters (I love you, my knives, don't stop, et cetera). Then the players race to see who can find the letters to spell their phrase first. You can take the letters you need from anywhere on any sign, but you *must* find them in the *right order*. Also, if another player spots a certain letter first, no other player can use that letter.

KEEP
HALT
CHEW
GUM
EAT
P
SMOKE
WATCH FOR KIDS
YIPE
BUMP A HEAD

For example, let's say you decide to look for the phrase 'I decided.' First you must find a sign with an I on it. The first sign you see says 'Bump ahead.' Oh well, keep looking. The next sign says 'Whispering Pines Motel, 2 mi. straight ahead.' Wow! What luck! Not only does that sign have the I you need, but it also has a D that you can use! You are well on your way to winning.

3 A few years ago, you could see a lot of cars with three silver holes in a row along the side. If you see one of these cars when you are with someone, touch something white and say, 'Three holes, touch white, you owe me a dime!'
4 It is generally considered bad luck to speak when you are in a train or car going through a tunnel.
5 It is very lucky to meet a wagon or truck with a load of hay, but unlucky to see the back of a hay wagon.
6 A paddiddle is a one-eyed car or truck, that is, one with only one working headlight, so spotting paddiddles is strictly a nighttime pastime. To play the game the way it was invented, you really need someone close that you feel like kissing, and who feels likewise about you. Otherwise, you could say that the first person who spots a paddiddle and says the word 'Paddiddle!' scores a point.
7 Just for the record, it is *very* lucky to collect a million bus tickets, and anyone who is able to do it is liable to be rewarded very generously by the Million Bus Tickets Fairy, a good friend of the Tooth Fairy.
8 When you drive over the railroad tracks, take your feet off the floor, touch the roof with both hands, and make a small wish.
9 When you see a graveyard, don't forget to hold your breath until you are past it. This superstition is older than history.

156
DIGGING FOR GOLD

two or more players

In this game, the players decide what kind of gold they are going to look for, and the first person to find his gold wins. The gold that you look for doesn't really have to be gold at all. Remember, all that glitters is not gold. For example, you may decide to look for a crosswalk, a white horse, and a train engine, while another player has to keep his eye out for a duck pond, a milk truck, and a hitch hiker. The first

DRIVE-IN
EXT LEFT

154
COLOR BY NUMBER
three players

If you don't already know about primary and secondary colors, it's time you did. The *primary* colors are red, blue and yellow, and they can be mixed in various ways to get the *secondary* colors which are purple, orange, and green.

Here it is in chart form:

Red + Yellow = Orange
Yellow + Blue = Green
Blue + Red = Purple
Blue + Red + Yellow = Brown or Gray (tertiary colors)
Black is the absence of color
White light contains *all* color

Now apply these principles to a game of car counting.

1 Each of the three players is given (or chooses) a primary color, and if anyone spots a car of that color, he receives one point.

2 What happens if a secondary color car comes along, you ask? Well, let's say it's a purple car. Since purple is made from red and blue, the players who are red and blue compete for it. They do this by trying to be the first one to point at it and say its color. This also applies for two-tone cars.

3 If a brown or gray one shows up, then all three players compete for it (unless it is the second color of a two-tone car: then it doesn't count).

4 An all-white car is a free point for everyone, but any white on a two-tone car doesn't count. A black car is no points.

This game can get fast and furious, and it's especially confusing if one of the players is color-blind!

155
WHITE LINE FEVER
any number of players

For as long as there have been people, there have been superstitions. Whether or not they are true depends on whether or not you believe in them. Here are a few of the superstitions, new and old, related to traveling and transportation. See how many you can spot in your travels, and keep track of them in your log book.

Superstitions tend to change from country to country, and from town to town, so don't be surprised if a few of the ones listed are different from how you remember them.

1 If you see a white horse, look around to see if you can spot a redheaded person. If you can, then any wish you make will come true.

2 If you see an ambulance, hold your collar until you see a four-legged animal, to avoid bad luck.

LOOK OUT!

Games for the motion sick

Look out everyone, I think I'm gonna ...!!

Are you sick of motion? Tired of losing your lunch every time you set foot in a car, plane or boat? Well, take heart, friends. This chapter is designed with you in mind.

You know, motion sickness has been with us for a long time, and almost everyone finds out about it at one time or another. Over the years, many folk 'cures' have sprung up to take care of motion sickness. The victims of these cures have had strings tied around their necks, have listened to chains rattling behind the car, have held their heads between their knees for hours, and have had to drink all kinds of vile concoctions, all in the name of science. Nowadays there are pills for motion sickness, but if you have neither your pills nor your voodoo charms with you, there are still a few things you can try.

Seasickness is caused by a combination of the rocking motion of the boat, and vertigo from watching the horizon shoot up and down. Find somewhere in the bottom of the boat near the keel where the up-and-down motion is not so bad, and don't look at the water. Play some games that will keep your mind off the up-and-down of the boat. (Old sailors play cards to ward off seasickness.)

Airsickness is caused by the fast motion of the plane, and is made worse if the plane is dipping up and down in rough weather. Avoid reading (drop this book!), watch the clouds roll by, or play some quiet games.

Carsickness is caused by vertigo from watching the ground near the car rush by, or from stuffy air. Roll down the window a bit, and don't do any reading. Look out the window, but don't look at the ground close to the car; keep your eyes on the distance. Or better yet, look out the front or back windows, where the scenery doesn't seem to rush by so fast.

And while you're looking out the window, you might as well be doing something besides just watching the scenery flash by. Why not try some of the looking-out games in this chapter? If you are the one who's carsick, have someone else read out the rules. Actually, you don't have to be carsick at all to enjoy these games, all you have to do is ... Look Out!

RPM

13
BELTRICK

As long as there have been fools and money, con men have been using this trick to separate one from the other.

All you need for the beltrick is a belt, a pencil, and someone to trick.

Fold your belt in half, roll it up (starting with the fold, so that the ends are on the outside), and lay it flat on the table or seat. Have a look at the picture to see if you've done it right. Now, tell your victim to put the pencil down in one of the two center loops. The idea is that he is trying to find the loop that will 'catch' the pencil when you pull the belt away, or in other words, the loop that is actually inside the folded belt.

If your victim puts the pencil down in loop A, you don't have to worry, because when you pull the belt away, the pencil will be outside anyway. But if he puts the pencil in loop B, which is the actual center of the belt, the pencil will be caught, *unless* you do this: let the outside end (in this case, the tongue end of the belt) uncurl one round, so it is now on the inside. Now, when you pull on the belt, the pencil will no longer be in the center. This means that no matter where your victim puts the pencil, it will never catch the belt, if you are on your toes. He will probably catch onto the trick after a few tries, so look out!

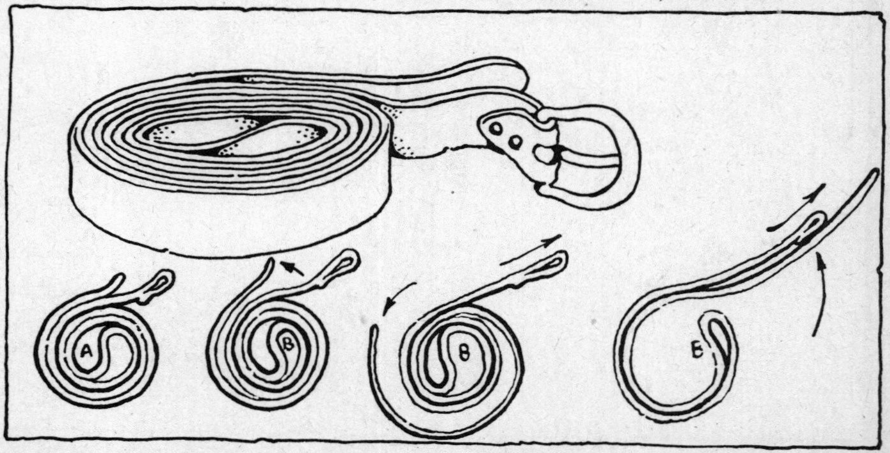
A
B
B
B

I CALL IT 'PAPER' HONORABLE MAJEST URK
HA HA HA! I'LL TAKE TEN BUSHELS!
105 AD
R.P.M

RIP AND WRINKLE

It shouldn't be hard for the determined traveler to find at least a few sheets of paper, even if you haven't brought any along. But if you were a wandering nomad on horseback in China 2000 years ago, you would have had to wait about 150 years for a guy called T'sai Lun to invent the stuff before you could play these intriguing paper games to while away the miles. The Egyptians couldn't wait, so thousands of years earlier they thought up papyrus, a writing material made from the pithy centers of a certain kind of reed. Papyrus didn't fold at all, but at least it was easier to write on than stone, which doesn't fold too well either. Of course, there was always vellum or parchment around to use in a pinch. If you wanted to jot down a quick shopping list, all you had to do was grab the nearest goat or calf and write on its skin, preferably after the goat or calf had been removed from it.

Nature, always slightly ahead of its time, had been making paper long before the Dawn of Man. In fact, one version goes as far back as the Dawn of Wasps, and even today you can still see paper wasp nests hanging in trees or under eaves. This is the most frightening kind of paper next to the kind they print report cards on.

The first honest to goodness man-made paper was manufactured from the inner bark of trees and rags. Centuries later, someone was watching a wasp at work, and realized that paper could also be made from the wood of the tree, which is what most paper today is made from, even though there are many other things, from cotton and flax to corn and esparto grass, that are easier to grow than trees and make better paper. Oh well, that's what we get from watching a wasp!

The ancient Japanese made their paper from the inner bark of the mulberry tree, and believed that paper was a god, so of course cutting it was considered a sin, if not downright disrespectful! Lucky for us, they thought of a lot of other things to do with paper besides cutting it, because using scissors in a moving vehicle can be very dangerous, especially with the way these crazy adults drive! Any cutting you need to do can be done by folding the paper first, then tearing along the crease.

The only other thing you may need to play the games in this chapter is a pencil, or, best of all, a fine felt-tipped pen.

14
ORIGAMI

Origami is the Japanese name for the art of paper folding. It has been practiced in the Far East almost as long as there has been paper, and the most beautiful figures come from that part of the world. There are hundreds of things that can be made by folding paper, and origami enthusiasts (there are lots!) are always discovering new ones.

All of the next four figures call for a square of paper. If you only have rectangular sheets, here's how to make squares from them:

1 Bring the bottom right-hand corner up, making sure that the right-hand edge of the sheet (A) lies exactly along the top edge (B).

2 Once you have lined up the two edges, crease the fold (C) with your finger.

3 Fold the part that sticks out beyond the edge (D) over that edge, and crease it with your finger.

4 Fold this part back again, and tear along the crease.

5 Unfold the sheet of paper, and you will see that it is a square.

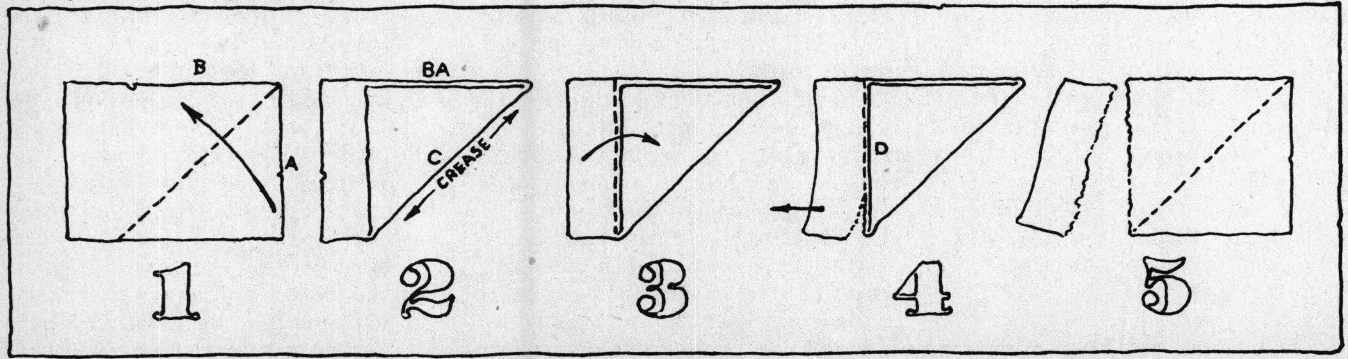
B
A
BA
C
CREASE
D
1
2
3
4
5

Paper Cup

To make a good sized cup, you need a square piece of paper about nine inches long by nine wide.

1 Fold corner D up to meet corner C, creasing along fold AB.

2 It should now look like the second picture. Next fold B over so it looks like the third picture.

3 Turn the paper over. Fold A over as you folded B, so that it looks like the fourth picture.

4 The two triangular flaps at the top (C and D) should be folded down in opposite directions and tucked under at E.

5 The almost finished cup should look like the next picture. All you have to do to finish it is open out the top. If you fold the two bottom corners under slightly, the cup will stand on its own.

The best kind of paper for this is shiny or wax paper.

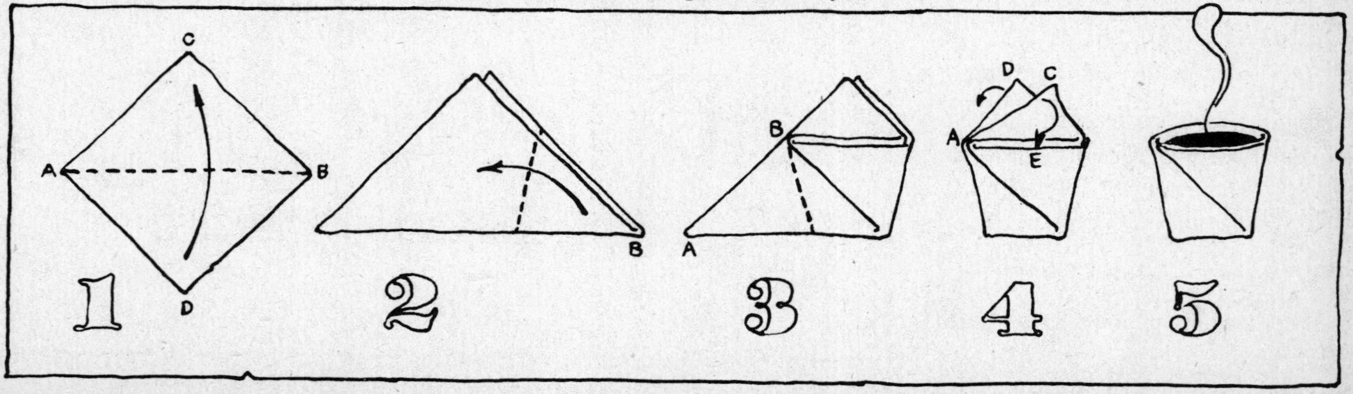
C
A
B
D
1
B
2
B
A
3
D
C
A
E
4
5

Wallet
This wallet should come in handy for holding your money or other valuables. It has one main compartment and a few secret ones for messages or other secret things.

1 You'll need a square piece of paper about 8 1/2 or 9 inches square to make a wallet that's about 2 by 4 inches.

2 Fold the bottom corner up to the top one, like the first fold for the paper cup.

3 Fold corner B over about two-thirds of the way along the bottom edge, but keep the bottom edge lined up.

4 Fold corner A over to meet the new corner E, then tuck it under into the folds.

5 Fold the bottom edge EF up to corners GH.

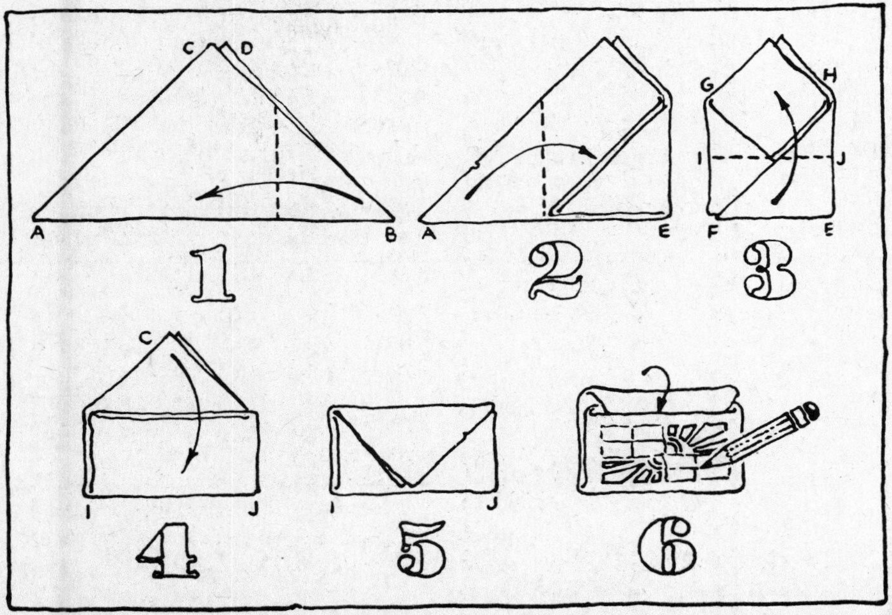
C
D
A
B
1
A
E
2
G
H
I
J
F
E
3
C
I
J
4
I
J
5
6

6 Fold the top triangles down to the new bottom edge IJ.
7 Your wallet is now finished. To close it up, tuck the triangular flap into the folds. If you open it out again and separate corners D and C of the triangular flap, you will see the main compartment. This is a good place to keep coins and heavy objects. The arrow on the drawing points into the secondary compartment, which is a good place to keep bills and notes. There are a few more compartments which you will have to find for yourself. I can't tell you because they are secret!

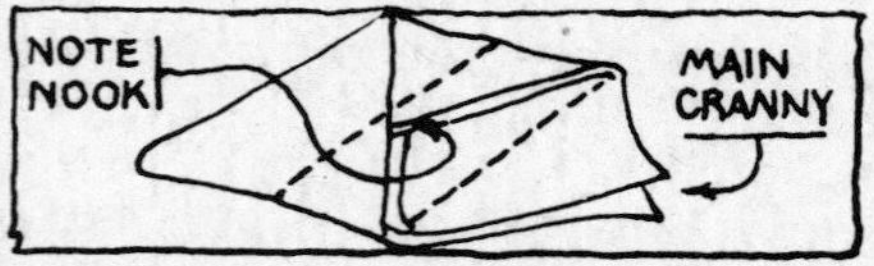
NOTE NOOK
MAIN CRANNY

Windmill
1 Start with a square of paper any size and fold corners A and B together and crease. Unfold again and fold the other two corners, C and D, together. Your square should now have two diagonal folds across it like the one in the first picture.
2 Fold corners A and B in so that they meet in the center where the two diagonal folds cross.
3 Turn the paper over and fold corners C and D together so they meet in the middle on the other side.
4 You now have a smaller square. Fold its corners, E and F, together at the center in the same way.
5 Turn the paper over again and repeat the process on the other side with corners G and H. You now have an even smaller square.

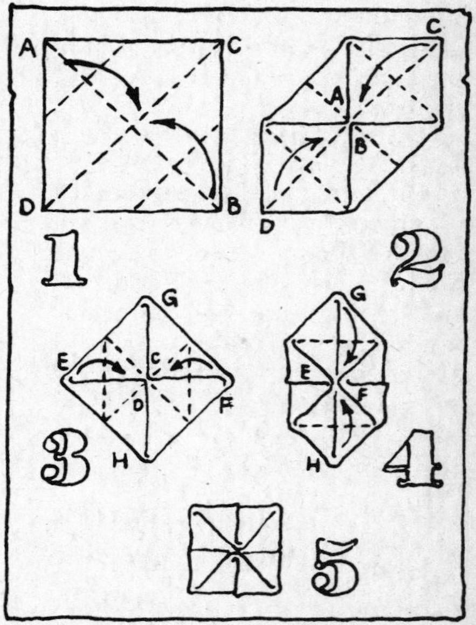
A
C
D
B
1
A
B
C
D
2
G
E
C
D
F
H
3
G
E
F
H
4
5

6 Open out the last small triangular flap (H) again, and pull on the corner exposed (A) until it looks like picture 6.

7 Do this with each of the other flaps (E, F, and G) and your windmill is complete. Poke the point of a pencil or pen through the center and thread a string through the hole. Hold the string by both ends and blow on the windmill, and it will spin incredibly fast!

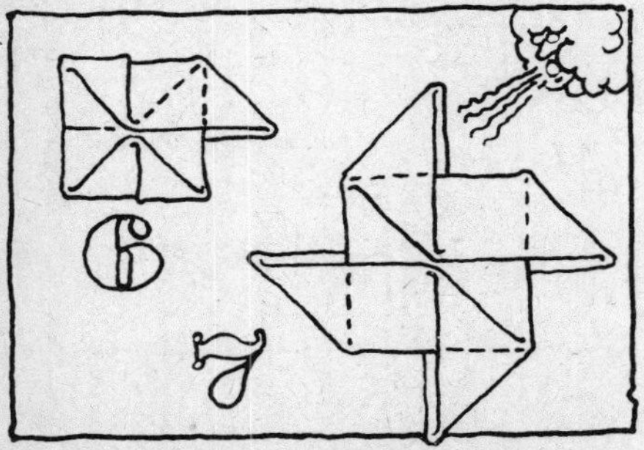
6
7

Bird

1 Fold a square of paper on the dotted line shown in the first picture, joining corners A and B.

2 Fold this triangle in half, joining corners C and D.

3 Fold the top point along the dotted line as shown in the drawing. Bend it back and forth a few times to loosen the paper, then straighten.

4 Push your thumb in between the two layers of the long side of the triangle and, with your index finger, push the folded point in and down, turning it inside out. This is the bird's head.

5 Fold the two left-hand corners down on opposite sides at the dotted line. These are the wings of the bird. Curve the tips down slightly.

If you hold your bird by the tail with your right hand, you can make its wings flap by shaking your hand.

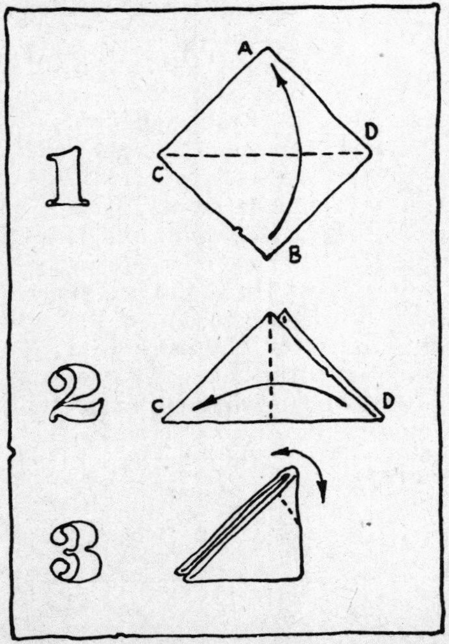
1
A
B
C
D
2
C
D
3

15

THINKING CAPS

Three paper head ornaments

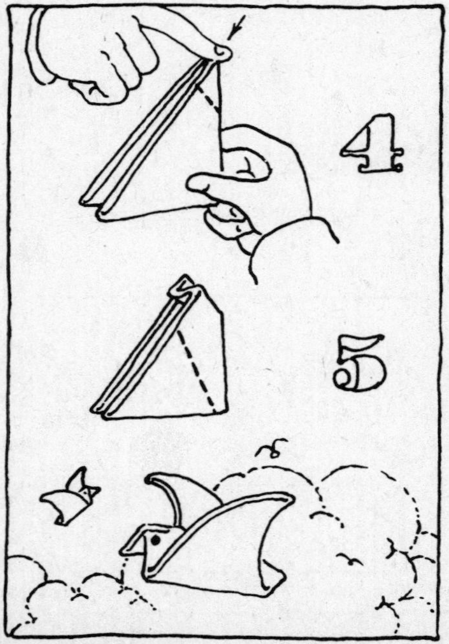
4
5

Extensive scientific tests and studies have proven beyond a doubt that the best kind of paper to use for thinking caps is a double sheet of newspaper, but any large sheets of paper will work just as well. So much for scientific studies.

Pirate's Hat

1 Fold a long rectangle of paper in half, folding side A down to meet side B. If you are using a double sheet of newspaper, this fold is already made.

2 Fold the top right and top left corners (C and D) down, as shown in the next two drawings.

3 You should now have two single-thickness flaps at the bottom. Fold these up on either side.

4 Open the bottom out and the pirate's hat is finished. Shiver me timbers!

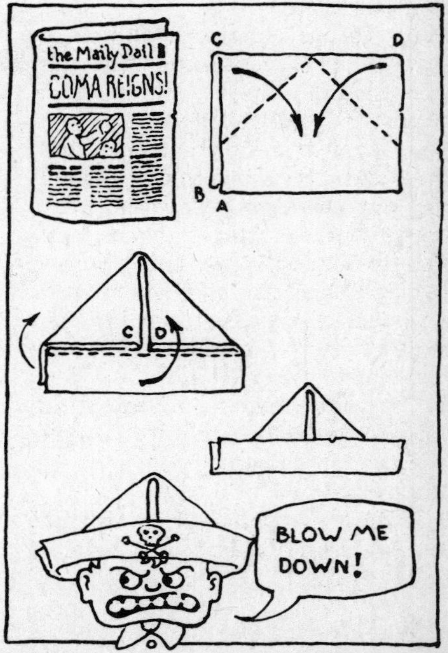
COMA REIGNS!
C
D
B
A
C
D
BLOW ME DOWN!

Printer's Cap

The printers who operate the large newspaper presses sometimes take one of the double sheets of newspaper and fold it into this hat to keep the ink out of their hair, and their hair out of the ink. Some of this nation's most respected thinkers have found that it also makes a good general purpose thinking cap.

1 It starts off just like the pirate's hat, with a large rectangular sheet folded in half, and the top left and right corners folded down.

2 Don't fold the bottom flap all the way up. Instead, fold it halfway up, and then fold it up again, as the second picture shows.

3 It should now look like the third picture. Don't fold up the second flap yet.

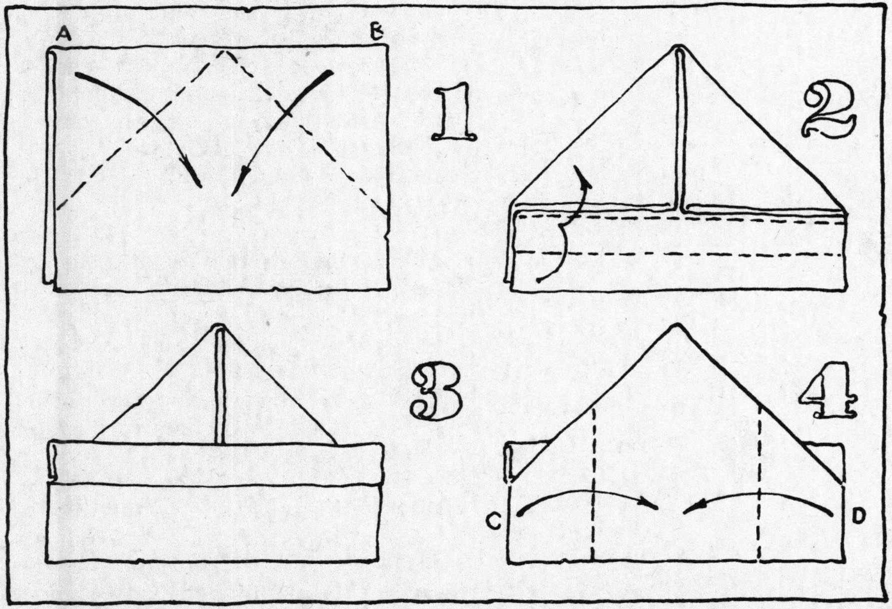
A
B
1
2
3
4
C
D

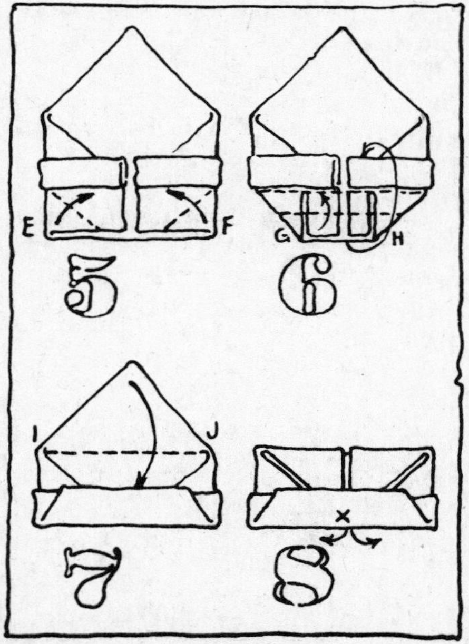
E
F
G
H
5
6
I
J
x
7
8

4 Turn your hat-to-be over. Fold the left and right ends (C and D) in on the dotted lines, so that they meet in the middle, as shown in the drawing.
5 Fold corners E and F up as shown.
6 Fold the bottom flap in half as shown.
7 Unfold the flap again, and this time fold the whole flap up and tuck the end GH in behind.
8 Fold the top triangle down at IJ and tuck the point in behind as well. Insert your thumbs in the bottom at point X and open out *all the way*.
9 Flatten it out a bit and it should look like picture 9.
10 Fold the top corners, X and Y, down to the middle and tuck them under the bands. Open it out at the middle and you are finally ready to get down to some serious cogitation!

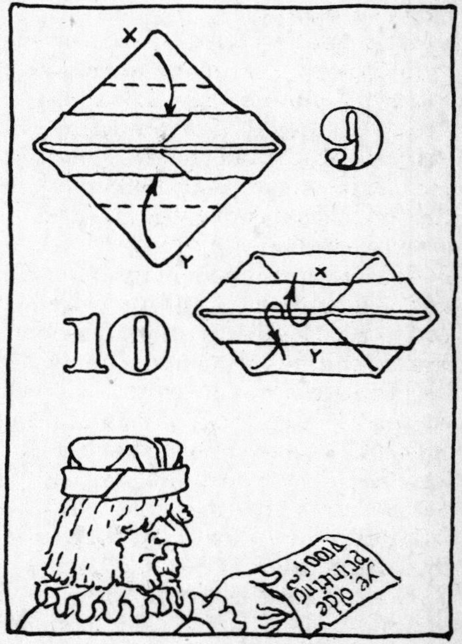
X
Y
9
X
Y
10
ye olde printing proofs

Pilot's Cap

Bzzzoooom! You'll feel like an old flying ace when you are wearing this cap. You will only need a single sheet of newspaper to make it, instead of a double sheet.

1 Fold the sheet in half, bringing the top edge (A) down to meet the bottom edge (B).

2 Fold the left and right corners (C and D) down, but not all the way down. See the picture.

3 Fold the front flap up halfway, like you did with the printer's cap (if you made one), then fold it the rest of the way up. Leave the back flap for now.

4 Turn the paper over and fold the left and right edges (E and F) over at the dotted lines.

5 You can see that in this case the left and right edges should *not* meet in the middle.

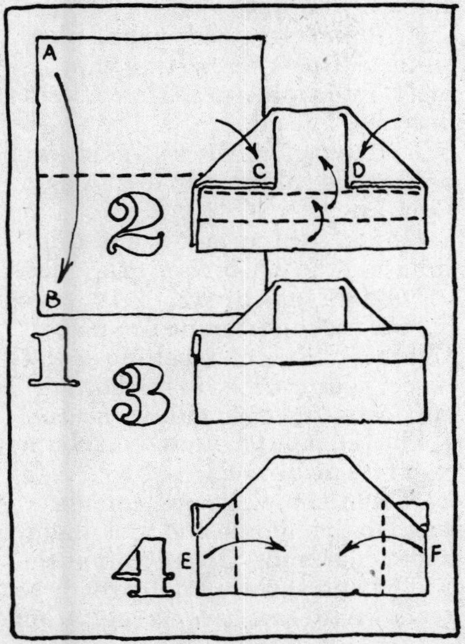
A
B
C
D
E
F
1
2
3
4

6 Fold the bottom flap up as you did the first one, by folding it halfway and then all the way. Tuck the bottom edge of the flap behind E and F. Open the hat out at the bottom and place at a rakish angle on your head.

Now that everyone has thinking caps, you are ready to try them out. Test them on some of these next games.

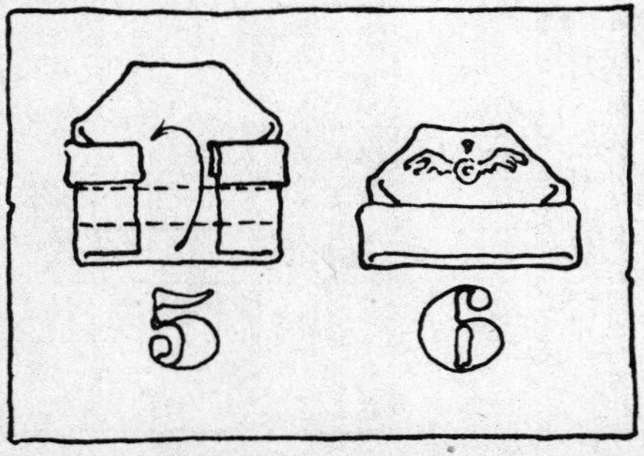
5
6

16
HANGMAN

two players, or more in rotation

This game is so old it's ancient, and the only reason it's been around so long is that it's a lot of fun! The rules

ANG AN
BYLDJFCPR
WRONG GUESSES
THE HANGED MAN

vary slightly from place to place, but the version here seems to be the most widely known. All you need are a sheet (or pad) of paper, a pen or pencil, and a pinch of ingenuity.

1 The basic idea of the game is this: one player thinks of a word (no names!) and the other player must guess what it is.

2 The first player must give the following hints to make the guessing easier. On the sheet of paper, the first player must put down a small dash for every letter of the word, and then fill in the vowels of the word (a,e,i,o,u) on the dashes where they should go. For example, the word 'hangman' would look like this:

__ a __ __ __ a __

3 Now the second player is ready to start guessing, one letter at a time. If he guesses a letter correctly, the first player must fill in the right dash with the letter guessed. For example, with the word 'hangman,' if the second player guesses 'n,' the first player must fill in the third and last dashes, so the word now looks like this:

__ a n __ __ a n

4 If a wrong guess is made, the first player writes the letter guessed down below (this is so the second player doesn't guess the same letter twice), and he draws the first stroke of the hanged man shown in the picture.

5 Two strokes make the gallows, one stroke the rope, one the head, one for the body, and two each for the arms and legs. So in all, the second player can make nine wrong guesses before he is hanged.

6 At any point the second player can make a stab at guessing the whole word, but, if he guesses wrong, two strokes are added to the hanged man.
7 If the whole man is completed before the second player guesses the word, he loses the game, and the first player wins one point.

Here are some hints for guessing:

If there are no u's in the word, then it stands to reason that there are also no q's.

If there are few or no vowels in the word, then chances are that there is a y in it.

If the third last and second last letters are i and o, then there is a good chance that the ending of the word is -tion or -sion.

If the third last letter is i, there is a chance that the ending of the word is -ing.

17
TORN JIGSAWS

two or more players

The title of this one just about says it all. Each person draws a picture or design, keeping it hidden from the other players. Make your picture as complicated and detailed as you can. When everyone has finished his masterpiece, each tears it up into an agreed-upon number of pieces, say thirty or thirty-five. The number depends on the size of your paper, of course. Now everyone passes the pieces to the player on his left, who tries to rearrange them into their original order. A point for the one who finishes first!

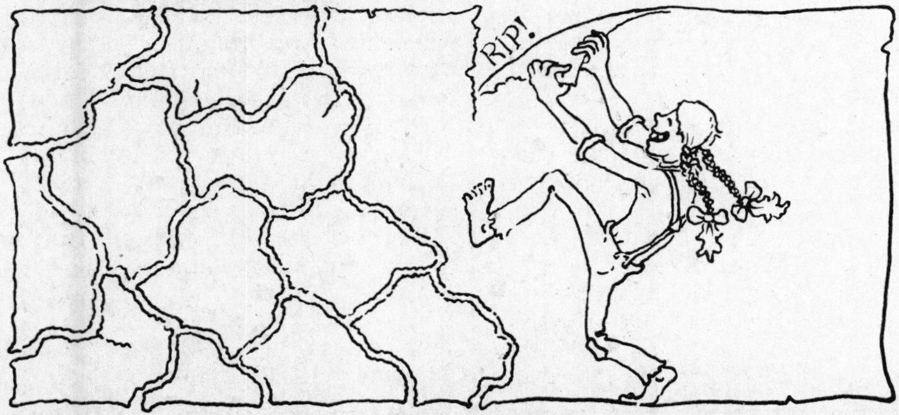
RIP!

18

MEMORIZATION

Kim's Game with a twist

two or more players

In Rudyard Kipling's great book, *Kim,* this game is taught to Kim by one of his employers, an Indian jewel merchant. The merchant teaches it to him using gems and precious stones in order to improve his powers of observation.

If you don't have any spare jewels kicking around, you can play this game with an assortment of small objects instead, such as a pen, some coins, a match, etc. However, since you will need fifteen or twenty objects in all, it is sometimes not practical to play this game in a vehicle.

So, instead, why not have the 'jewel merchant' draw the objects on a sheet of paper. The other players get thirty seconds or one minute to look over the assortment of objects drawn and then the sheet is covered up. If you don't have a watch, count up to 200. The players each must try to write down a list of all the objects they saw on the paper, keeping their lists hidden from each other. If you want, you can set a time limit on this, say two minutes or so. The player with the highest number of objects guessed correctly wins a point and becomes the jewel merchant for the next round.

19

SCRIBBLES

any number of players

You can't win any points with this game, but that doesn't make it any less fun. It can be played alone, or with any number of players.

The object of the exercise is to turn the most meandering scribble into something recognizable. Each player draws a simple squiggle on a sheet of paper and passes it on to another person, who must include the squiggle as one of the lines in a drawing of a scene or object of some kind.

The pictures make it clear. The thick lines are the original scribbles, which must be drawn without lifting the pen from the paper.

If you want, you can make the game more difficult by making a rule that the finished drawing must be made without lifting the pen.

20
SPROUTS

two players

This is an amazing game. The rules are so simple that you can learn them in five minutes, and remember them always, and yet it's challenging enough that you can play it for hours.

1 Start with any number of spots (at least six spots works best) or dots, placed on the page at random or in any pattern. Leave plenty of space around them.

2 Players take turns at drawing lines, straight or curved, connecting two spots, or looping back to the same spot. A new spot is placed anywhere on this new line after it is drawn. In a game of two spots, the first player can make any one of the five moves shown in the drawing.

3 The two basic rules of play are these:

a) The line drawn can be any size or shape, but it can't cross itself or any other line, and should stop at the spots, and not pass *through* them.

b) No spot can have more than three lines coming out of it. Each new spot that's drawn on a line already has two lines coming out of it, one on either side, and only one more can be added before it is 'dead.'

4 The player to make the last legal move is the winner. Watch out for those illegal moves – those which cross lines or use dead spots. In the picture are two sample six-spot games showing some of the strange and beautiful patterns that sprout out of a scattering of random spots. Note that even though there are some spots that are not dead (that is, they don't have three lines coming out of them), they cannot be reached without crossing a line, or they have no partner spots to join, so the games are finished.

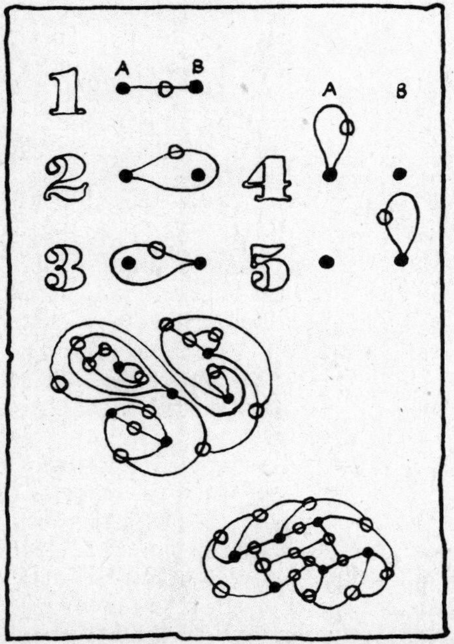
1
A
B
2
3
4
5
A
B

21
CONNECTIONS

two or more players

B
A
A
B

To play this exciting game you need to be sharp and alert! On your toes! You have to have the eye of an artist, the hand of a surgeon, the mind of a chess champion, and a pencil and paper.

1 Draw an even square grid of dots, any number to a side, like the one in this drawing.

2 Players take turns drawing one short line between two dots that are side-by-side.

3 The object of the game is to complete as many squares as you can, and to prevent the other players from doing the same thing. Each square must have only one line per side, and when you complete one you put your initial in it, and take an extra turn. If you finish another square you take another turn, etc. If you make two boxes by adding one line, you only get one extra turn. If you finish a square you *must* take another turn, whether you can finish another square or not.

4 When all the dots are used up, count up the number of squares each player has initialed to determine the winner. The player with the highest score subtracts the next highest score to get his final number of points.

Always try to avoid making the third side of a square because that means that the next player can complete the square and put his own initial on it. When you first start out this is easy enough to do, but as the game goes on it becomes harder and harder to avoid making the dreaded third side. One consolation is that it is also harder for your opponent to avoid setting up a square for you to complete.

22
POSSIBILITIES

two or more players

This has been a favorite game for ages. It was old in Queen Elizabeth I's time, for what it's worth. What it involves is using the letters of a large word to form smaller words. You can't use a letter twice in the forming of a new word unless it occurs twice in the original word.

For example, let's say you decide on the word 'bridge.' Each player takes a pencil and paper, and keeping his sheets hidden from the other players, starts to write down all the words he can think of, using the letters b,r,i,d,g and e. These are some of the many (more than you would think!) words that can be made from the word bridge: Ride, bride, ridge, red, die, dig, rig, big, bed, dirge, id, erg, gird, grid, rid, bid, bide, rib, ire, dire, brig ... the list goes on. Do you see any that I've missed?

The winner is the player with the most real words made from the original. If you win, you receive one point for every word you thought of that no one else did.

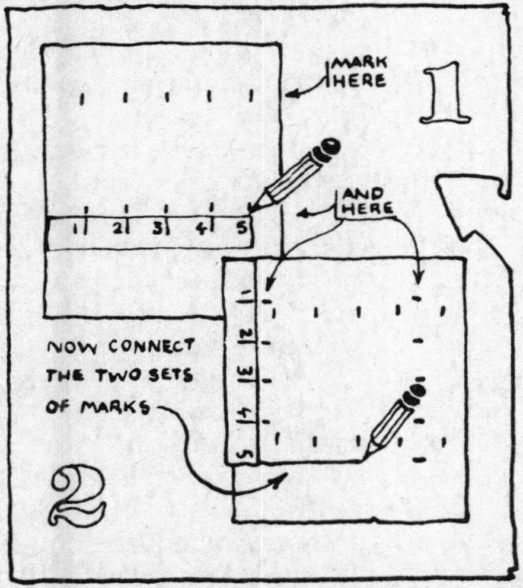
MARK HERE
1
AND HERE
1 2 3 4 5
NOW CONNECT THE TWO SETS OF MARKS
2

23
PAPER DICE

One dice is called a 'die', and you are about to manufacture one.

If you don't already have a ruler, you will need to make one. Put a mark on the edge of a sheet of paper about one inch from the corner. Using this as a one-inch ruler, mark off six equal divisions along the edge of another sheet of paper, starting at one corner. You now have a six 'inch' ruler.

1 Use your ruler to mark off a five-square grid, as shown in the first two pictures. When finished, you should have a perfect square marked off into 25 smaller squares.

2 Using your pencil to thicken the lines, copy the diagram shown in the third picture onto your grid. The thick lines show where to tear, and the dotted ones where to fold.

3 Using the crease-and-tear method, *carefully* rip along all thick

lines. If your vehicle has stopped you can use scissors.

4 Fold the side tabs A,B,C, and D so they point straight up.

5 Fold tab G up and continue folding up the middle row of squares until you have a cube sitting in the center of a long strip.

6 Fold the two ends of the strip (tabs Y and Z) up and tuck tabs Y and Z into the slits on each side of the top. You should now have a cube that sits still without flying apart.

7 To convert this innocent looking cube into a die, all that needs to be done is the spotting. The spots on the opposite sides of a die always add up to seven, which means that when you put your spots on, be sure to put the 6 opposite the 1, 5 opposite 2, and 4 opposite 3.

If you want to use your die, look

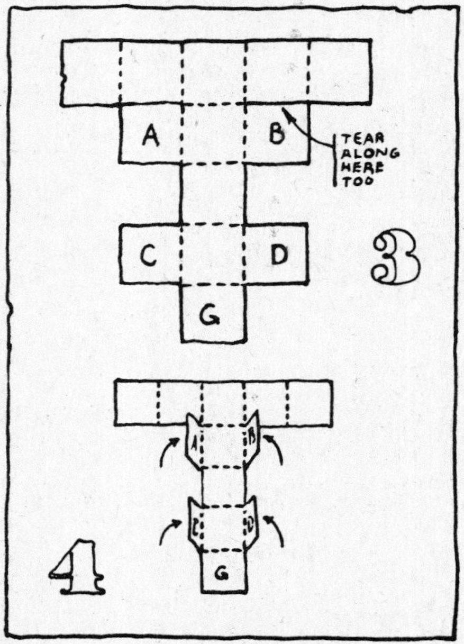
A
B
TEAR ALONG HERE TOO
C
D
G
3
4
G

up the dice games at the end of the What to Do with the Loot chapter, and the board games in the chapter before that, and *get shaking!*

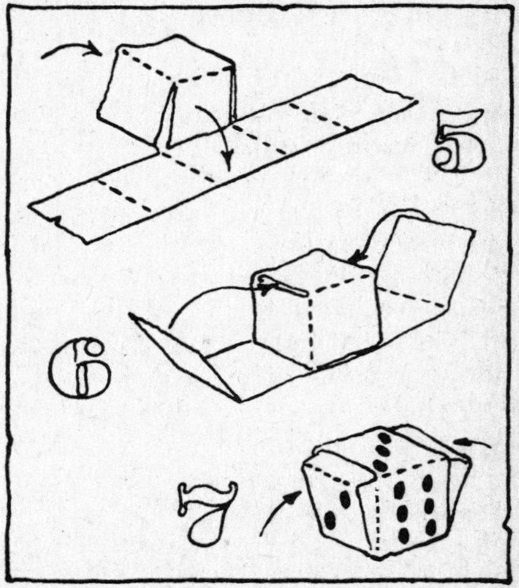
5
6
7

24
S.O.X.

two or three players

Everybody must know the game of Tic Tac Toe (Noughts and Crosses, x's and o's ...) by now, and it seems that people are constantly inventing and re-inventing a way for three people to play it. This version of three-handed Tic Tac Toe, called s.o.x., has been invented at least twice, without either inventor knowing about the other.

s.o.x. is played on a grid made of six crossing lines, three going up and down, and three going across, instead of the usual four lines used in Tic Tac Toe. This gives a total of 16 squares instead of nine.

If three people are playing, the rules are simple:

1 Each player chooses one of the three letters, s, o, or x. The game is played on a larger grid, in the same manner as Tic Tac Toe. You try to make a straight or diagonal line of three of your own letters, at the same time trying to prevent the other player from doing the same thing.

2 The first move by each player must be made in one of the *outside* squares. Only after each player has placed one letter on the grid can any letters go into the inside squares.

3 The winner is the first person to get a row of three, be it straight or diagonal, of his/her own letter. If it's a draw the cat gets one point.

If there are only two players, a slightly different set of rules comes into play:

1 Each of the two players decides which of the three letters he wants to be. The one not chosen is the cat's.

2 Using a grid of six lines, the first player places the letter s in one of the outside squares. The second player puts the letter o in one of the outside squares. Players do this no matter what letter they have chosen as their own.

3 Back to the first player again. He/she places the letter x in one of the outside squares. The second player now must place the letter s anywhere on the grid. The first player then places the letter o, and so on, repeating the series s.o.x. in order, over and over. This means that every so often, each player plays the other player's letter!

4 If there is an opening for a letter which will complete a row of three, the player who must play that letter at the moment *must* fill that opening, or automatically lose the game. It's hard to place a letter that belongs to the other player in a spot that will lose the game for you! This is what makes the game so interesting.

5 Of course, the winner is the player whose letter has formed a row of three, even if the other person played the last letter that formed the row. If it's a draw, the cat wins one point.

S O
S X X X
S
O O

25
BLIND DARTS

two or more players

What!? Blind darts! It sounds positively *dangerous!*

Actually, there are no darts involved in this game, in fact, no pointy objects of any kind, unless you count your pointing finger, which is what you use instead of darts.

Make your dartboard by drawing a large circle on a sheet of paper. In the dead center of the circle draw a smaller circle about an inch across. This is the bull's-eye, which is worth a big 100 points. Draw as many spokes as you want, and have them radiating from the central circle, until the dartboard looks a little like a tricycle wheel. Number the spaces between the spokes, but don't use a number higher than 20.

Now for the blind part. Close your eyes (no peeking), or look at the ceiling, and swing your finger around in a circle three times over the dartboard, which is resting on the seat, or on your suitcase table. Bring your finger down on the board. If it lands anywhere in the circle, you score the number of points marked in the space where your fingertip rests. If your fingertip hits one of the spokes, you score the higher of the two numbers on either side. If it lands completely inside the bull's-eye you have automatically won, because the first player to reach 100 points is the winner. Each win is worth two points on your overall trip score.

1
5
6
7
100
8
9
10
14

26

BLIND ART

any number of players

The only thing about this game which is similar to Blind Darts is the blind part! Each player puts a book on top of his head, and then a sheet of paper on top of that. Now try to draw the pig shown in the picture as a warm up. You'll be surprised at the results, to say the least! Try drawing something else besides the pig, and don't tell anyone else what it's supposed to be. See if they can guess!

27

WALKING BLIND

two or more players

If you tried playing the last two games, you should be getting quite used to doing things blind. By now you should be able to walk around sightless without bumping into things. Want to find out how well you'd actually do?

On a sheet of paper that is fairly large draw ten circles, each about the size of a penny, scattered over the paper. These represent the obstacles of which a blind person must be wary. If you like you can label them 'chair,' 'coffee table,' 'skate board,' or whatever, or you could draw the objects on the paper instead of circles.

The players then take turns. Look at the ceiling and close your eyes – no peeking! Swing a pencil around three times and plunk it down on the paper. Still looking at the ceiling, move your pencil in any direction in a straight or curved line, or any combination of both, until your pencil runs off the paper.

Take a look. How many of the obstacles did you hit? Now it's the next player's turn. The first person to reach the edge of the paper from a point at least three inches inside, without bumping his nose on a telephone pole or stepping on a dog's tail, is the winner, and scores one point.

28
SETS
two or more players

On a large sheet of paper write the numbers from one to twenty scattered at random all over the sheet, and put a small circle around each. Leave as much room as possible around each number. Now write the same numbers again on the same sheet, scattering them far and wide. Make sure that duplicate numbers are far from each other.

The object of this crazy game is to link each pair of the same number together with a line which does not cross or touch any other line. Each player makes up a sheet which he passes to the player next to him. The first player to properly complete his sets scores one point, and wins the round.

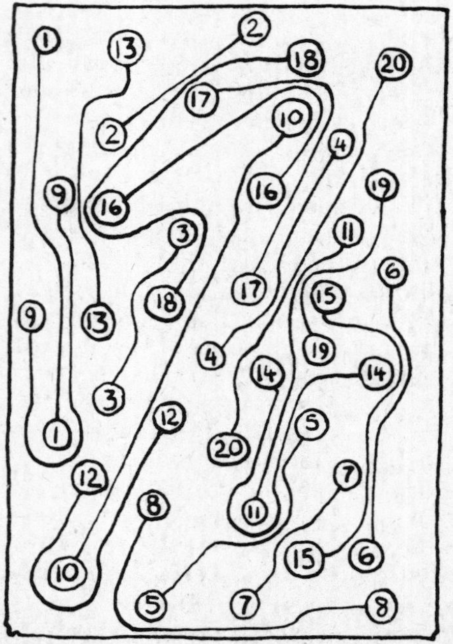
1
13
2
18
20
17
2
10
4
9
16
16
19
3
11
6
17
15
18
9
13
19
4
14
14
3
5
12
1
20
12
7
8
11
15
6
10
5
7
8

29
MÖBIUS MADNESS

Möbius may have been a mad mathematician, but since his discovery of the strip that bears his name, things have never been quite the same. Who would have thought that by giving a long strip of paper a twist or two, and forming a loop, you would be making a device capable of antics beyond your wildest imaginings? Mathematicians get tickled positively pink when you give them a chance to talk about the topological twists of this comical strip, but the talk is mostly numbers, so let's leave the technical stuff out and just stick to the fun part.

Take a strip of paper about two inches wide by a foot or two long. Hold the ends of the strip together so that it forms a big loop, then give one of the ends a half-twist. Although tape is ideal, you can join the ends together by putting tiny

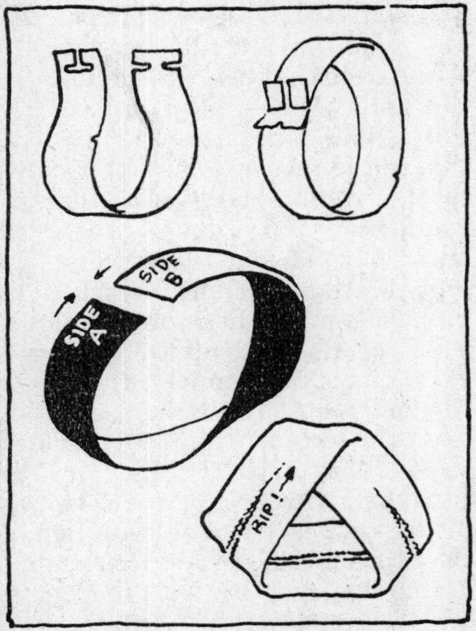
SIDE B
SIDE A
RIP!

tears in them like the ones in the first picture, and sliding the tabs of one end into the slots of the other. If handled carefully, this join will hold the strip together even when you tear it in half, but don't do that just yet.

You are now holding an honest-to-goodness Möbius strip, model A. Make like you are going to draw a line around the inside of the strip with your pencil. This seems to take longer than it should, but when you look at the strip, you see why.

Instead of just going around the inside of the strip, the line seems to also go around the outside! In actual fact, the Möbius strip no longer *has* an inside or an outside, it only has one side, and one edge! That half-twist you gave the piece of paper is the culprit in this caper. All this is perfectly natural to mathematicians but I promised to leave them out of this.

Take your new loop and tear it along the center (along the line you drew, if it's in the center). Instead of turning into two loops like any normal loop would, this twisted strip turns into one long loop! If you make your tear over to one side, it turns into two loops, one longer than the other. If you give the paper one *full* twist before you join the ends, it turns into two joined loops when you cut it in half! Try making and tearing loops with one and a half and two twists and, for added madness, try tearing some of these off-center.

30
HEXAFLEXAGONS
Plain and fancy

Hexa- flexa- *what!?*

If you are baffled now, just wait till you read the explanation of these weird and wonderful inter-dimensional doors. It might help confuse you to know that a hexa-flexagon is a flat polygon of six equal sides which is usually folded from a straight strip of paper, although other shapes can be used. When this strange but innocent looking hexagon is 'flexed' (hence the name), the two outside faces change! Messages or designs drawn on one face disappear, only to reappear later, garbled and rearranged, much like this explanation.

Luckily the things are much easier to make than to explain. The only catch is that you need something sticky to hold them together, like tape, glue or bubble gum.

The first hexaflexagon we are going to make is called a (are you ready?) trihexaflexagon because it has three faces, two visible and one hidden. To make it, you will need a strip of paper at least one inch wide by ten inches long. When you are creasing and tearing the paper to make this strip, be sure that it is exactly the same width all the way along.

1 The first drawing shows a 60-degree angle, which is the angle you find in all three corners of what's called an equilateral triangle, which is one with all sides of equal length, and all corners of equal size. These triangles are the essence of our hexaflexa-friends.

2 Lay your strip of paper on the 60-degree angle so that the bottom long side of the strip rests along the thick line, and the corner of the

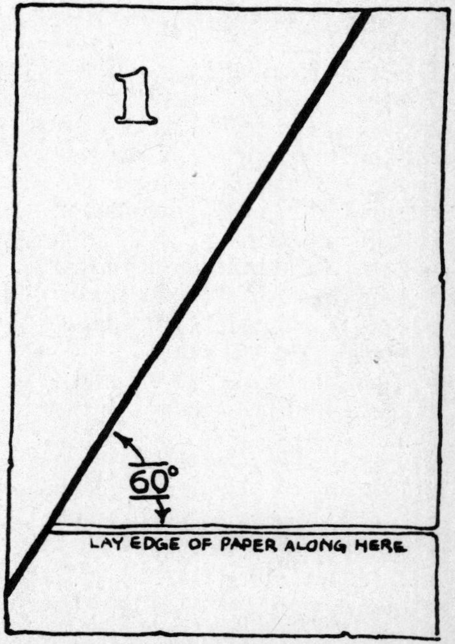
1
60°
LAY EDGE OF PAPER ALONG HERE

strip just touches the corner of the angle.

3 With a pencil and a ruler (or anything with a straight edge) join the two ends of the thin line that stick out on either side of the strip of paper. You now have a 60-degree angle marked off on the left-hand end of your strip.

4 Crease and tear along line AB.

5 Fold the corner A up so that it touches the top side, and edge AB lays along the top side.

6 Turn the strip over and fold corner B up till it touches the top side.

7 Continue rolling the strip over and folding the bottom left corner up until you reach the end of the strip. It's very important to do this folding part very carefully, so that all the edges and corners meet just so.

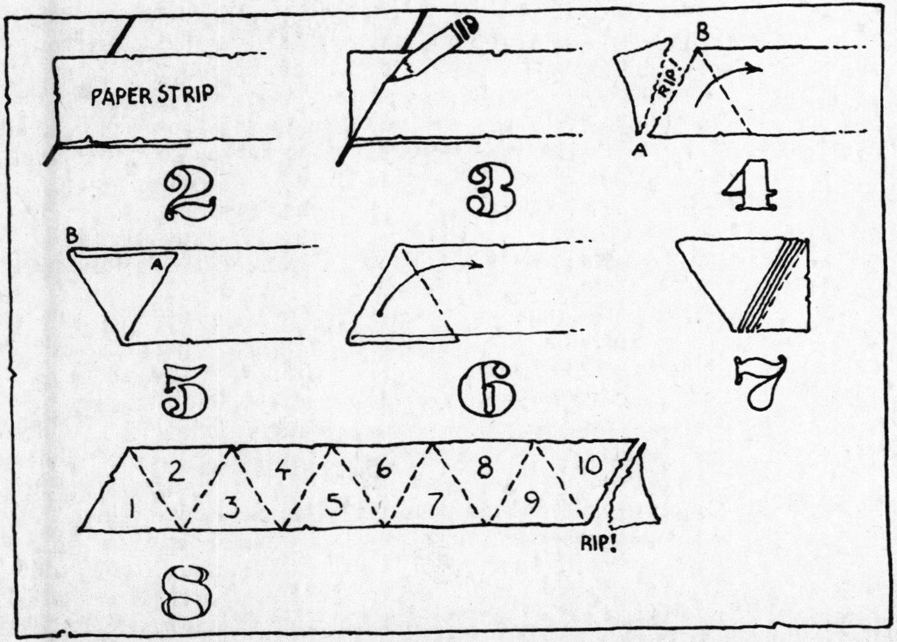
PAPER STRIP
2
3
B
RIP!
A
4
B
A
5
6
7
1
2
3
4
5
6
7
8
9
10
RIP!
8

8 Unfold your strip. Count off ten triangles, and tear off the extra ones from the right-hand end.
9 Now comes the fun part. Fold the long part of the strip down, along line AB, after the third triangle from the left.
10 Fold the last four triangles up, along line CD.
11 The second last triangle, number nine, is laying over the first triangle. Pull the first one out so that it now lays over nine.
12 Fold the last triangle over on top of the first and stick it down with bubblegum, or whatever else is lying around.
13 You are now the proud owner of a trihexaflexagon. You can see that it has six sides and two visible faces (one face is hidden). Decorate the two faces with geometrical designs. You may be wondering why you

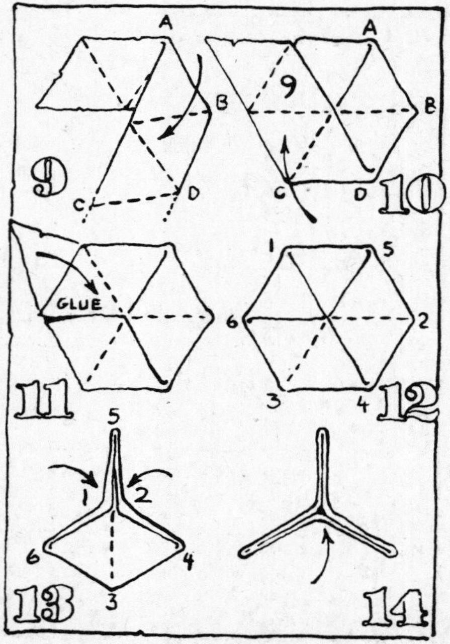
A
B
C
D
9
GLUE
1
2
3
4
5
6
10
11
12
13
14

went to all the trouble of folding the dad-blasted thing, when all it does is lay there with a smug look on its faces. Read on.
14 To make the little critter spring into action and start performing its multidimensional tricks, you merely bring every *second* corner up together to a point and turn the figure over. Open out the bottom point, and there is a whole new face! Look at the other face. Your original design has split up and shifted into the corners! Gadzooks!

This part is easier to figure out if you number the corners of one face from 1 to 6. Lay the flexagon flat and bring corners 1 and 3 together until they touch. Then bring corner 5 up to the other two. Turn the figure over, and open out the other face by pushing the point with your finger. If your flexagon *won't* flex,

don't despair. You have formed what's known in the business as a 'node.' All you have to do to banish the nasty node is open the trihexaflexagon again and bring corners 2, 4 and 6, together, instead of 1, 3 and 5.

You may have noticed that your flexagon looks a lot like a flattened Möbius strip. That's because it *is* a flattened Möbius strip! You could put your pencil on it and run a line all the way around and back to your starting point, and it would cover all sides of the thing.

Be careful that you don't lose your pencil in it, for hexaflexagons are a little like Alice's looking glass. They are doors to other worlds and dimensions. Anything idly dropped or dripped into a flexagon may just end up in someone's lap in the fourth dimension! How would you like it if a fourth-dimensional car full of fourth-dimensional people suddenly appeared in *your* lap?!

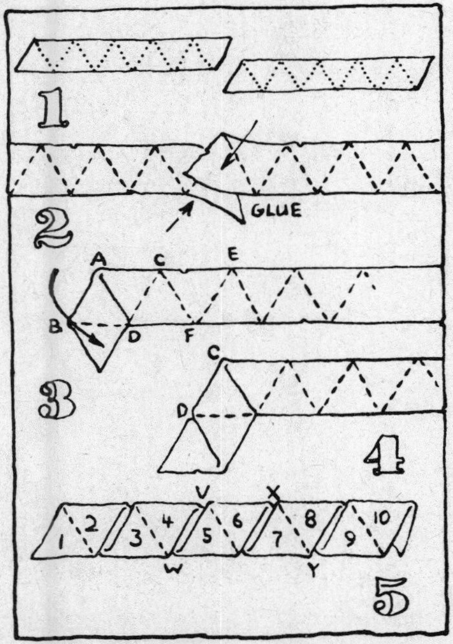
1
2
GLUE
A
C
E
B
D
F
3
C
D
4
V
X
1
2
3
4
5
6
7
8
9
10
W
Y
5

If you feel the urge to move on to more advanced interdimensional gymnastics, try making a full-fledged hexaflexagon, which has *six* faces, instead of the trihexa's three.

1 Start off the same way you did with the trihexaflexagon, but this time make two strips of ten triangles for each hexahexaflexagon.
2 Stick the first triangle of one strip on top of the last triangle of the other strip. Tape or glue them together. You should now have a strip of 19 triangles.
3 Fold the first two triangles on the left side down along line AB.
4 Next fold the first *four* over along CD.

5 Continue rolling over the left-hand set of triangles in this manner, folding along lines EF, GH, and so on, until you are left with a strip ten triangles long. One end of this strip is only one thickness of paper, while the rest of it is two layers thick. Make sure that the strip lies flat with the one-thickness end on the left, as shown in the fifth drawing.

6 Fold the first four triangles over and down along line VW.

7 Fold the last three triangles (on the right side) *under* and down line XY.

8 Pull the last triangle out from underneath the second triangle and lay it on top.

9 Tuck the triangular flap (the one-thickness end) in between the two layers of paper that form triangle ten, and stick the two loose flaps together with anything sticky. Your hexaflexagon is complete. Decorate the two faces showing.

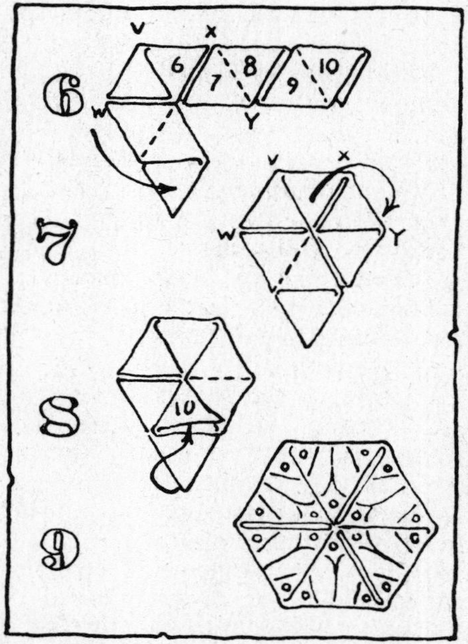
6
V
X
6
7
8
9
10
W
Y
7
V
X
W
Y
8
10
9

The hexaflexagon can be flexed the same way as your trihexaflexagon, by bringing every second corner up to a point, turning the whole thing over, and unflexing the other end. The difference is that this new flexagon has six faces instead of three. Faces one, two, and three tend to show up more than four, five, and especially six. In fact, it may take a long time and a lot of furious flexing for you to find the sixth face. And for heaven's sake, don't drop anything into this one!

31
S.O.S.

two or three players

s.o.s. is the international distress code that can be used to call for help in any emergency situation. It was originally chosen in 1912 as a world-wide code because it was easy to transmit in Morse Code (three dots, three dashes, three dots) and the letters do *not* stand for anything, not even Save Our Souls.

Like the distress code of the same name, the game s.o.s. is internationally known, and certainly a lot more fun. These are the rules:

1 Draw a grid a little like a Tic Tac Toe grid, only with a lot more lines, at least five by five. See the drawing.

2 Each player can write either an s *or* an o in any empty square on the grid, the object being, like Tic Tac Toe, to form three letters in a straight or diagonal line so that they spell out the international distress signal, s.o.s., and to prevent the other players from doing the same thing.

3 Once you have formed an s.o.s., draw a line through it, give yourself one point, and move again. Again, you can write an s or an o in any empty square on the board.

4 If two lines of s.o.s. are formed when you put one letter on the grid, you count two points, but only get one extra move.

5 Any letter can be used as often as you want to form a line of s.o.s. This means that an s in the center of the grid could have an s.o.s. above it, below it, to the left and right, and on each of the four diagonals.

6 When every space on the grid is filled up, the winner is the person with the highest number of s.o.s.'s formed. For each game you win, score one point on your overall scoresheet.

7 If you see an s.o.s. anywhere on the grid that has been there for a while and is unclaimed, you can claim it and score a point for it, whether you formed it or not.

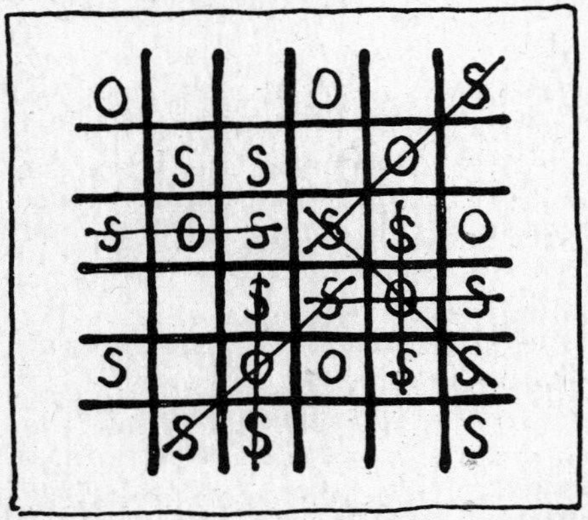
O O S
S S O
S O S S S O
S S O S
S O O S S
S S S

32
DOT-TO-DOT

any number of players

You have probably seen those books filled with page after page of numbered dots, which, when connected in the right order, make a picture of something. This game uses the same idea except that nobody (and I mean *nobody*) knows beforehand what the picture will turn out to be.

Each player draws a group of ten to twenty random dots anywhere on a sheet of paper. Make the dots large and easy to see. Players then pass the sheets of paper to the persons on their left. When the papers have all been passed, the players start trying to connect the dots to form a picture of something. This is not as easy as it seems. Sometimes, no matter which way you turn the paper, you can't seem to make head or tail of the mess of spots. In extreme cases like this, stumped players are allowed to add two extra dots to their papers to help make sense of things.

Players who finish their drawings without adding any extra dots score three points. If a player adds one dot, he scores two points, and if he adds two dots, he scores only one point for his finished drawing.

GARS
OPEN
FAST FILM
drink SPREE!
BUS STOP
NO
EVER GET THE FEELING YOU'RE BEING WATCHED?
B.P.M.

DIGITAL PLAY

FOR FINGERS

Finger tricks

Let's hear it for fingers, fine friends in weather fair and foul! Constant companions ever at our beck and call, ready to help out with any task. 'No job too small' seems to be their motto, for they can handle anything from chopping bricks karate-style to the most delicate brain surgery. Without fingers, humanity would be a lost cause, another forgotten species, for it was fingers that built the pyramids, fingers that wrote the great works of music and literature, fingers that painted the masterpieces and raised the mighty skyscrapers. And don't let any foot tell you different.

Besides being helpful, fun and musical, our digits are intelligent too. Our ten fingers are the basis for the entire number and counting system. If you turn to the chapter called Count Me In!, you'll find out how to use an ancient finger system to multiply and divide large numbers quickly. Fingers can talk too – speechless and deaf people use a finger alphabet to communicate. North American Indians used to talk with folks from other tribes by means of a sign language using the fingers and hands, and Doctor Doolittle would be proud of the psychologists who have taught chimps to talk using sign language.

There are many more examples of fingers being helpful to humans:

Little Jack Horner's Thumb Plum, for example, or Sherlock Holmes' Famous Fingerprint Clue, King Midas' Touch of Gold, and the Little Dutch Boy's Finger in the Leaking Dyke.

All in all, you must admit that fingers are pretty swell guys and that they deserve a break for a change – don't get so nervous, it's only a figure of speech! How about treating them to some of the finger fun in this chapter? They will have a chance to build up their muscles, to perform a couple of corny magic tricks, to put on makeup and act on stage and in the movies, to make friends with other fingers, to play games of chance and skill against each other, and to try out their reflexes. Sound like fun? Okay, all you have to do now is get your fingers to agree to turn the page!

33
LIMBER UP YOUR DIGITS!

Before you start any of the games, loosen up the old meat hooks with a few of these finger excercises.

1 **Finger Push-ups** Hold your hands in front of you and close them into fists. Start with the index fingers and uncurl them so they point straight up. Curl the indexes back up into the fists and then uncurl them again, this time pointing to the side, towards each other. Do this five times, and then move on to the next set of fingers in line and do the same thing. Do this with all four fingers, and lastly but not leastly, the thumbs.

2 **The Splits** Hold your hands out in front of you with the fingers pointing straight ahead and the palms facing downward, as if you are going to slap your knees. Hold all your fingers and thumbs close together so they are touching. Move the thumbs as far from the other fingers as you can, being sure to hold those fingers together. Move the thumbs back again. Do this five times. Now move the thumbs *and* the index fingers away from the other fingers, making sure that they touch each other at all times, and that the other fingers still touch each other. Do this five times, and then do the same thing with the thumb, index and middle fingers. Next hold all the fingers together, and then try to move the little fingers away from the others without separating them.

3 **Finger Wiggle** The title says it all. Keep moving every finger in all directions, wiggling them every which way as if you are trying to play honky-tonk piano and your fingers won't obey orders. After doing this for a few minutes, you begin to feel the effects, and when you stop, your fingers will feel like they can take on anything!

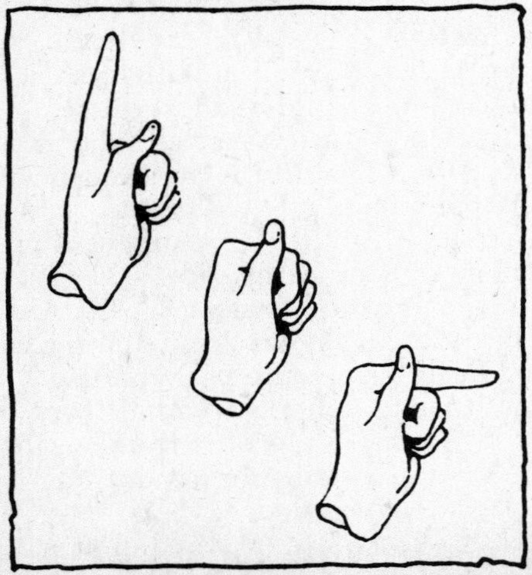

34
SHADOW PLAY

About a hundred years ago people went to see performers do this kind of thing on stage. With the help of your ever ready fingers, though, you should be able to see a shadow play right where you are.

If you have a strong light source, such as a patch of sunlight on the seat, or a flashlight at night, try out a few of the shadow friends shown here, to brighten things up a bit!

With a whole menagerie of shady animals and strange-looking people to choose from, you should be able to find a few characters for your play. Use a sheet of paper as a backdrop if the seat is too bumpy, and get set to hear the sound of applause when the curtain goes up!

35
FINGER PUPPETS

Here are a few more chances for your fingers to become stars of the silver screen. If you have a fine-point, washable, felt-tipped pen (the best kind to use when traveling, by the way), use it to draw some tiny faces on each of your fingertips. Now you have five or ten well-trained actors ready to perform! If you like larger puppets with more life in them, try the hand puppet shown in the second picture. Bunch your hand into a fist, add eyes and a nose and all the trimmings, and *presto!* instant puppet with a big mouth! All the better to eat you with! This one makes a good monster or giant, but is also capable of playing funny roles in comedy plays. With the other hand, you could make a cowboy (or football player, or ballet dancer, or . . .) like the one in the picture.

How about some paper costumes and tiny folded hats?

If you don't like the idea of drawing on your hands, try some of the puppets described on the next page.

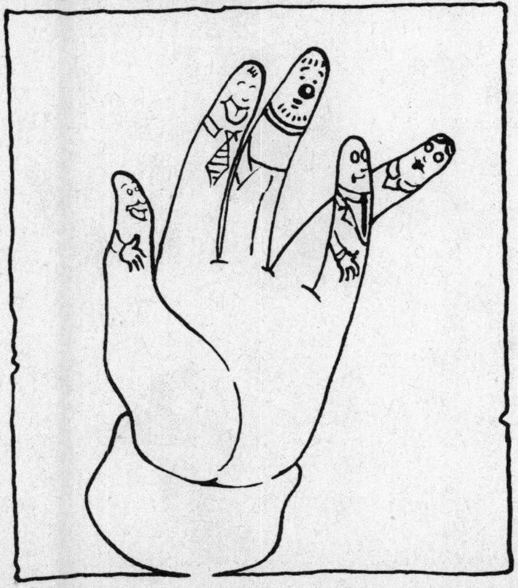

36
MORE PUPPETS

The Hanky People
You might think twice about blowing your nose after seeing the strange people that can be made out of an ordinary handkerchief or tissue.

Tie a medium-sized knot in the center of one side of the hanky, then tie a small knot in each of the two corners on the same side, and you

have a wizened old witch with a long flowing dress, or a kindly old gypsy woman. Slip a finger ring or loop of string on for a girdle and adjust the nose a bit, and the old woman can become a beautiful girl. You can hold her up by putting the tip of your finger in the back of the girdle, from below.

If you tie the bottom corners of her dress around each other, and tie small knots on the corners, the girl becomes that well-traveled rogue Sinbad, or, with slight adjustments in his costume and posture, the Villain.

You will find the whole cast to be very versatile actors, able to become many different people at will, a little like the old theater, where every actor played several parts.

Rabbit and Donkey
These two kaleidoscopic characters make good smart aleck sidekicks for the other performers, but they can also take on a lead part with the greatest of ease. They are both masters of disguise, and by shortening their ears or adjusting their faces, they can look like anything from a horse, dog, kangaroo or giraffe.

They are both formed with one simple knot. Fold the hanky in half, bringing the two top corners together (A and B). Hold the handkerchief in the right hand by the corner AB, and let the rest hang limp. Tie a half hitch just below the corners and adjust the ears, and you have Rabbit. By pulling on his nose and shortening his ears, you can turn Rabbit into Donkey. By shortening the ears even more, Donkey becomes a horse or whatever your imagination declares. After all, that's who's in charge here!

All of these characters can be held from underneath by the hand or index finger. With Rabbit, your index finger can hold up the head and your thumb and middle fingers can form the front paws, underneath the cloth.

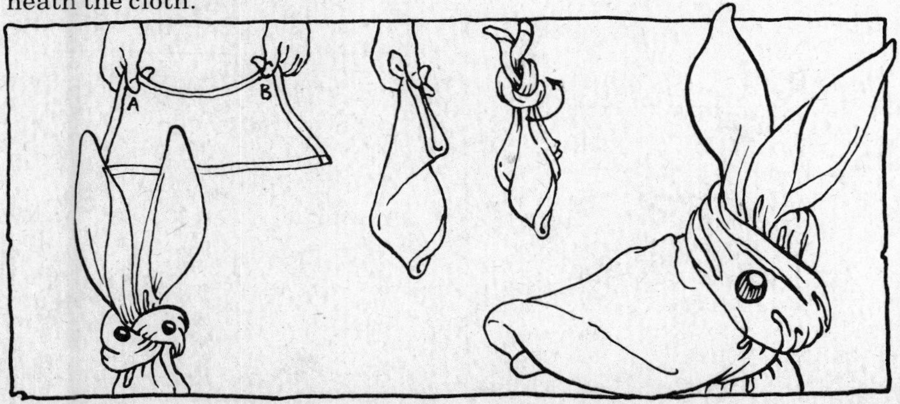
A
B

When you've got your cast of characters all lined up, you are ready for the curtain call! You can rehearse if you want, or just let them play it by ear – this is called free improvisation, and can lead to some hilarious scenes.

37

ODDS AND EVENS

two or three players

This is one of a group of very old hand games that all involve the same basic play. All at once, the players quickly raise and lower one fist three times, opening out a certain number of fingers on the third 'throw.' This motion is done as if they were knocking on a table three times with their knuckles, then opening out their fingers on the third knock.

1 In the game of Odds and Evens, the players open out either one or two fingers on the third shake of the fist.

2 The first player calls out 'Odd!' or 'Even!' as the hands come down, but *just before the fingers open.* The object is to guess whether both players will open out the same number of fingers (Even) or a different number (Odd).

ODD...

3 If you guess correctly, you score one point and get another turn at guessing. If you guess incorrectly, you lose your turn, and the other player calls odd or even on the next round.

4 If there are three players, you can play 'odd man out.' Players stick out one or two fingers on the third shake as before, but this time, no one calls odd or even. Instead, the player with a different number of fingers from the other two is the 'odd' man, and the other players each score one point.

38
ANIMAL CRACK-UPS
two, three or four players

Animal Crack-ups is a new version of Odds and Evens that is guaranteed to have you cracking up with laughter in no time flat. Each player decides on an animal he wants to imitate (or you could draw names from a hat) and what the animal's call-of-the-wild sounds like. The call should be short and simple, like 'meow,' 'arf arf,' 'oink,' 'blub blub,' or whatever. Pay close attention to everyone else's call.

1 All at once the players bring their hands down three times, Odd and Even fashion (see the last game) and open out one, two or three fingers on the third throw.

2 If two players have the same number of fingers out, they try to be the first to say the other's animal call. The first one to say the other's call wins the round and scores one point.

39
MORA
two players

In order to play the ancient Roman game of Mora, your mind will need to be as sharp as your eyes and reflexes.

1 The two players open out any number of fingers on the third throw (see Odds and Evens if you don't understand this part).

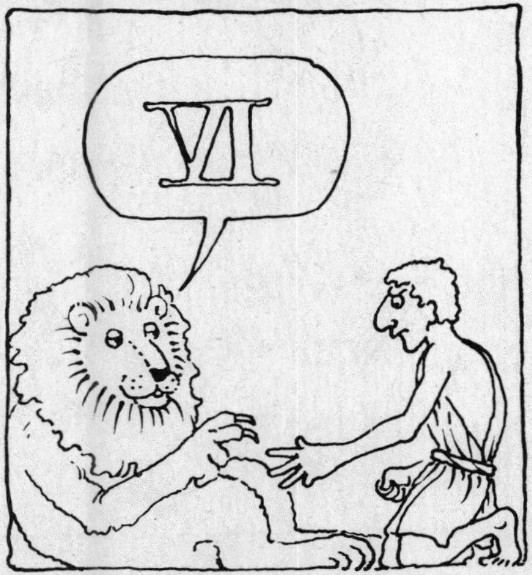
VII

2 The first player must call out the number that he thinks will be the *sum* of all the fingers extended by both players. This calling out must be done on the third throw, but before the fingers open out. Otherwise, you lose your turn.

3 If you guess right, you win that round, score one point, and guess again on the next round. If you guess wrong, the other player guesses on the next round, although he doesn't get a point for your wrong guess.

By watching carefully you can sometimes see certain patterns in the other player's style of play, and by doing some quick calculating in your head, you have a good chance of guessing the correct sum of fingers.

40
SCISSORS, PAPER, ROCK

two or three players

This is another hand game that seems to be Italian or Roman in origin, but it has also been known for centuries in Japan as the game of Janken. It has traveled all around the globe in the hands of young travelers like yourselves, and kids everywhere seem to know of it.

1 It is played in the same manner as the last three games; on the count of three, players extend one hand and open a certain number of fingers.

2 Players can open out either all five fingers, two fingers, or no fingers at all. Five fingers represent *paper,* two fingers represent *scissors,* and no fingers (the fist) represent *rock.*

3 In a game of two players, if both players open out the same sign, it's a draw, and a point goes to the cat. If they open out different signs, this is how they score:

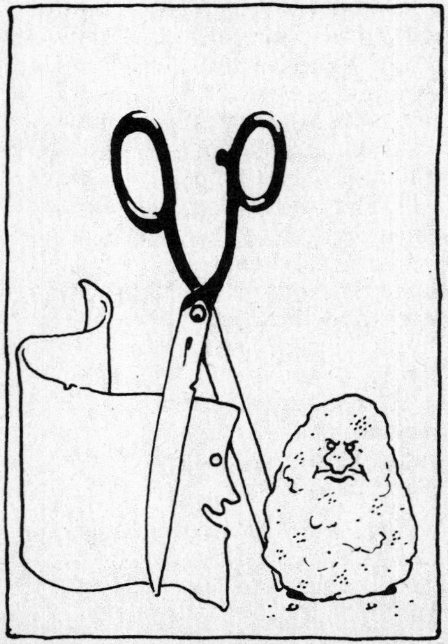

Scissors wins over *paper* because they can cut it.
Paper wins over *rock* because it can wrap it.
Rock wins over *scissors* because it can break them.
The winner of the round scores one point.

4 If there are three players, each scores according to what the other players have. For example, if each player has a different sign, no one wins because they cancel each other out. One point for the cat. If the other two players have paper and you have scissors, you win the round and score *two* points. If two players have rock, and you have scissors, they both win over you, but it is a draw between them, so they get only one point each instead of two.

41
SUPER VISION

three or more players

If you learn to play this game well, you will find yourself in possession of a very useful skill. However, it will take plenty of practice to get good at it.

The first player writes a short message on a slip of paper, keeping it hidden from the other players. He then attempts to communicate his message – but using only his fingers! How? You may well ask. Well, as you know, at last count there were 26 letters in the alphabet. A is the first letter, B the second, K the eleventh, and so on. The first player tries to spell his message out by showing the other players the *number* of the letters, one by one. He shows the number by 'flashing' the appropriate number of fingers on one hand. The first letter of each word is counted off on the left hand, the second letter on the right hand, the third on the left, and so on. Confused yet? Well, here's an example to clear things up:

Suppose (just suppose) that the message in question is 'A pail of air.' The first player holds up one finger on his left hand for A, then starts off the next word by flashing 16 fingers (three fives, then a one) on his left hand for P, one on the right for A, nine (five, then four) on the left for I, 12 on the right for L, then 15 on the left for O, and so on.

Here is a number chart of the alphabet to help the first player out in the beginning. After a while you won't need it.

A1 B2 C3 D4 E5 F6 G7 H8 I9 J10 K11 L12 M13 N14 O15 P16 Q17 R18 S19 T20 U21 V22 W23 X24 Y25 Z26.

The first person to guess what it is that the first player is trying to 'say' is the winner, and gets to try to recite a message for the next round. With a little practice, you can turn this into a quick code for speaking to your friends when they are within sight but not sound.

HUH?

42

RIGHT, WRONG!

any number of players

Touch your nose with your right hand, and your right ear with your left hand. Now clap your hands in front of you, and touch your nose with your *left* hand and your *left* ear with your *right* hand.

See how fast you can keep this up. As soon as you slip, it's the other player's turn to make a fool of himself!

43

SEVEN OLD COUNTING-OUT GAMES

two or three players

These games are like the classic 'Eeny meeny minie moe ...' and the more players you can get in on them the better. These rhymes can be used for deciding who is 'It' or who is the first player, or you could use them as games of their own.

The players gather in a circle, and the person reciting the rhyme points at each player, one after the other, at the same time as he says each word of the poem. (Sometimes it is every two syllables, as in Eeny meeny minie.) The last person pointed at is out. If the person reciting goes out, he still carries on the counting. This goes on until only one player is left. This person is 'It.' You could even say that this player is the winner, and scores one point. In some games, the players hold out two hands, which must both be counted off before the player is out.

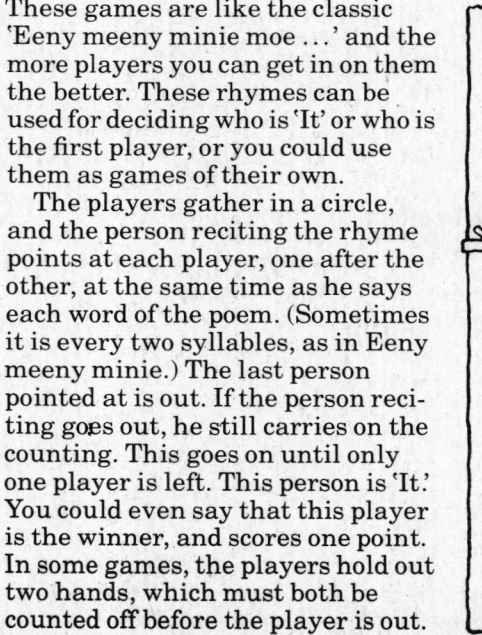

EENY, MEENY, MINIE....

Sometimes the person saying the rhyme has to slap the finger of the person he points to last, as he says the last word. If he succeeds, the person hit has to become the reciter.

The combinations seem unlimited, and so do the number of rhymes and rhyming games, but here are seven of the best:

One Potato
Players put forward both fists. These are the potatoes. If you are doing the counting out, tap each player's two potatoes, one at a time with one of your own potatoes, as you say each *number* in the rhyme. Count your own two fists as well. On the last word of the rhyme ('more'), the potato touched must be taken away. This goes on until only one is left. Here is the rhyme:

One potato, two potatoes,
Three potatoes, four;
Five potatoes, six potatoes,
Seven potatoes, *more*.

1
2

Letter Out
This version of the counting-out game tends to go on for quite a while because there is less chance of getting caught. The person counting recites the alphabet, pointing to one player after the other as he recites each letter. If the person counting happens to be pointing at you when he says the first letter of your first name (J for John, etc.), then you are out.

A
EH?

Engine, Engine

Engine, engine, number nine,
Rollin' down Chicago line;
If that train should jump the track,
Do you want your money back?

The player pointed to on the word 'back' answers either yes or no, and the person counting out recites this next verse, pointing at players as before.

Y. E. S. spells yes (or N. O. spells no)
So out you must *go!*

The player pointed to on the word 'go' is out.

These next four rhymes are counted out in the usual way; point at one player after another as you say each section of the rhyme. The lines are marked off so you can see how to do it, except for this first one, which counts out on each word.

My Mother

My mother and your mother live
across the way,
One fifty-five North Broadway.
Every night they have a fight
And this is what they say:
Acka backa, soda cracka,
Acka backa boo.
If your daddy chews tobacco,
Out go Y. O. U. !!

Dickery Dickery

Dickery / dickery / dare,/
The pig / flew up / in the air;/
The man / in brown/
Soon brought / him down,/
Dickery / dickery / dare./

Ibbity Bibbity

Ibbity / bibbity / sibbity / Sam,/
Ibbity / bibbity / steamboat./
Up the river, / down the river,/
Out / goes / *you!* /

Intry Mintry

Intry / mintry / peppery / corn,/
Apple / seed and / apple / thorn./
Wire, / briar, / limber lock,/
Three / geese / to make / a flock./
One / flew east / and one / flew west,/
One / flew over / the cuckoo's / nest./

44
BREAKING YOUR THUMB, SNAPPING YOUR NOSE

Yeow! Your friends will grimace with sympathy as they watch you voluntarily tear your thumb off – and yet, you don't even seem to notice! As a matter of fact, when they open their eyes again and look closely, your thumb is still there, unharmed and wiggling happily!

'How can this be?' your awe-struck friends will gasp. Startle them some more by breaking your thumb again, and then, just to keep them on the edge, reach up and crack the bone in your nose. Snap! Crackle! Pop! Before they start looking for a phone to call an ambulance you'd better show them that you are, in fact, undamaged. You have merely performed a couple of simple, and impressive, finger tricks.

For the first one, you need only two hands. Hold the left hand in

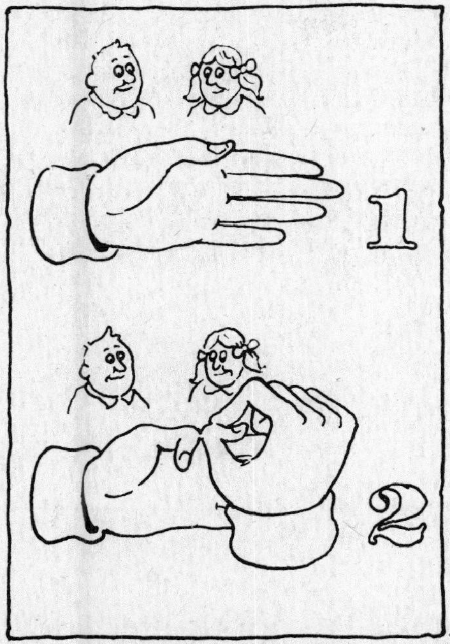
1
2

front of you, as if you were reading your palm, with the fingers pointing to the right, and the palm toward you. Tell your friends that you are going to break your thumb off, and if anyone has a queasy stomach he should jump out of the vehicle at the first opportunity. Your right hand then reaches over and appears to grasp the joint of the left thumb between right index and thumb.

In reality, as your right hand hides your left from view for a moment, you bend the left thumb down at the joint as shown in the picture. It appears as if you're holding the left thumb between your right thumb and index finger. Wiggle the 'thumb' for a second, then slowly move your right hand to the right. To the audience, who sees only the back of the left hand, it

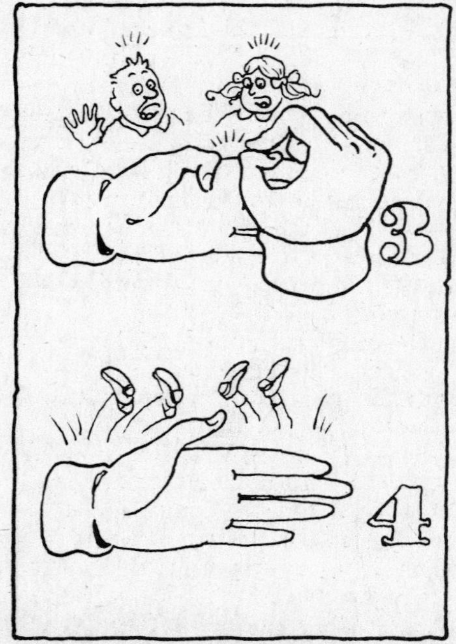
3
4

appears you are pulling your left thumb right off!

Before they get a chance to recover, spring the nose-cracking stunt on them. Hold your nose with both hands as shown in the picture, and face your friends. In this position, your thumbs should be in front of your mouth and hidden by your hands. Move your nose from side to side with your hands, and at the same time click your thumbnails against your teeth. To your friends it will look and sound as if you are tearing your nose right off!

POP

PROFESSOR ZTINCK! YOU'RE JUST IN TIME TO HELP US IN OUR SEARCH FOR THE MIND!
PSYCHO-LOGY
X-RAY

MIND GAMES

For eggheads

Caution! We are now entering the mysterious realm of the mind! In this cave of echoes, you must be ever on the lookout for wandering psychosis, hungry paranoia, and lurking nightmares and frightmares. Heaven only knows how we found it in the first place – psychologists (the folks who study the mind) and thinkers down through the ages have typically disagreed on the position, function and meaning of the mind, and even its very existence. It hides out somewhere in the region of our brain, sometimes letting us catch a few vague glimpses of its workings, but more often than not keeping us totally in the dark. Or maybe we keep *it* in the dark – who knows? If the mind does, it's not telling.

The study of the mind is filled with burning questions, of which 'Why?' is perhaps the most burning. 'Why me?' is the next most burning. 'How high is the sky?' has also been heard echoing through the halls of learning, along with 'Is there really a Santa Claus?' I'll say one thing for these psychologists, they're a curious bunch ....

The only thing that all the experts seem able to agree on is that the mind can be a lot of fun when it puts its mind to it. Mind you, it can also be a downright nuisance; cranky, selfish, forgetful, and ... uh ... I forget what else ...

What it really needs, when it gets like this, is a spot of mental gymnastics to get the juices flowing. A stiff shot of sanity sanitation never hurts, either. If this sounds like your prescription, try out some of the hard and soft-boiled mindgames in this chapter. You will soon have the pesky critter jumping through mental hoops and eating out of your hand. These games help to develop your powers of observation and deduction, sharpen your mental reflexes, put muscle on your neocortex, and generally improve your outlook on life. Try them! Your mind will thank you.

45
EYE SPY
two or more players

I spy with my little eye something that is ... blue!

This game must be the goldenest oldie in the book, but if you don't already know it, it's never too late to learn.

One player is chosen to start. If it's you, look around the inside (and *only* the inside) of your means of transportation and secretly choose an object or patch of color. It could be anything from a thin pink stripe on a scarf to the color of the seat, or someone's eyes. Say the rhyme above ('I spy ...') and let the others know the color. The other players can only make guesses about which object they think you spy, and you must answer their guesses with only 'yes' or 'no.' The player who first guesses the correct object wins that round and scores one point. For the next round the winner becomes the spy who chooses an object that everyone else must guess ....

You say aloud 'I spy with my little eye something that is pink!' Don't give it away by looking at what you spy. The other players then ask questions like 'Is it Dad's nose?' 'Is it the cap on the thermos?' 'Is it my lucky rabbit's foot?' until someone guesses correctly. That player 'spies' for the next round.

There is another way to play this game, and that is to give the first letter of the object's name as a clue instead of its color. In this case you say, 'I spy with my little eye something that starts with ... x?!'

46
TABOO
two or more players

You probably already know about certain words that are considered 'taboo' in some places. Some words are fine for general use on the playground or among friends, but you would never shout them out in the classroom or church!

This game utilizes the same principles. There are several ways to play it, but the basic idea is that you decide on a letter of the alphabet which will be taboo in conversation, and from then on, anyone caught using it will be dealt with severely.

1 In the first version of this game, the first player decides on the taboo letter, and then asks questions of the other players, trying to trick them into using the poison letter. The first player can use the letter as often as he likes, but the other players must either not speak words with that letter in them, or sub-

stitute a high-pitched squeak for the letter in the word. For instance, if the taboo letter is R, and the first player asks, 'What time is it?' a typical answer might go like this: 'Why, I believe it's fou(squeak) o'clock, si(squeak).' The first player to use the wrong letter loses that round and becomes 'It' for the next round. In other words, the loser must take over the first player's role.

2 Another way to play this game is to have everyone trying not to say the taboo letter. All players must carry on a conversation, but if any one of them uses the taboo letter, he must drop out. The last player left wins the round and scores one point.

47

HOW MANY BIRDS IN THE BUSH?

two or more players

You know what they say, 'A bird in the hand is worth two in the bush.' The problem with counting birds in bushes is that often you can't see the birds for the leaves, even though you know they're there because you can hear their chirping and chattering. Just try to count birds by listening to their songs and you'll see what I mean.

Try this: use coins instead of birds and your hands instead of a bush. One player puts an unknown number of coins (more than three) in his cupped hands and shakes them until they chatter like a flock of gossiping blackbirds. 'How many birds in the bush?' the player asks, and all the other players guess, one at a time. The ones who guess correctly win one point. If only one person guesses right, he gets to shake the 'birds' for the next round.

48
IN THE ATTIC

two or more players

All kinds of crazy things go on in the attic when the lights are out and the people asleep. You can find anything there, from an allomorph alliterating to a zygote zigzagging. What else can you think of that goes on in the attic?

Start the game off by saying something like, 'In the attic there's an acrobat admiring.' The next player starts his sentence off in the same way, but the last two words must begin with B. The third player ends his sentence with two words starting with C, and so on through the alphabet. If you had your English teacher with you, she might tell you that the last two words in each sentence must be a noun and a participle, but who brings his English teacher along on a trip, anyway?

Here's a sample game among three players just starting:

1 In the attic there's an aardvark applauding.
2 In the attic there's a bird beaming.
3 In the attic there's a cat calling.
1 In the attic there's a dog digging.
2 In the attic there's an elf eating.
3 In the attic there's a philosopher frying.

Oops! Hold it! That last one doesn't count because philosopher does *not* start with an F even though it starts with an F sound. Player three loses one point and player one starts off again at F. You also lose a point if you can't think of anything to say right away, and break the rhythm of the game. Keep the game moving very quickly all the way to zipping zebras, and then start back at A again. If you want, you can leave out the last three letters, X, Y, and Z, to make the game move even faster.

49
THAT'S GOOD!

two or more players

What kind of bad things can you think of to say about something you especially love, like bubble gum? You might say that it gets very sticky when wet, and that you wouldn't want to have it dropped down your shirt. After a while it loses its flavor and gets hard as a rock. It's very unpleasant to step on and is often found under desks.

To someone who didn't know what you were describing, it could be anything from concrete to cockroaches. One would never think that you were talking about something as scrumptious as bubble gum!

Think of something that everyone likes, or thinks of as nice or beautiful. Now try to describe this thing to your friends, without telling them what it is, and saying only

bad things about it. Try to make the thing you are describing sound as ugly and as awful as you can, but don't say anything untrue, or anything that will give it away. The other players try to guess what it is that you're talking about. The first player to guess correctly scores a point and gets a chance to describe something in the next round. If no one can guess what it is, tell them and then take another turn describing something in 'glowing' terms!

50 SIMON SAYS

two or more players

This old game has many versions and variations, and is so popular that people are named after it! When our great-grandparents played it as children, they probably said 'The Sultan says . . .' but the basic game has remained unchanged for years and years. In its simplest form, it's played like this:

One player is chosen to be Simon. This player must perform actions which the others copy. With each action, Simon says, 'Simon says do this!' or 'Simon says touch your head!' or whatever. If Simon says only 'Do this!' you must not do it. If he says one thing and does another, you must only do what Simon *says*. For example, Simon might say, 'Simon says touch your left elbow' and instead touch his *right* elbow. If *you* touch your right elbow, you are out of the game. If you copy Simon's action when he says only 'Do this,' you are out of the game. The last player left in the game scores one point and becomes Simon for the next round.

SIMON SAYS DO THIS!

51
GEOGRAPHY

two or more players

The first player says the name of a village, town, city, state, province, country, continent, river, lake, ocean, or planet that first springs into his or her mind. The second player must then say the name of a village, town, city, etc., which begins with the same letter that the first name *ended* with.

For instance, let's say that the first player says 'Saskatchewan.' The next player must then say the name of someplace geographic that starts with letter N. The game might go like this: Nicaragua ... Africa ... Allansville ... Europe ... Egypt ... Toronto ... Oxford ... and so on. Using a map will make the game go much faster.

If you can't think of anything that hasn't already been said, you are out of the game. The last person left wins the round and scores one point.

52
BACKSEAT HIDE AND SEEK

two or more players

You might think that there aren't a heck of a lot of places to hide in the backseat of a car, or even on a train or bus, but in this game, it's not your body that you hide from the other players, it's your imagination! It's a very versatile fellow, your imagination, and if it sets its mind to it, it could hide virtually anywhere, from under a stray molecule, to behind the last star of the outermost galaxy of the universe, or in even stranger places than that! At that rate, the other players might spend several eternities searching under every atom for it, so you'd better set some limits before you start looking for a hiding place. For instance you should let your imagination hide only in places that all the other players are familiar with, such as your home town, or cities or towns that you all have visited. If they can narrow it down and guess what room you are in, that's close enough to count (there are zillions of places your imagination could hide in the smallest closet!)

Here are some more limits: the players get only 25 questions to find out where you are, and you can answer their questions with only 'yes' or 'no.' If they can't guess where you are with 25 questions, you win the round and get another chance to hide. If someone guesses where you are, he gets a chance to hide next round.

All set? Okay, send your imagination winging out over the pavement, back along the road to town, and tuck it away in some dark corner, then let the guessing begin!

53

OPEN IT!

four or more players

This is an old guessing game like 'Button, Button.' The players divide into two teams, and sit on opposite sides of the seat. The players of one team go into a huddle and pass a coin or other small object from one hand to another. When they have secretly decided which hand the coin should remain in, they hold their closed fists in front of them and face their opponents, who have to guess which fist holds the coin.

If Team Two thinks a hand is empty, one of them gives the order 'Take it away' and that hand is put behind its owner's back. If Team Two thinks it knows which of the hands holds the coin, a player gives the order 'Open it' to the hand, which must immediately do so.

If the second team orders an empty hand to open, or if it orders the coin-holding hand taken away, it loses that round, and Team One scores one point and gets another turn.

If they find the coin, they score one point and it is their turn to shuffle the coin from fist to fist, and hide it from the other team.

OPEN IT!

54

FRANTIC ANTICS

one or more players

This old drinking game, otherwise known as Cardinal Puff, is sure to give you a severe case of athlete's brain, if nothing else. You don't have to be drinking root beer to derive the full benefits of the game, but it helps. Actually, you don't have to be drinking anything at all, you can carry out all the actions with an empty cup full of Symbolic Ambrosia, favorite drink of Cardinals.

If you can go through the whole string of actions about to be described without flinching or making one mistake, you become a full-fledged, card-carrying member of the Secret Order of Cardinals, and henceforth from this date may use its initials after your signature. If, however, you make one slip, you must begin at the beginning again.

Cardinal Puff is the Great Grand Mufti of the order, and whenever any member is enjoying Symbolic Ambrosia with friends, they must all drink the following Secret Toast to Cardinal Puff:

'This is to Cardinal Puff for the first time tonight!' says the toastmaster (or the first person to think of it) in a loud theatrical voice. Then, while everyone sits with their empty cupfuls of Ambrosia sitting on the table in front of them, or held between their knees, the toastmaster goes through the following rhythmic actions:

1 Tap the right side of the nose once with the right index finger.
2 Tap the left side of the nose once with the left index finger.
3 Tap the right side of the glass' rim once with the right index finger.

4 Tap the left side of the rim once with the left index finger.
5 Tap the table (or your knee) on the right side of the glass once with your right index finger.
6 Tap the table on the left side of the glass once with the left index.

The toastmaster then picks up the glass between thumb and index finger, takes one sip, says 'This was to Cardinal Puff for the first time tonight,' taps the glass once on the table, then sets it down.

Whew! Everyone else must then go through the same set of actions. Watch carefully! If someone makes a mistake, he must wait till the next round before trying again. If the toastmaster makes a mistake, the person on his right becomes the toastmaster. When everyone has finished, the toastmaster starts the next round.

'This is to Cardinal Puff for the second time tonight!' you say (assuming you are the toastmaster). Now repeat the same sequence of actions that you went through in the first round, except this time you tap everything *twice* with your index fingers. For instance, you tap the right side of your glass twice with your right index, then the left side twice with your left index, and so on, right through the whole series. When you get to the last part, pick up your glass with the thumb and *two* fingers, take *two* sips and say 'This was to Cardinal Puff for the second time tonight,' then tap your glass twice on the table and set it down.

It's starting to get complicated. Well, you've only just begun! In the next round, you must do everything

three times, and in the round after that, *four* times.

If you think all this is next to impossible, just try to get through the fifth and final round without making a slip-up! 'This is to Cardinal Puff for the fifth and final time tonight!' you say, and instead of using your index fingers to tap everything five times, you must use all five fingers held together. Go through the actions as before, tapping everything five times, pick up your glass with all five fingers, drain it, and say 'This was to Cardinal Puff for the fifth and final time tonight!' Then tap your glass five times on the table and turn it upside down.

If you managed to get through all that, congratulations! You *deserve* to be a member of the Secret Order of Cardinals.

55
BACKWORDS
any number of players

Hang on everyone! It's time to put your mind in reverse! All the sentences shown below must be recited backward after hearing them read once forward. The first player reads one of the sentences aloud and then points at one of the other players. That player must recite the phrase from memory, but backward! For example, 'Cat's in the cupboard' would come out as 'Cupboard the in cat's.' If the player who is doing the reverse reciting makes a slip of the lip, the first player points at another player. The first person to get it right wins the round and scores one point. The winner reads a sentence aloud for the next round. If no one gets it right, the first player reads another sentence.

It's best to start off with one of the first five shorter sentences until everyone's motor warms up a bit.

1 I went to the movies tomorrow.
2 The flowers were brightly singing.
3 I'm a knock-kneed chicken.
4 I saw Esau sitting on the seesaw.
5 Everyone is in the best seat.
6 Have you seen Pa smoking a cigar, riding on a bicycle, ha ha ha.
7 The train I came in has not arrived.
8 Acka backa soda cracka, acka backa boo.
9 Some men are wise and some are otherwise.
10 Mary had a little lamb, a little toast, a little jam.
11 Things are more like they are now than they ever were before.
12 I can't figure out where I leave off and everyone else begins.
13 Would you rather be a bigger fool than you look, or look a bigger fool than you are?

56
VERSE-ATILITY
any number of players

This game is just the thing to sweep the cobwebs out of the corners of your cerebrum.

Each player chooses a different one of the four-line verses below and memorizes it.

Jack and Jill
Went up the hill
To fetch a pail
Of water.

I eat my peas with honey,
I've done it all my life.
It makes the peas taste funny,
But it keeps them on the knife.

Nothing to do but work!
Nothing! Alas! Alack!
Nowhere to go but out!
Nowhere to come but back!

As I was sitting in my chair
I *knew* the bottom wasn't there.
Nor legs nor back, but *I just sat,*
Ignoring little things like that.

Humpty Dumpty
Sat on the wall
Humpty Dumpty
Had a great fall.

As I was going up the stair,
I met a man who wasn't there.
He wasn't there again today!
I wish that man would go away!

I put my hat upon my head
And walked into the strand,
And there I met another man
Whose hat was in his hand.

I've never had a piece of toast
Particularly long and wide,
But fell upon the sanded floor
And always on the buttered side.

Some of the verses are harder to memorize than others, so younger players should choose an easy one. Save the last one till the very end. Once everyone has thoroughly memorized a chosen verse, take turns trying the following antics with it:

1 In your head, count the number of words in your verse. Have someone else check it with the one in the book.

2 Now say your verse out loud, numbering each word. For example, if your verse is Jack and Jill, start reciting like this: 1 Jack 2 and 3 Jill 4 went 5 up …

3 Now say your poem backward. (Water of pail a fetch to …)

4 Now, as if all that weren't enough already, try saying your verse out loud, clapping on each second word and snapping you fingers on each third word. For example, 'Jack and(clap) Jill(snap) went up(clap) the(snap) hill …'

5 By now, everyone's mind should be going soft around the edges. To finish the job, have all players recite their verses at once.

For each of the above antics that you performed correctly, give yourself one point. Everyone is bound to make plenty of mistakes on the first round, so give it a couple more tries with the same verse, then try another one.

57

MEMORY?

two or more players

This game will test your powers of memory like Kim's Game, but it's much simpler and faster moving, and especially fun with a large group of people.

Make a list of ten simple words, numbering them from one to ten. Read the list, including numbers, out loud to the group. Now say any number from one to ten. The first player to tell you what word on the list corresponds to that number scores one point.

After a few rounds of this, you might want to try something different. Make a new list and read it out loud, but this time, read it in any order but the right order. The first player who can recite the list in the proper order scores a big five (count 'em!) points and wins the game!

58

CONVERSATION

three or more players

Anyone who listened in on this conversation without realizing that it was a game would think that the people talking were pretty strange, because the words just don't seem to make sense! For one thing, none of the sentences are more than two words long, and, for another thing, it sounds more like some kind of weird poem than an actual conversation.

Actually, if our eager eavesdropper listened more carefully he might notice a strange pattern in this nonsense conversation. For instance, the first word of each two word sentence starts with the same sound as the second word of the last sentence. He might also notice that each sentence made sense by itself, even though the whole string of sentences sounded like so much gibberish. At this point he might catch on and realize that you were not actually carrying on a conversation, but playing a game!

1 The first player starts by saying a two word sentence made up of one noun and one verb, in that order (e.g. Rain falls).

2 The second player also says a two word sentence, but the first word (the noun) must start with the *same two letters* as the second word (the verb) of the last player's sentence.

3 A sample 'conversation' might go like this:

Time flies.
Fleas jump.
Jugglers toss.
Toast burns.
Birds fly.

Oops! That last sentence just won't do! That player is out! The last player left in the game scores two points and wins the round.

59
IF TOESES WERE ROSES...

two or more players

There is a great old movie called *Singing in the Rain*. In one classic scene, several actors chant 'Moses supposes his toeses are roses, but Moses supposes erroneously!' while frantically tapdancing. Luckily, you don't have to know how to tapdance to play this great game.

1 All you really need to know is how to make up a certain kind of sentence. The same form of sentence must be used throughout the game. 'If *(something)* were *(something)* you could *(do something to)* them.' For instance, the first player might say 'If *toeses* were *roses* you could *water* them.'

2 The second player says the same type of sentence, but fills in the blanks with different words. But not just any words will do. The first blank must be filled with a word that would go with the last blank-filler in the previous player's sentence. Meaning, the second player has to think of something else you could also *water* (using the last example), then use that word to fill the first blank in his own sentence.

3 A sample game would start out like this:

If *petunias* were *horses* you could *ride* them.

(The next player has to think of something else you can ride.)

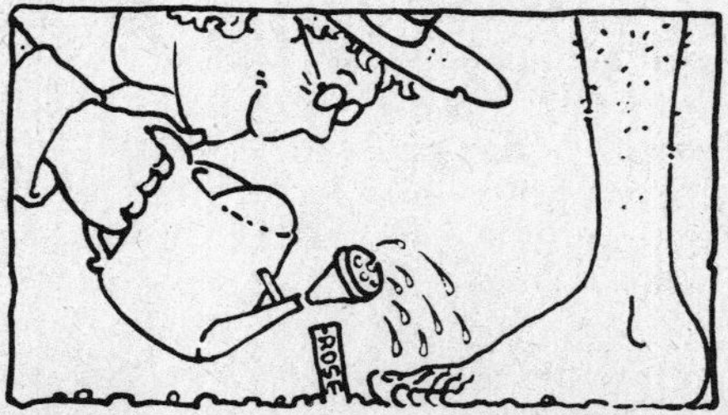
ROSE

If *bicycles* were *baseballs* you could *catch* them.

If *measles* were *socks* you could *wear* them.

If *hats* were *cats* you could *pet* them.

If *dogs* were *candies* you could *eat* them.

And so on ...

Are you beginning to get the idea? The first noun in every sentence goes with the verb in the last sentence.

4 If you can't think of any words to fill the blanks, you are out of the game. You are also out if your first noun does not fit the last player's verb, or if both of your nouns fit your own verb, for example, 'If peanuts were pies you could eat them.'

5 The last player left in the game is the winner, and scores two points.

60
JOTTO

two players or two teams

If you are planning on playing Jotto, you'd better get out your thinking caps and lucky charms, because you'll need all the help you can get. The object of the game is to guess the five letter word that the other player is thinking of, while that player is at the same time trying to guess your own secret word. If you like, you can use a paper and pencil to help you figure out the word.

1 Each player thinks of, or writes down a five letter word whose letters are all different.

2 Players take turns guessing which five letter word they think the other player has written down.

3 You can answer each other's guesses only by saying *how many letters* in the word guessed are also in your secret word. Don't say which letters they are, just how many. For instance, if your word is *words,* and the other player guesses *guest,* you tell him that one letter in *guest* is also in your word.

4 On a piece of paper write down all the words you guess, with the number of letters right. At the bottom of the sheet write out the alphabet. If you guess a word that has *no* letters common to the other player's word, cross out the letters that are in the word you guessed from the alphabet ... These clues will help you in your word detective work. By looking carefully at the words you've guessed, you should be able to eliminate the letters that are not in the other player's secret word. For example, let's say you guess *jerks,* and the other player tells you that there is one letter in *jerks* that is also in his secret word. Then you guess *jerky* and the other player tells you that there are no letters in *jerky* that are in his secret word. Well, you can deduce that the J, E, R, and K in jerks are not in the secret word because they are also in *jerky,* which has no letters in the secret word. Therefore, the letter in *jerks* that is in the other player's secret word must be the S.

5 The first player to guess the other player's word is the winner!

WORD

61

TWENTY QUESTIONS

two or more players

The object of this game is to guess the secret object chosen by the first player by asking 20 questions that the first player must answer with only 'yes' or 'no.'

1 The first player thinks of an object or thing, and announces to the other players whether the thing he is thinking of is animal, mineral, or vegetable. It must be something that fits one of the three categories, but it can't fit in more than one category. For example, you can't think of anything like a house, which is made up of vegetable (wood) and mineral (metal) substances. Things made from rubber or plastic, because they are usually made from petrochemicals, should be classified as vegetable for the sake of the game, even though they are actually on a fine dividing line between vegetable and mineral. Other petroleum-based substances are oil and gasoline, most paint, paraffin wax, solvents, and thousands of other things.

2 After the first player has chosen a word, the other players then take turns asking questions that can be answered by 'yes' or 'no.' In the beginning, it's best to ask very general questions and narrow it down later.

3 The first player keeps track of the number of questions asked, and if no one has correctly guessed the secret object by the twentieth question, the first player wins the game and scores one point, and thinks of another object for the next round. The player who correctly guesses the object wins one point and takes the place of the first player.

DON'T TELL ME...
IT'S..UH..MINERAL!
NOPE.
SPHINX

62
GHOSTS
two to five players

Who's afraid of ghosts? Not me! Especially since the Ghosts I'm talking about is the name of this great game:

1 The first player thinks of any word, then says the first letter of that word out loud.

2 The second player must then think of a word beginning with that letter, and name the word's *second* letter out loud.

3 The next player then thinks of any word beginning with the first two letters that have already been named, and says this new word's *third* letter.

4 The game goes on like this. The object of the game is to avoid being the first person to finish spelling out any complete word of five letters or more.

5 If you finish any word five letters long or longer, you lose that round and score the letter G. The next time you lose a round, you score the letter H, and the next round you lose you score an O, then an S, then a T,

G
H
O

which, when put together spell GHOST. Anyone who loses five rounds and becomes a Ghost drops out of the game. The last person left is the winner!

6 A sample game among three players might go like this:
1 'G' (Thinking of the word *ghost*)
2 'I' (Thinking of the word *give*)
3 'A' (Thinking of the word *giant*)
1 'N' (Also thinking of *giant*)
2 'T' (Finishes the word)
Player two loses the round and scores a G.

7 If you have a reason to believe that a player was bluffing and did not have a real word in mind when saying his letter, you may challenge him. If he can't tell you what word he had in mind, he loses the round. If, however, he really *did* have a word in mind and you challenge him, you lose the round.

63
BOUTES-RIMES

two or more players

One version of this game goes all the way back to 1648, when it was invented in France by the poet Dulos. It became fashionable as a parlor game among the folks rich enough to have parlors, and it spread like hot butter to parlors all over Europe.

Having been invented by a poet, it is, naturally enough, a very poetic game. It goes like this:

1 The first player says four words out loud. The first and third words must rhyme with each other, and the second and fourth words must rhyme with each other. For example, the four words might be 'try, can, pry, and pan.'

2 The other players will each need a pencil and paper. They try to write

a four-line poem using each of the four words as the last word of each line.

3 The first person to finish the poem is the winner, but only if the poem makes some kind of sense. If it doesn't, then the second player to finish is the winner, if *his* poem makes sense. Let everyone finish his poem, and then read them all out loud.

Here is an example, using the four words above:

Oh, everything did I try
To get my lunch from its can.
For I've nothing with which to pry,
Just a rusty old dust pan . . .

Well, it's a bit rough around the edges, but it fills the bill.

64

HEAD TO FEET

any number of players

This is another mindgame that requires pencil and paper.

1 The only other things you'll need are two short words, both with the same number of letters. Everyone writes down the two agreed-upon words on his sheet of paper.

2 The object of the game is to magically transform the first word into the second word, one step at a time. With each step, you can only change one letter, and each new step must also be a real word.

3 Whoever changes the first word into the second word in the fewest steps is the winner. In the event of a tie, both players win.

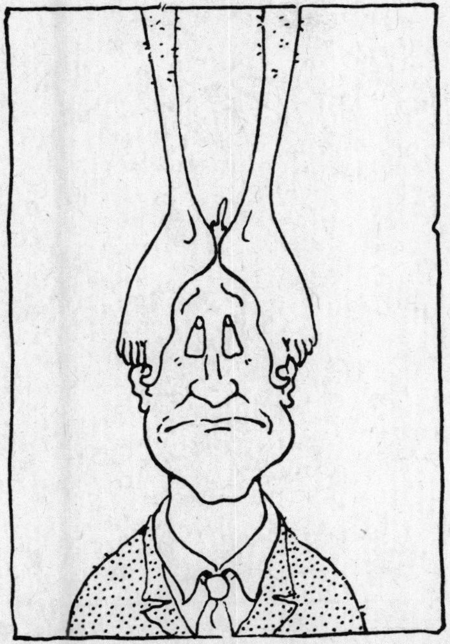

4 For example, this is how to change the word *head* into *feet* in the fewest possible steps:

head
heed
feed
feet

In each step, only one letter has been changed, and each is a real word.

Other combinations you might try are: *dog* to *cat, boy* to *man, word* to *rock, flour* to *bread,* and *wind* to *calm.*

65
ALPHABETICAL

any number of players

The first player starts out by saying 'I have an ____________.' The blank must be filled with a word that starts with the letter A. The second player repeats the first player's sentence, adding on a phrase that contains a noun beginning with the letter B. The third player repeats the second player's sentence and adds on a phrase containing a noun or verb that begins with C.

For example, a game among three players might start like this:

1 I have an *aardvark.*

2 I have an aardvark with a *balloon.*

3 I have an aardvark with a balloon in a *can.*

1 I have an aardvark with a balloon in a can for my *Dad.*

PICKLED
BALLOON
IN
AARDVARK
SAUCE

2 I have an aardvark with a balloon in a can for my Dad to *eat.*

The game goes on like this until you have gone right through the alphabet. If you want to make the game a little simpler, leave off the last three letters of the alphabet, X, Y, and Z.

This is the kind of game where a dictionary would come in handy. Also a very good memory, as it becomes harder and harder to remember the whole sentence. If you make a mistake you are out of the game. The last player left wins that round and scores one point.

EUREKA! I'VE DISCOVERED A WHOLE NEW BRANCH OF MATHEMATICS!

COUNT ME IN!

Numbers. Where did they come from? Where are they going to? Who cares anyway? These are the questions which have puzzled mathematicians for centuries.

Like almost everything else, the discovery of numbers is blamed on our lovable but clumsy ancestor, the caveperson, who found them very handy for keeping track of how many fingers and toes were on each hand and foot. Not to be outdone, the ancient Egyptians had to think up their own number system, then the Babylonians and Greeks and Romans decided to join in, and the whole thing turned into a free-for-all. If only they had known about modern day arithmetic tests they might not have bothered.

Most of the ancient number systems and symbols were clumsy and difficult to use, so they gradually died out. One of the more sensible systems did manage to survive, though – the Arabic numerals which are the numbers that most of the world uses today. You'll recognize them when you see them; they look like this: 1,2,3,4,5,6,7,8,9, and 0. These are called the 'digits,' and all the other numbers are made from them. Please note that there are the same number of digits as there are fingers on two normal hands, which is why fingers are also called digits. Don't even *think* about what would happen if we all had 7 1/2 fingers! People discovered all kinds of amazing things about numbers, so they gave them a science all their own, and called it 'mathematics.' At this point the mathematicians went ape and began to realize that there were many different and stranger kinds of numbers than the ones you use to count apples and oranges.

'Look here!' these mathematical types said, 'Start with two ordinary hands, and you've got your *digits.* Stir well, salt to taste, and – presto! – you have all the *counting numbers* up to infinity. Take them all away and you have the *negative numbers* down to infinity. Throw these in with the counting numbers, and you have the *integers.* Look in between each integer and you'll see an infinity of *fractions.* Add these to the integers and you have what are called the *rational numbers.* These, together with the notorious *irrational numbers,* form what we know as the *real number system,* with which we can add, subtract, multiply, divide, count, describe, and measure.

ABRACA – ALGEBRA

Four numbertricks

'Now we are into the weird realm of number theory. Mutter a few magic axioms, and you get the *prime numbers, composite numbers, complex numbers,* and a lot of other strange things. Wave an equation or two over the whole batch and in a twinkling of an eye, *transinfinite numbers* appear, along with their funny little friends, the *infinite* and *infinitesimal numbers*. Next thing you know, you've got more square roots, geometry, algebra, congruences, set theory and reciprocals than you can shake a fistful of digits at!'

There's an old saying that goes 'You only have to show that something is impossible, and some mathematician will go and do it!' It's very true. They are constantly discovering things that don't exist. They are always looking for the answers to questions like 'How many rabbits in an empty hat?' Occasionally they stumble upon a new galaxy or star or planet or element or theory of the universe in their equations, and when the other scientists go looking for them, sure enough, there they are!

But aside from playing a large part in almost everything, from the pyramids and space flight to money and time, numbers can also be a lot of fun, as this chapter sets out to prove, and don't you let any arithmetic teacher tell you different!

Here is some helpful magic that you can perform with ordinary everyday numbers. Besides the aforementioned numbers, all you need is an understanding of basic arithmetic and a willing audience.

Age Calculator

This one is easy. Tell a friend that you are going to guess his or her age.

1 Ask this friend to multiply his age by three, without letting you see the calculations.

2 Then ask him to add six to the result, then divide the sum by three.

3 Have him tell you the final answer.

4 Subtract two from that number, and the result is the person's age!

Magic Multiplication

There is one heck of a funny number going around the neighborhood, namely number 12345679. If you see this number, try the following antics with it:

1 Write the number 12345679 (note that there is no 8) on a piece of paper.

2 Ask a friend to choose one of the digits of the number 12345679.

3 Multiply the chosen digit by nine.

4 Multiply the number 12345679 by the result, and lo! – you have a string of numbers, all the same as the original digit chosen!

5 For example, if your friend chose the number 7, your calculations would look like this:

```
  7      12345679
 x9           x63
 —      ——————————
 63      37037037
        740740740
        ——————————
        777777777
```

Counting Up to a Billion

How long do you think it would take to count up to a billion? A day? A week? A *year?* What would you say if I told you that if you counted at the rate of 200 numbers per minute for twenty-four hours every day without stopping to eat, sleep or catch your breath, it would take you hundreds of lifetimes to count a billion? Impossible, you say?

Well, get a sheet of paper and a pencil. To start, let's say that a billion is a million million (in some countries, it's a thousand million). If you count 200 numbers a minute, how many will you count in an hour, day, or year? Your formula for figuring all this out looks like this:

(number counted per minute) x (60 minutes in an hour) = (number counted per hour) x (24 hours in a day) = (number counted per day) x (365 days in a year) = (number counted in a year).

What did your calculations come out to? For all that effort, counting night and day without rest for a year, you have only counted just over one hundred and five million. When you divide this number into a billion it will give you the number of years it will take to count to a billion at this rate. The answer will surprise you!

Dates, Events and Ages

This trick will make your friends wonder if you don't have some sort of magical properties after all.

Ask your traveling companion to write down the following things, keeping them hidden from you:

1 The year of his birth.

2 The year that any memorable event happened in his life.

3 The number of people in the car.

4 How old he will be on December 31 of this year.

5 The number of years ago that the memorable event took place.

6 Now ask your friend to add up all the numbers.

Close your eyes and mumble some mystic equations. Write a number on a piece of paper and hand it to your friend. When he opens it, the total for all his numbers is written on it!

'How did I do it?' you ask, and rightly so. Well, the answer to that is really very simple. The year of your birth plus your age as of December 31 of this year always equals the present year. The same goes for the year that an event happened, plus how many years ago it was. For example, if you were born on June 23, 1967, you will be 13 on December 31, 1980 (which, for the sake of argument, we will say is the present year). Add 13 to 1967 and you get 1980, the 'present' year. If an important event happened in 1974, and you add 6 to that, which is the number of years ago 1974 is, you get 1980 again.

So far, you know that your friend's total is going to be twice the present year, plus the number of people in the car. Here is the whole thing in formula:

2 x (present year) + (number of people in car) = ?

The question mark in the formula above is your answer, which you will have to figure out. For a really spectacular effect, you could write the answer on a slip of paper beforehand, hand it to your friend to hold, and then have him work out the calculation the long way round. After he is done, let him open out the paper to see that you have already beaten him to the answer, before he even started!

67
UP TO A HUNDRED

two or more players

This is an adding-up game, and is great fun for the mathematically inclined. You can play it by doing the sums on paper or, if you're feeling especially supple-minded today, you can work them out in your head.

1 The first player writes down any number from one to nine. The next player adds any other number from one to nine and writes the sum underneath the first number.

2 The players continue like this, each one adding any number from one to nine. The object of the game is to be the person whose final addition brings the sum to *exactly* 100. This requires quite a lot of strategy and foresight. You are trying to be the first person to bring it up to 100, and you are also trying to keep all the other players from finishing before you do.

Once you've tried this game on for size and are familiar with it, try playing it in reverse – subtract one digit numbers from 100, and the first player to reach zero is the winner. Or, once you've limbered up your brain cells a bit, you could try with numbers between one and 20 to reach a final sum of 517 or 739 or whatever. Try doing *these* sums in your head!

68
JUMBLE YOUR NUMBERS

two or more players

If you have a few friends traveling with you who are all near the same age, then Jumble Your Numbers is a great game to enliven your living. If you are slow in the beginning, don't worry. After a few rounds, everyone's brain will be as sharp as a whip.

1 The first player starts off by giving a mathematical calculation as fast as he can. This is a kind of race. The idea is to try to calculate it faster than anyone else can follow.

2 If at the end of the calculation no one can give the first player the right answer, the first player scores one point, and tries out another calculation on the gang.

3 The first person to give the right answer out loud scores *two* points, and takes over from the first player.

4 At any time you can challenge the player who is saying the calculation. If it turns out that this player has *no idea* what the right answer is, he *loses* two points, and the player who challenges wins two points, and takes over.

5 A calculation can have no more than twelve steps. If it does, it is disqualified, and the player who said it must give another one.

6 A sample calculation might go like this:

'Take the number 68, divide by two, divide by two, subtract one, divide by four, add one, multiply by five, add one, divide by two, and what do you get?

The answer is 13.

That calculation has nine steps.

7 At no time can any player use paper to figure out a calculation!

69
FINGER COMPUTER

In school you might be learning one of these new finger-arithmetic systems that are taking the world of mathematics by storm. Ever since that old caveperson started giving number-names to fingers and toes, people have been using them to do more complicated math. Well, fingers anyway, the invention of shoes having made toes useless as calculators.

The finger computer described here is a very ancient system. It was used in Europe during the Middle Ages, but probably goes back a lot further than that. People in those days usually knew the multiplication tables up to 5 x 5, and found that this system could come in very 'handy' for figuring out more complicated calculations.

For multiplying numbers between 6 and 10, they used the following method:

1 Starting with the little fingers, the fingers on each hand are given the values 6 through 10, as shown in the first picture.

2 To multiply, for example, 6 x 8, touch the '6' finger on one hand (it doesn't matter which one you use) to the '8' finger on the other hand.

3 Count the lower fingers, *including the two touching fingers,* and multiply the total by 10.

4 Multiply the number of upper fingers on the left hand by the number of upper fingers on the right hand.

5 Add the two results, 40 and 8, together to get your final answer, 48. Always remember that any number times zero equals zero, so if there are no upper numbers on one hand (as when multiplying any number by 10) the result is zero, plus the number of lower fingers times ten.

There is a complicated way to use this finger computer to multiply numbers higher than 10, but if you can multiply the digits by themselves and by 10, you can usually break down larger calculations into smaller bits and figure them out, or do the calculation on paper.

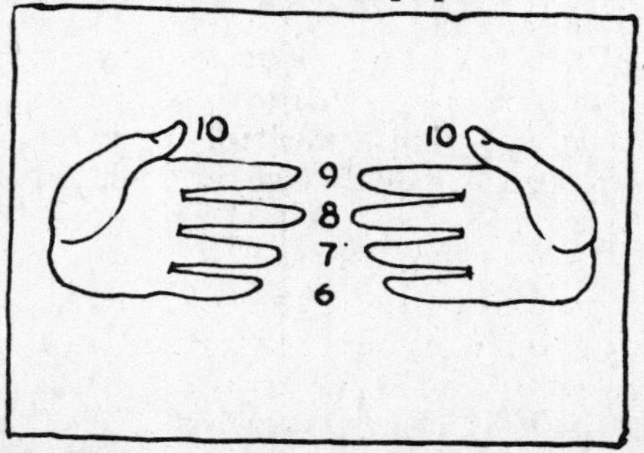
10
10
9
8
7
6

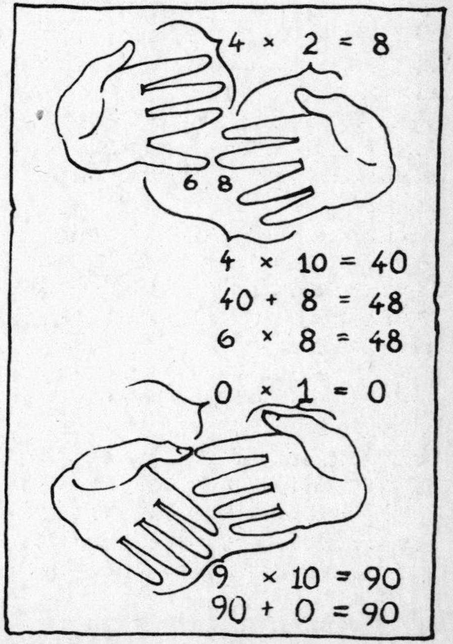
4 × 2 = 8
6 8
4 × 10 = 40
40 + 8 = 48
6 × 8 = 48
0 × 1 = 0
9 × 10 = 90
90 + 0 = 90

CHECK!
RPM
C.

BORED GAMES

Board stiff? Try these!

People in ancient times didn't have much time to be bored; they were too busy surviving. If a cave dweller ever thought of anything new, he quickly forgot it when he heard the roar of a cave bear, or the roar of his stomach. The only new thoughts he had time for were the ones that would help catch the next meal, or help keep him from being someone else's next meal.

So ancient people developed strategic board games, not out of boredom, but as a kind of magic ritual to try to bring about good hunting, or to keep hungry beasts away from the herds. Even today people try to act out the ageless problems of life on the game board, and who can blame them? Sometimes life itself seems like a game, with everyone planning the next move, or rushing blindly from square to square, driven by Chance. In these games, Chance also plays a leading part, in the form of dice, otherwise known as the Devil's Bones.

People in every corner of the Earth play these games, amazing in their similarity. In fact, there are only a few types of games, from which all the other games have developed.

Before you start reading the rules for the games, there are a few things you should know.

1 The playing pieces are known as *counters*.

2 In many games, the players start their counters on the side of the board nearest them, which is known as *home*.

3 This diagram shows the four types of moves that are used in these games:

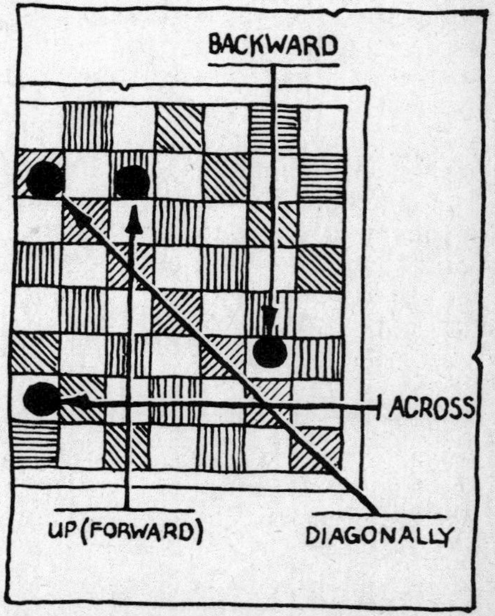
BACKWARD
ACROSS
UP (FORWARD)
DIAGONALLY

4 In checkers, you jump over a counter to take it off the board. In chess, you land on the same square. There are other ways to take or trap counters, and the following standard names are used to describe them:

Short Jump This is the one used in checkers, where you jump from the square or point right next to the opponent's counter, to the empty point or square right next to it on the other side.

Multiple Short Jump If, when you 'short jump' an opponent's counter, there is another one right next to your counter again, you may jump this one as well, as long as the square on the other side of it is empty. This is called the multiple short jump.

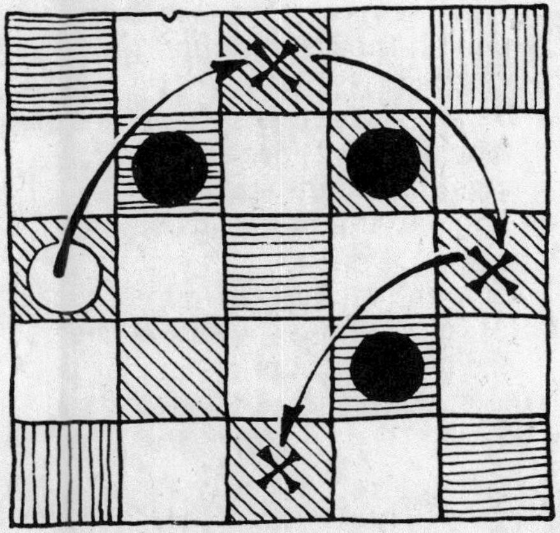

Trap In some games, when you have two counters, one on each side of an opponent's counter, and in line with it, you have 'trapped' it and can remove it from the board.

70
MAKING DICE AND COUNTERS

Dice have been around for a long time in many different shapes and sizes. Luckily for us, the most popular one is also the easiest one to make – the good old ivory cube. The oldest known cubic dice are over 4,000 years old, and look just like the dice we use today. Although ivory *is* the best thing to make them from, they can be and are made from plastic, wood, paper (see number 26), glass, and, easiest of all, sugar cubes. When you are marking your dice, always remember that opposite faces of the cube should be numbered so they add up to seven. That is, the one should go opposite the six, the two opposite the five, and three opposite the four.

Counters can be made from almost anything. Coins make good

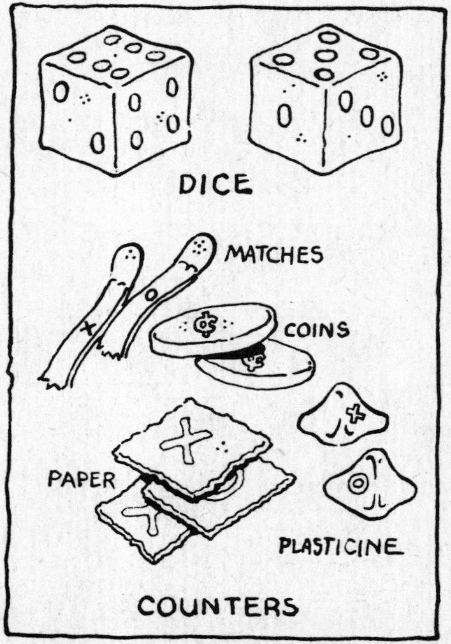
DICE
MATCHES
COINS
PAPER
PLASTICINE
COUNTERS

'men,' but they are too easy to spend. You could also try matches, squares of paper, or anything that can be marked in different colors, or with an x and an o, for different players. The very best thing of all is different colors of plasticine, which will stick to the board over rough terrain. If you find that your counters keep shifting and sliding every time you hang a left, try licking the bottom. The moisture will help hold them in place. Or, if worse comes to worst, you could stick little bits of chewing gum or tape on the bottom. If you have drawn your own game board on stiff paper, you could punch a hole in each square with a match, and then use matches or toothpicks as counters, and anchor them in the holes.

71
CHECKERS

two players

Checkers, also known as Dames or Draughts, has been around for a long time.

1 Each player has 12 counters, and the board is eight squares wide by eight squares long.

2 The game starts with the counters in the position shown in the picture.

3 Players take turns moving one counter at a time. They can move *forward* only, onto any black square that touches the one they are on. The white squares are not used.

4 Captures are made with the short jump and the multiple short jump, in the forward direction only. If you have the opportunity to capture an opponent's counter and don't take it, your opponent can remove your counter from the board. This is called 'huffing' a counter. After huffing your piece, he then takes his regular turn.

5 If one of your counters reaches the opposite side (your opponent's home base), it is 'crowned' a King. Crowning occurs when you put one counter on top of another counter of the same color and move them as one piece. Kings can move and capture forward *and* backward, on black squares only. Otherwise they move just like ordinary counters, and can capture like them too!

6 Kings can also be captured by ordinary pieces.

7 The object of the game is to take all your opponent's counters off the board, or block them so they can't move. The player who does this is the winner.

72

SNAKES AND LADDERS

two to six players

This is a great old game that has been with us in many different forms for many different years.

1 Each player starts with only one counter, placed on square one. The basic object of the game is to be the first player to get your counter 'home.'

2 Moves are determined by the roll of one die. Whatever number you roll on the top of the die is the number of squares you move your counter forward on the board. If you like, you don't even have to use counters, providing you can remember the number of the square you are on.

3 If you land on a square that has a ladder on it, climb that ladder to the top.

4 If you land on a square that has the *head* of a snake on it, you are swallowed by the snake, and must move down to the end of the snake's tail.

5 If you land on a square that has another counter on it, that counter must go back to square one.

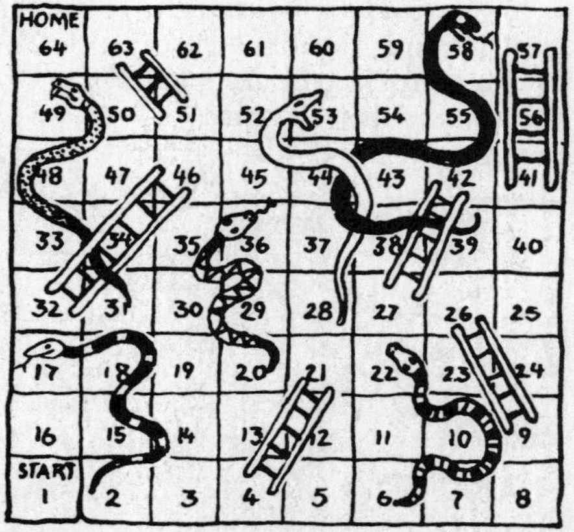
HOME
64 63 62 61 60 59 58 57
49 50 51 52 53 54 55 56
48 47 46 45 44 43 42 41
33 34 35 36 37 38 39 40
32 31 30 29 28 27 26 25
17 18 19 20 21 22 23 24
16 15 14 13 12 11 10 9
START
1 2 3 4 5 6 7 8

6 You must shake exactly the right number to get home. For example, if you are on the third square from home, and you shake a three, you win. But if you shake a five, you move forward three squares and back two, to make a total of five squares moved, so now you are on the second square from home.

7 The first person to land on the home square wins!

The board game shown here is just a small sample board. After you have tried the game out on it, move on to a larger and more complicated game board, which you draw yourself. All you need is a pencil and a sheet of paper, plus a generous supply of snakes, and of course, ladders!

73

H_2O

two, three or four players

H_2O, as you know, is the chemical term for water, also known as ice and steam. Water is found all over the planet, and in some of the strangest places. For example, you yourself are made up of 75% water! But when modern man wants water, where does he look first? The tap of course! And we all know that the water comes to the tap via a pipe. But how many of us really know what happens to the water traveling through those dark pipes? It can't be an easy ride. There are millions of bends, settling pools, traps, taps, tanks, heaters, coolers and drains along the way to watch out for, just like in this game.

And yet, despite all that, it's an easy game to play. Winning, however, is another matter. Each player needs only one counter, and only one die is used. The player with the highest first roll of the die starts.

1 Players take turns rolling the die and moving forward the number of squares dictated by the die.

2 If you stop on a square that has a trap or speed-up on it, you must follow the directions given in the square.

3 If you land on a square that has another counter already on it, that counter must go back to the first square and start again.

4 You must roll exactly the right number to reach home, as in Snakes and Ladders. If you are on the third square from home, and you shake a three, you win. But if you roll a five, you move forward three squares and back two, to make a total of five squares moved, so you are now on the second square from home.

5 The first player to reach home wins.

DOWNHILL— TAKE EXTRA TURN...
PIPE MAZE LOSE 1 TURN
SETTLING TANK— LOSE 1 TURN
TAKE SHORT CUT
LOSE TWO TURNS
TAKE 1 MORE TURN
TURN INTO TWISTED TRAP
BACK TO THE START...
OOPS
FINISH!

74
BATTLESHIPS

two players

War is heck. And war at sea is worst of all. You never know when a submarine or destroyer is going to sneak up and start taking pot shots at you. A safer version of war, nearly as exciting as the real thing, is called Battleships. Each player has two grids like the ones shown, with 100 small squares (10 squares on a side). One grid is for positioning your own ships, and the other grid is for keeping a record of the shots fired at your opponent's ships. The rules are very simple:

1 Each player gets the following ships:

1 battleship 5 squares long
1 cruiser 4 squares long
2 destroyers 3 squares long
2 submarines 2 squares long

They can be positioned anywhere on the first grid. To show where they are, shade the squares with a pencil, but keep their positions hidden from the other player!

2 Both grids are marked off with letters along the top and numbers along the side. This is so every

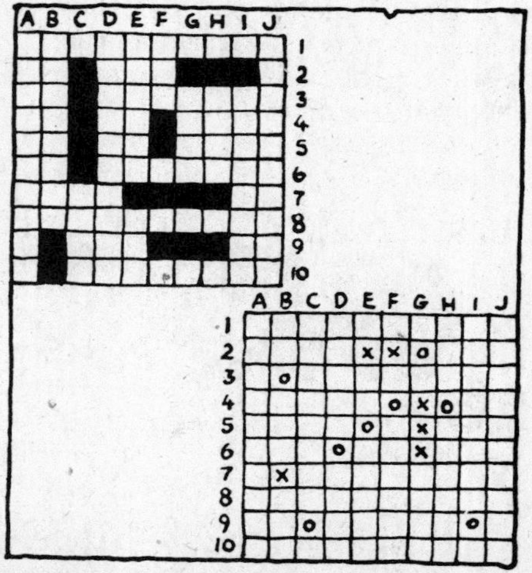

A B C D E F G H I J
1 2 3 4 5 6 7 8 9 10
A B C D E F G H I J
1 2 3 4 5 6 7 8 9 10

square in the grid can be given a name which tells its position. For example, square F5 is in the F column, 5th row down.

3 Players take turns calling out shots, one at a time. To do this, you call out the letter-number of a square, such as F5, B9, etc. If the other player calls out a square that makes up part of one of your ships, it scores a 'hit,' and you must tell him which ship he hit. For example, on the grid shown, if he called out F5, you must say, 'You hit my sub!'

4 Keep track of the shots you've fired by marking them on the other grid. You could mark an x for hits and an o for misses.

5 A ship is sunk when it has been hit on *all* its squares. The first person to sink all the other player's ships is the winner.

75
VICE VERSA
one or two players

As you can see from the picture, this game (actually it's more of a puzzle) is played on a strip of seven squares.
1 Three markers of one color are placed on one end, and three markers of another color on the other end (you could use three pennies and three dimes). The middle square is left empty.
2 The object of the game is to reverse the position of the counters, so that they are at opposite ends, in as few moves as possible.
3 First a counter of one color is moved, then a counter of the other color. They can be moved one square forward, or jumped over another counter onto an empty square, but *they cannot move backward.*
4 If two people are playing, they play on separate boards, and the winner is the person who reverses the positions of the counters in the fewest moves.

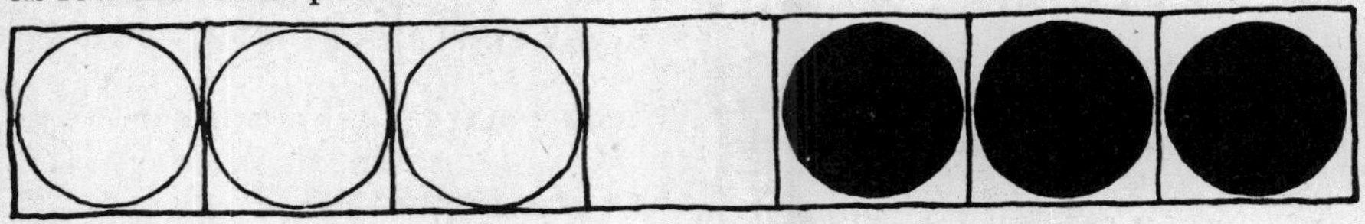

76
STEEPLECHASE
two to five players

A steeplechase is a type of horse race where the horses have to jump over obstacles called hurdles.

The game is a small version, played on a track like the one shown. In addition to that, you'll need two dice, and each player needs one 'horse,' or counter, of a different color.
1 The players place their horses on 'start' and the first player rolls the dice.
2 If you roll two numbers lower than five, the lower one is the number of spaces you move your horse forward.

If you roll a five and a six, you lose your turn.

If you roll one number five or over, and one under, you move one space.

If you roll double one, two, three, or four, you move only the number of one die.

If you roll double fives, you go *back* five spaces.

If you roll double sixes, you fall off your horse and go back to the beginning.

3 If, when you are moving forward, *or* backward, you stop on one of the spaces with an **x** in it (these are the hurdles), you lose one turn.

4 Needless to say, the first person to reach the finish line is the winner!

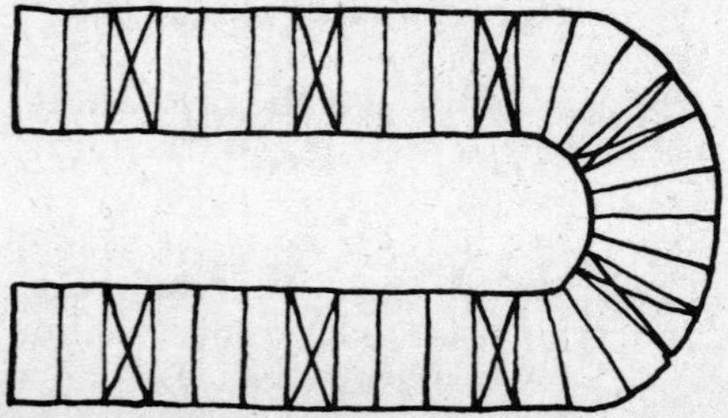

77
LATRUNCULI

two players

Latrunculi (Latin for bandits or robbers) is an early form of checkers that goes back to the heyday of Rome.

The playing board, as shown in the picture, has only 16 squares, but every square can be played on.

1 Each player has four counters, which start on the back row, as shown.

2 As in Checkers, players take turns moving the counters forward (but not backward) diagonally, one square at a time. They can't move straight up or across, but must move diagonally.

3 Captures are made with the short jump or multiple short jump, and, as in Checkers, counters *can't jump backward!*

4 When a counter reaches the opposite side of the board, it is crowned a King (the other player places one of the captured counters of the same color on top). The King can move and jump forward *and* backward, but still only diagonally.

5 The winner is the player who blocks or captures all the other player's counters, so that player can no longer move.

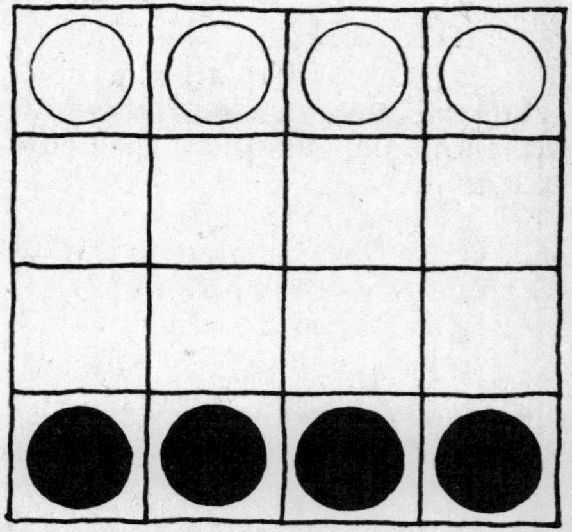

78

FIVE IN A ROW

two players

This is one of many variations of the Latrunculi game. Tic Tac Toe is another. This one is played on a board that is five squares wide by five long.

1 Instead of starting at opposite ends, the two players alternate their counters at both ends as shown.

2 Players take turns moving their own counters one square at a time. They can move forward, backward, across, or diagonally, but they cannot jump.

3 The object of the game is to get all five of your own counters in a straight row, either up and down, across, or diagonally. The first player to get a row of five wins!

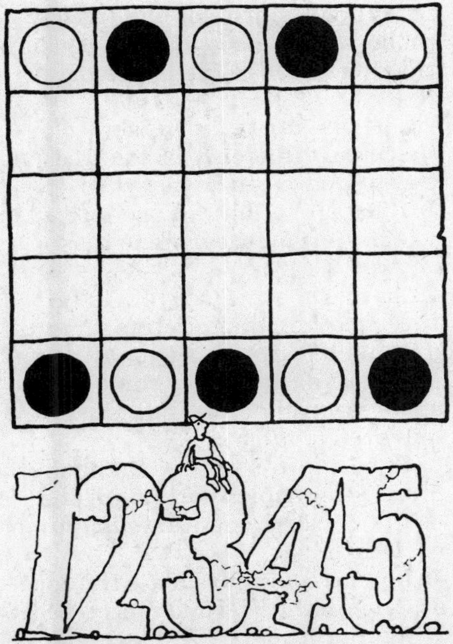

12345

79

BUSHWHACKERS!

two players

Being a trapper in the days of the pioneers was not an easy job. Besides all the dangers from wild critters, there was always the chance of running into a tribe of unfriendly Indians, who did not take kindly to the paleface strangers moving in and taking over their hunting and fishing grounds. Sometimes Indian braves would lie in ambush, and bushwhack unsuspecting trappers.

This game is played in much the same way as the Indian braves and the paleface trappers played their little game of life and death. The trapper knows that the brave may be waiting somewhere in the forest to jump him, but has no way of knowing where the brave is hiding. The brave, on the other hand, has an intimate knowledge of stalking and the way of the woods. He can

see and hear the trapper coming, but can't predict what path or direction he will take, and hence where to wait in ambush for him.

1 Each player has one counter. One is the brave, and the other is the trapper.

2 Each player has his own playing board. The brave is allowed to look at the trapper's board, but the trapper must *not* look at the brave's playing board. Other than this, the boards are the same.

3 The brave starts on any one of the three black squares at the top of his own board, and the trapper starts on one of the black squares at the bottom of the other board.

4 Counters move only on the black squares. They move diagonally, in both directions, and can jump *sideways* (but *not* forward or back!) across a white square.

5 The trapper moves first. His object is to get to one of the three black squares at the other end of the board without landing on a square which the brave is already on, on the other board.

6 The brave's objective is to lie in wait for the trapper, on any square. He can move around or stay put on his turn, but may not 'attack' the trapper by moving onto a square that the trapper is already on.

7 If the trapper lands on a square which, on the other board, is inhabited by the brave, then the trapper is 'bushwhacked' and the brave wins the game. But if the trapper makes it safely to the other end of the board without bumping into the sneaky brave, the trapper wins!

80
ALQUERQUE

two players

The Egyptians played this game over two thousand years ago. From there it moved into Arabia, then into Spain. The Spaniards took it to the New World with them and taught it to the natives of Central America, who still play it to this day.

The board has five points to a side. The counters play on the points (the places where the lines cross).

1 Each player has twelve counters, arranged as shown in the picture.

2 White moves first.

3 Players take turns moving onto any empty point. The counters move along the lines, forward, across, and diagonally, but they can't move backward.

4 Players must capture, by the short jump or multiple short jump. The counters can jump in any direction except backward.

5 If one of your counters reaches the other player's home base, it must stay there until it can jump one of the other player's counters. Once it has done this it is crowned a King, and can move around again in any direction.

6 The winner is the player who captures or blocks all the other player's counters so they can't move. If neither player can move, the game is a draw or tie.

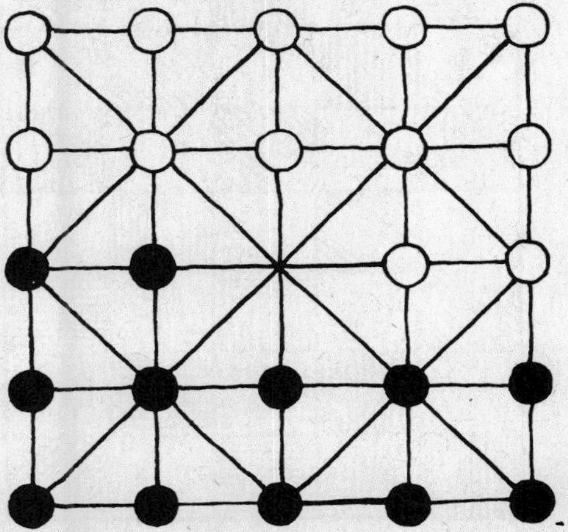

(YOUR MOVE)

81
COYOTE AND CHICKEN

two players

This is another game that is common to the East and West, from Spain to Japan. The chicken in the game is no dumb bird! It single-handedly takes on a pack of twelve ferocious coyotes! The knock-kneed chicken jumps around the board on its skinny legs, knocking coyotes out left and right!

The board, as shown, is four by four squares big, with two diagonal lines running from corner to corner. The game is played on the points where the lines cross, and the counters move along the lines.

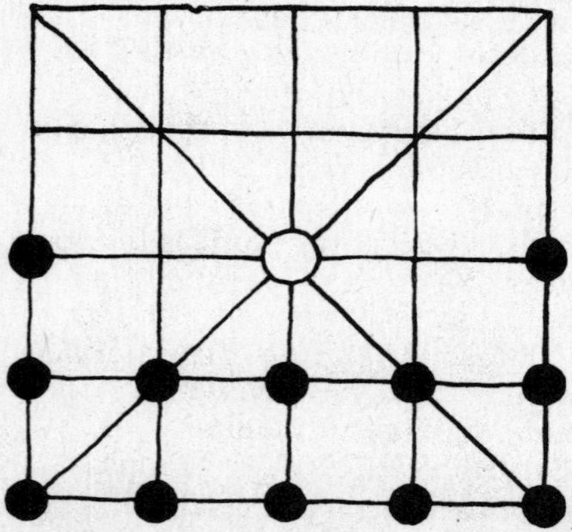

1 The chicken player has only one counter, while the coyote player has 12. They are arranged on the board as shown, to start the game. The chicken moves first.

2 The chicken can move one space in any direction (along the lines) onto an empty space, and can capture by the short jump or the multiple short jump in *any* direction, as long as the counter moves only along the lines from point to point.

3 The coyote can move one counter at a time, one space in any direction along the lines, but he *can't jump or capture*.

4 The coyotes try to block the chicken so that it can't move. If the coyotes manage this, they win.

5 The chicken wins if it captures so many coyotes that they can no longer block it.

82
SENAT

two players

Anthropologists, the people who study people, had to do a little detective work with the help of a few archeologists to put together the rules of this game, because it is one of the most ancient games around – over *three thousand* years old! And, of course, in that length of time, people are bound to forget a few of the rules. So these anthropologists looked at some old Egyptian paintings of people playing Senat, and by comparing it with games (like Block and Jump) played today that are descendants of this most noble, most ancient game, they were able to figure out the original old Egyptian rules! And guess what else these dusty old professors found out about the game of Senat? It's fun!

The playing board is five squares wide by five long, and all squares can be played on. Each player needs twelve counters.

1 Players take turns putting *two* counters at a time down on any squares on the board except the center one, until all counters are on the board.

2 The player who put down the final two counters starts. If this player can't move, he can move one of the other player's counters out of the way, so he can move.

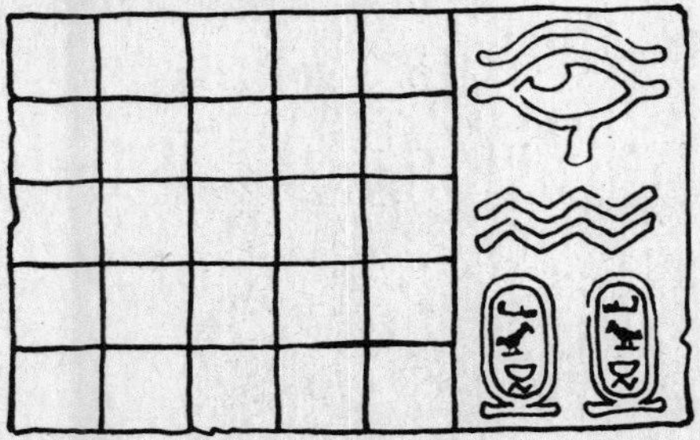

3 Players take turns moving one counter at a time, one square up, down or across, but *not* diagonally.

4 Counters are captured by *trapping* (see the introduction to this chapter for a description of trapping) but captures made before all the counters are on the board don't count. Captured counters are removed from the board.

5 If a player *voluntarily* moves a counter between two of the other player's counters, it can't be trapped.

6 The object of the game is to capture or block all of the other player's counters.

7 Later in the game, if neither side can move, players count the number of counters left on the board. The player with the most counters left wins.

83
BLOCK AND JUMP
two players

This is one of the many variations of Senat that have been handed down over the years. It is also similar to Checkers, and it goes to show how easy it is to invent games by taking rules from other games and mixing them together. Not all of these 'mixed-up' games are successful, but Block and Jump is one that has managed to survive the test of time mainly because it is simple, and, best of all, fun.

It is played on a Senat board, five squares wide by five long, with all squares in use.

1 Each player uses 12 counters, as in Senat, but all are placed on the board at the beginning of the game, as shown in the picture.

2 Players take turns moving one counter at a time, one square up, down, or across, but not diagonally.

3 Captures are made by the short jump or the multiple short jump. Unlike Checkers, captures don't *have* to be made. That is, if you miss a chance to capture, or decide not to, your opponent *cannot* remove your counter from the board, like he can in Checkers.

4 The object of the game, funnily enough, is to block or capture all of the other player's counters.

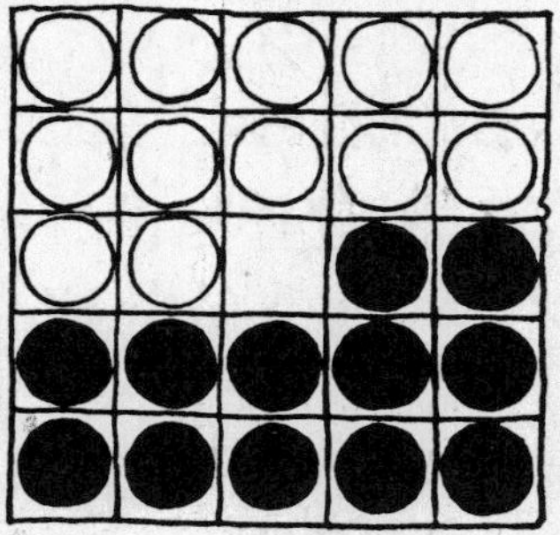

84
MORRIS
Three-man & nine-man
two players

You don't need three or nine people to play Morris. That's only the number of counters! Morris boards have been found scratched into the floors of ancient Egyptian temples, and in the streets of Greek and Roman cities. They have been carved in the decks of Viking ships, and in the tops of school desks. If you are traveling in Europe or Asia, kids will know this game everywhere you go. Why, even William Shakespeare played Nine-man Morris! So, I'd like to take this opportunity to introduce you to a really great game, your friend and mine, Morris!

Three-man Morris
This is a simple version. It is played on the funny-looking board shown in the first picture.
1 Each of the two players has three counters.
2 Players take turns putting counters, one at a time, on any three points (where the lines cross) on the board.
3 Players can't move until all counters are on the board. Then they take turns moving one counter at a time along the lines, one point at a time (no fair jumping over a point), to any empty point.
4 The object of the game is to get three of your own counters in a row on any straight line on the board (horizontally, vertically, or diagonally) while at the same time trying to keep the other player from doing the same thing. How you place the counters right at the beginning of the game is important – pay close attention to what the other player is doing, and try to block as much as possible, as in Tic Tac Toe.

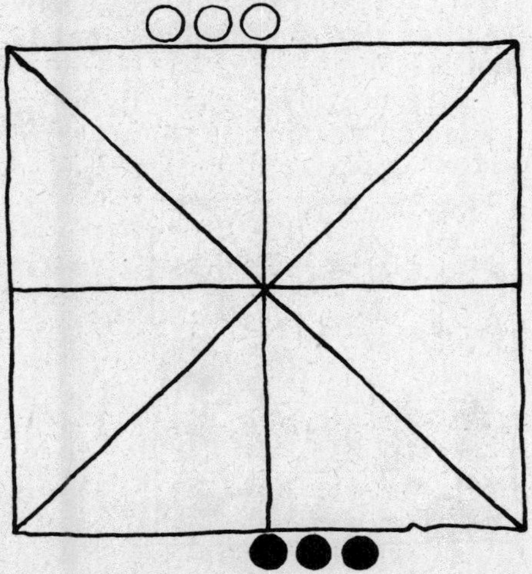

Nine-man Morris
The rules for this version of Morris are slightly more complicated, which makes for a more exciting game. It is played on the points of the board shown, with each player having nine counters.
1 Players take turns putting one counter at a time on any point on the board.
2 No moves can be made until all the counters are on the board.
3 When all counters are down, players take turns moving one counter at a time, along the lines, one point at a time.
4 When a row of three counters is made on any line, that player can remove any one of the other player's counters. This rule also applies when the counters are being placed on the board during the first part of the game.

5 The object of the game is to block the other player so that he can't move, or to capture seven of the other player's counters. The first player who does either is the winner.

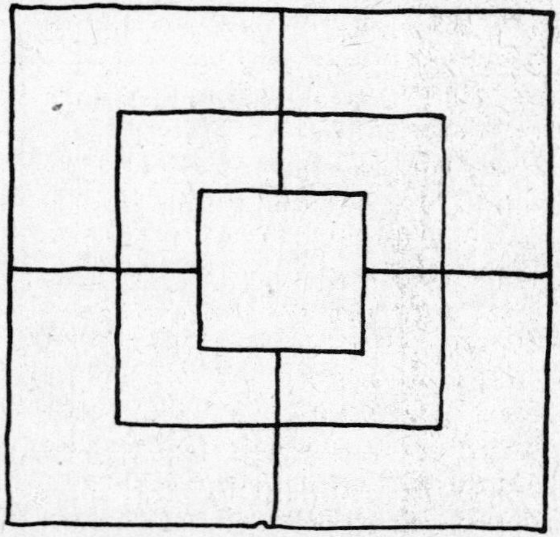

85
KONO
two players

Kono is a game that comes originally from Korea. In this version, no pieces are captured or taken off the board, but the game is still as exciting as a good comic book, or a game of Kick-the-Can.

It is played on the crisscross board shown in the picture, on the points where the lines cross. Counters move along the lines.

1 Each of the two players has seven counters, which start out on the board in the arrangement shown.
2 Players take turns moving one counter at a time in any direction, one point at a time. Counters can move up or down, across, or diagonally.
3 Counters can jump over any other counters, including their teammates, by the short jump or the multiple short jump, but no other counters are captured or removed from the board.
4 The first player to get all seven counters arranged in the starting position at the opposite side of the board is the winner.

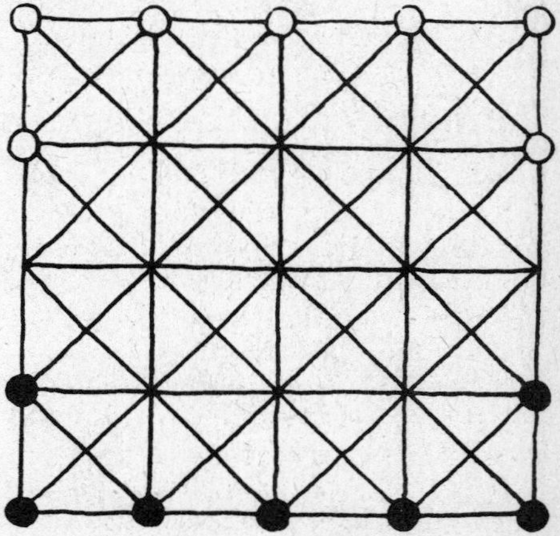

DAD! LOOK WHAT I FOUND!
RIGHT! TOSS IT IN THE TRUNK WITH THE REST OF THIS JUNK...
ROCKS
RPM

WHAT TO DO WITH THE LOOT

Yo ho ho and a bottle of pop!

You don't have to be a pirate to find loot en route. Any salty seadog can dig up a few bottle caps or straws, and with a little bit of scrounging you might find anything from a candy wrapper to a lime-green, twelve-masted schooner! Just try to get *that* in the trunk of your dinghy!

Here's a few things to keep an eye out for:

- bottle caps
- bubble gum
- drinking straws
- paper bags and plates
- disposable cups
- small pebbles
- candy wrappers (especially tin-foil)
- string (see chapter Why Knot?)
- toothpicks
- sugar cubes (ask first!)

Sounds like about the most worthless collection of junk you've ever heard of, doesn't it? Well, in actual fact, you can have more fun with that 'worthless junk' than you can with a suitcase full of expensive toys and games. And what's more, it can be found anywhere, fits into a pocket and costs not a red rum-dipped cent. Want to find out more? Read on, read on ...

GUM
POP
POP
GUM

RIP OFF

three or more players

The more players you can round up for this game, the better. Choose one player (draw straws, count out, or whatever . . .) to be the Banker. The rest of the players each get a number. For instance, the first player is called Number One, the second player is called Number Two, and so on. Each player is given three toothpicks, matches, or whatever is handy.

1 The object of the game is for each player to try to hang onto his or her loot, and for the Banker to try to collect all the loot, in order to go out.

2 The Banker takes the loot away like this: if he calls out your number, and snaps his fingers before you do, you must give him one toothpick (or whatever you're using as loot).

3 If a player snaps his fingers by mistake, he or she loses one toothpick. For example, if the Banker says 'One!' and Number Three snaps his fingers, Number Three must give the Banker a toothpick, whether the Banker snapped first or not.

4 A good way for the Banker to rip off loot is to tell a story, or get into a conversation with one of the players, and somehow work one of the numbers into the story.

5 When players lose all their loot, they are out.

6 When the Banker has ripped off all the loot, the first player to go out becomes the Banker for the next round.

DISGUISES

Have you ever wanted to be a Frankenstein monster, an Indian brave, a pirate, a space cowboy, a robot, or a witch? You finally have your big chance. With a few paper bags and plates, some pens or markers, and a little ingenuity, you are well on your way to taking on the role of your choice.

Before you even start, make sure that the bags and/or plates are clean. Always tear out a large nose or mouth hole, because breathing is important to living, and living is what life is all about!

There are hundreds of ways you can use your paper bags – smaller ones make good hats, and larger ones can be worn covering your whole head. You can even tear off the bottom of the bag to produce a 'convertible' mask that lets the real you show through. Paper plates can

be used as either hats or faces, or torn in half to make weird glasses, goggles or eye masks. Poke holes in the edge of the plate with a pencil point, and tie a string 'harness' to the plate to hold it on your head. Paper plate accessories may be worn alone or with your bag masks.

To make holes and alterations in the paper bags, wet the tip of your finger and draw a wet line on the paper where you want the hole to be. The paper will tear easily and cleanly along this line. The paper plates will be easier to tear if you draw the holes with a pen or pencil.

If you are chewing some gum, you can use it to stick things like bottle caps, tinfoil, or straws to your masks. The rest of the detail (things like warts, wrinkles, eyebrows, hair, bolts, etc.) can be drawn on with a pen or marker.

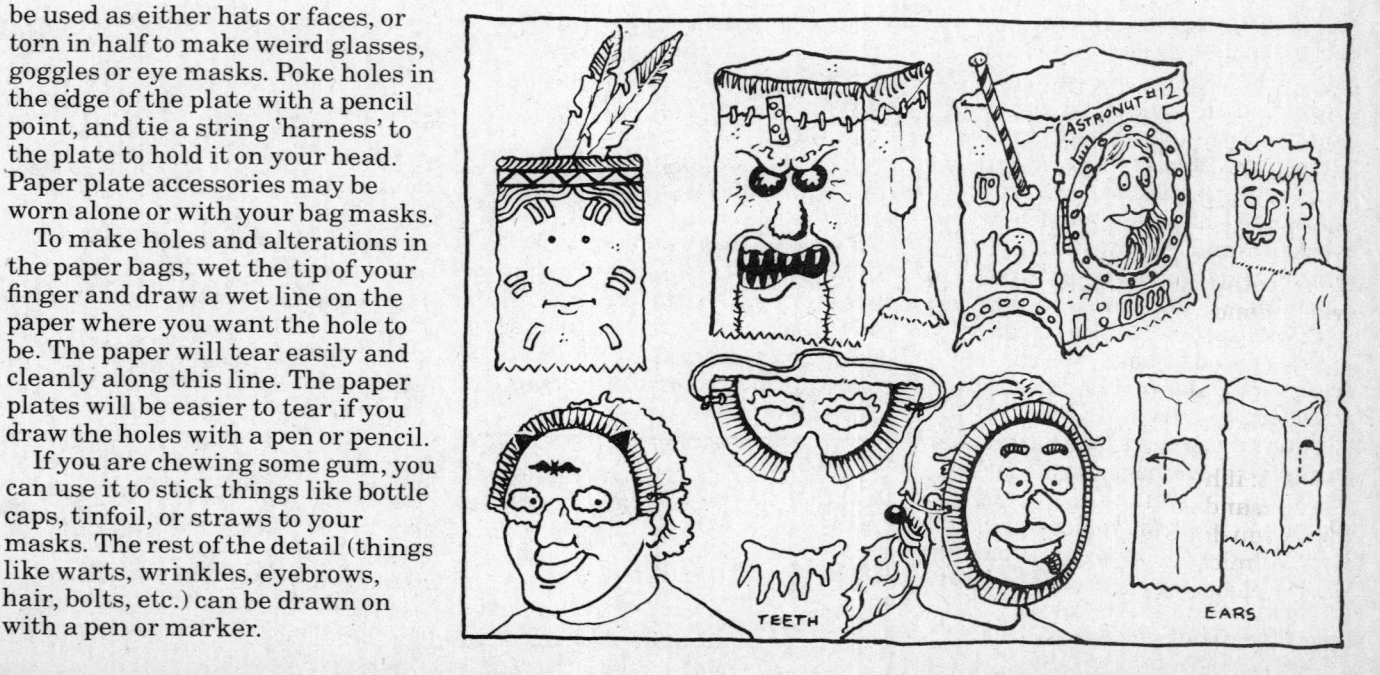

ASTRONUT #12
12
TEETH
EARS

88
FOIL ART

Not all sculpture is done in stone, bronze or clay. Artists have used some pretty weird things to get their ideas into the third dimension. Bread dough, plastic, rubber, tin cans, plaster, string and rope have all been tried with varying amounts of success. If you want to try your hand at being a sculptor, and you don't have any of these exotic materials, don't despair. You can sculpt with something you can probably find in your own car or train (or *whatever* it is that you're traveling in) – tinfoil!

You can use the kind that comes in cigarette packages and chocolate bar wrappings. If there is some paper on the back, you can remove it by wetting the corner and peeling the paper off. You'll probably need at least a couple of pieces, so scrounge up all you can get!

The rest is up to you. What you can make is limited only by what you can think of! An easy one to start out with is the ever-popular wine glass. Mold the cup part around your fingertip, then twist the stem and flatten out the base. Trim the edges, and voila! Cheers!

If you are lucky enough to find a tinfoil pie plate, you can draw a picture on it with a pen or pencil. The lines that you draw sink into the foil creating a raised effect. You can color this foil picture with some kinds of markers.

89
BUBBLES

To make lots of bubbles you need only a little bit of soap solution, and if you take proper precautions, and are very careful, you shouldn't even have to worry about spilling any.

You can make a 'swell' bubble solution (if you'll excuse the pun) out of that liquid soap you sometimes find in gas station washrooms. You only need about as much as you use to wash your hands. Mix it half-and-half with water. If you are resourceful, it isn't too hard to figure out how to use bar or powdered soap or even shampoo. Pour about two fingers (one inch) of your soapy solution into the bottom of a disposable cup with a lid and add just *one drop* of soda pop, or the tiniest pinch of sugar, for holding power. This should be more than enough for at least a zillion (count 'em!) bubbles. The less of this stuff

you splash around in the car, the more the all-important driver will like it.

The next thing to keep an eye out for is a drinking straw. If it is paper, tear a small slit in one side of one end and fold back the paper along the slit. Dip this end in the bubble brew through the hole in the lid of the cup. After a few practice attempts at blowing bubbles, you should be able to get more than just wet!

If you want to make bigger bubbles, you'll need some kind of hoop with a handle. A finger ring with a string tied to it works great. You could also make a bubbler out of another straw. Flatten it out, form a loop in the middle, and twist the ends together into a handle. These kinds of bigger and better bubble-makers work best outside when you are stopped. Just dip them into your soap potion and blow. Wow! First prize goes to the biggest bubble!

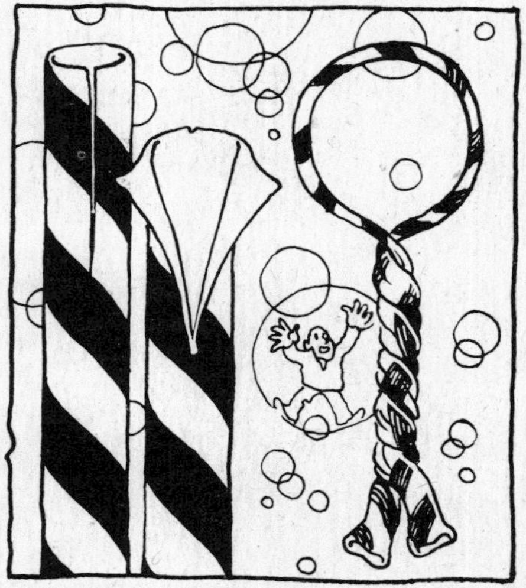

90
COINSPIN

Try this trick sometime when you're feeling relaxed. You'll need nerves of steel, two toothpicks and a coin. Put the coin down on a flat surface. Place the points of the toothpicks on either side of the edge and try to pick the coin up with the toothpicks, as shown in the picture. Coins with ridged edges work best.

With a little practice, you should be able to hold the coin steady. This is the easy part of the trick. The next part is what requires the nerves of steel! Lean close to the coin and blow on it. If it doesn't fall from the toothpicks, it should spin around at high speeds, humming as it spins.

91
RUBBINGS

Have you ever seen rubbings of tombstones, brass plaques or other monuments? To produce these beautiful rubbings, the 'rubbers' lay a sheet of paper over what they wish to copy, then rub the paper with a special large wax crayon. The crayon picks up only the raised parts of the stone or brass.

If you've brought along a soft lead pencil or a crayon, as well as a supply of paper, you are nearly set to produce some rubbings of your own. All that you need now are some things to make rubbings of! You probably already know that you can produce rubbings of coins, but what you may not know is that you can also use leaves, cloth, textured paper, sandpaper, string, the grill of your radio, etc. In short, anything that's fairly flat with some kind of texture on the surface.

Lay the thing to be 'rubbed' on a hard flat surface, lay a sheet of paper over top, and carefully rub

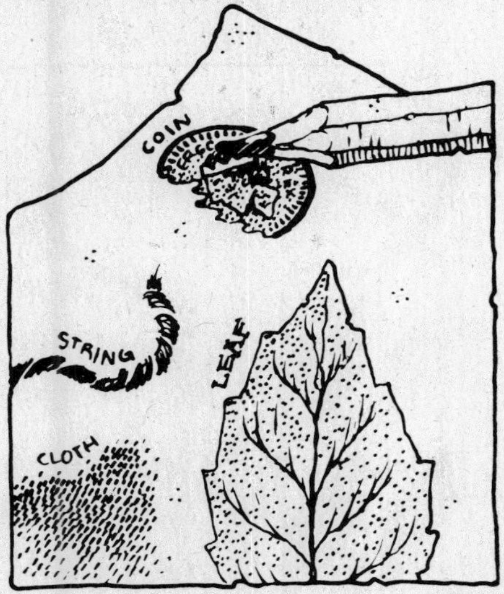
COIN
STRING
LEAF
CLOTH

over the paper with the side of the pencil lead, or with a crayon. Don't press too hard. If you are careful, you can even get some cloth texture off the side of your sneaker, or from the upholstery of the car seat. Experiment with other things like the tread of your shoe, textured plastic, different kinds of plants, and bottle caps (a rubbing of a bottle cap looks like a sun or a flower).

After you have tried out a few different things, and maybe made a collection of rubbings of all the different leaves you can find, try using all the different textures you've discovered to build up a whole picture. You could use a cloth texture for the ground in a landscape, and use leaves as trees, etc. Or you could arrange a piece of string into a picture, and make a rubbing of that. The possibilities are unlimited.

92

PUZZLES WITH A POINT

Toothpick mindbenders, four in all

These puzzles are designed to sharpen your wits to a needle point. Give them a good try before you peek at the answers. You'll feel 100% better if you figure them out yourself.

1 If anyone told you that six plus five equals nine, you would think he was crazy! But, strangely enough, this impossible statement can be proven, using a few toothpicks.

Problem: Lay six toothpicks down as shown. Add five more to make only nine.

2 Lay down seventeen toothpicks as shown to make six squares.

Problem: Take away only five toothpicks, and, without moving any other toothpicks, leave three of the original squares.

3 Lay down twenty-four toothpicks to make nine squares as shown in the picture.

Problem: Remove only eight toothpicks, and, without moving any other toothpicks, leave only two squares.

4 Form an equal-sided triangle with three toothpicks as shown.

Problem: By adding only three more toothpicks, form a total of four equal-sided triangles. This is a tough one!

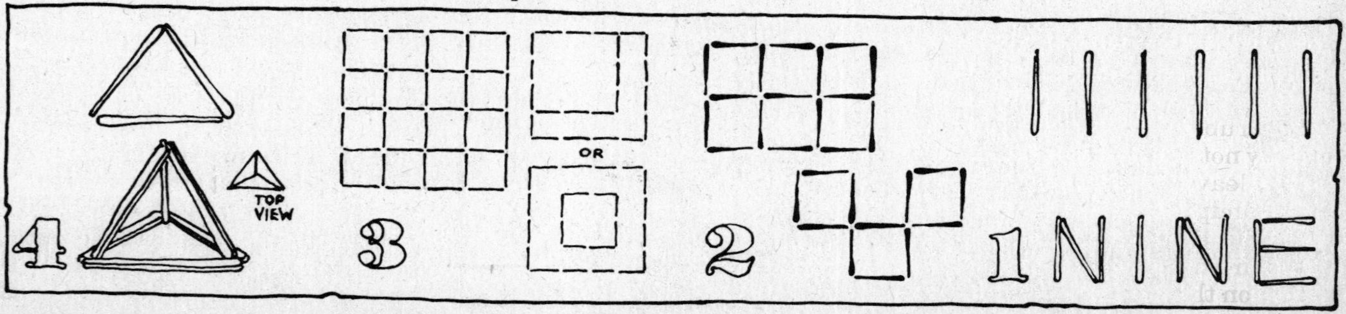
TOP VIEW
4
3
OR
2
1
NINE

93

CUPCATCHER

Take one disposable cup (plastic, paper or styrofoam), one piece of string, and a wad of tinfoil or paper, and you have all the fixin's for a real good time! The Cupcatcher is a traveler's version of a toy that is older than the hills. Way before your time.

The picture just about tells it all. Poke a hole in the bottom of the cup with a pencil or pen, and push the end of your piece of string through. Tie a knot in the end of the string, or better yet, tie it around a match or toothpick. Tie the other end of your string (which should be about two feet long or so) around the wad of paper or tinfoil, and you are ready to go! Hold the cup in one hand, with the string hanging down below. If you give the cup a quick jerk upward, the wad at the end of the string will fly up in the air. The idea is to try to catch this flying wad in the cup. This is not as easy as it sounds! But keep practicing. If you are traveling with other people, have a Cupcatcher tournament!

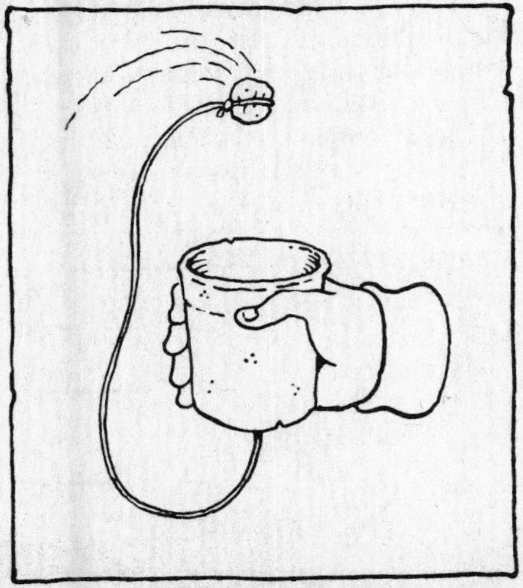

94

HUL GUL

two or more players

This game has been popular ever since children played it in ancient Greece. Each player needs the same number of counters. You can use anything small, such as coins, bits of paper, pebbles, or whatever you can find. Ten counters each is a good number to start with.

1 Hide a few counters in your fist.

2 Turn to another player and say 'Hul Gul.' The other player replies 'Handful!' Then you say 'How many?'

3 The other player then tries to guess how many counters you have in your fist.

4 If he guesses right, he gets to keep all the counters.

5 If the other player guesses too high, he must give you some of his counters to make up the difference between his guess and the real number of counters. For example, if

you have five counters in your hand, and the other player guesses twelve, he must give you seven counters.
6 If the second player guesses too low, he must give you five counters, or the small half of his counters if he has less than ten.
7 Now it is the other player's turn to hide some counters in his fist.
8 The game is over when one player has won all the counters.

HULGUL
HANDFUL!!

95
ODD WINS

two players

In this game, the odd person wins. All you need to play is an odd number of toothpicks, coins, pebbles, or whatever. You should have at least 15 altogether.
1 Throw the counters in a heap on the seat.
2 Players take turns taking counters from the pile. They can take one, two, or three counters at a time.
3 This continues until there are no counters left in the pile.
4 The winner is the player who has picked up an odd number of counters. Like I told you, the odd person wins!

96
SPINNER!

A hundred years ago, toys were scarce for most kids, and the existing toys were mostly simple unbattery-operated, unspeaking, unbionic, everyday toys. In those days, kids often made their own toys, like this spinner.

You can make the same toy today out of a big button and a piece of string about three feet long. You can make a button out of cardboard if you don't have one handy. Tear the cardboard into a rough circle or square about two inches across. With the point of a pencil, poke two holes near the center of the cardboard, about a quarter inch apart. Push one end of the string through one of the holes, then back through the other hole, and then tie the two ends together. If you like, decorate your spinner with designs or pictures.

Hold the string as shown in the picture, with the index fingers through the loops. Push the button into the center of the two strings and give it a few turns. Keeping the spinner spinning takes a little practice. Keep turning the button until the strings on both sides have a few twists in them. Pull out on the ends of the string. This will start the button spinning as the strings start to unwind. As it begins to slow down, bring your hands together a bit, and the string will twist up again. Pull your hands apart again, and the button will spin in the other direction. This is a bit like learning to use a yo-yo. After a while, you should be able to keep it going *almost* forever.

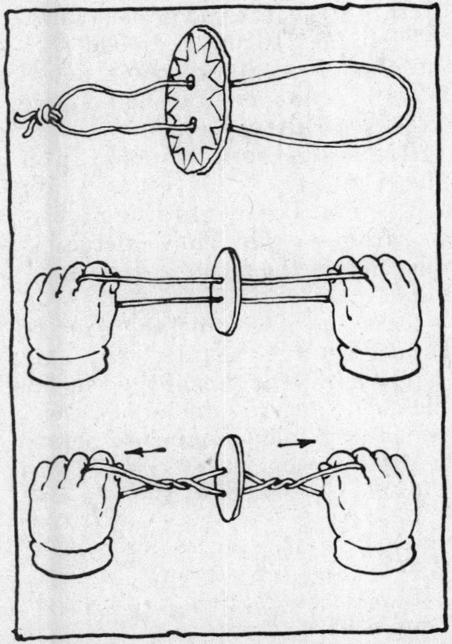

NIM

two or three players

This is one member of a large family of take-away games. These games are usually very simple to play, and yet they can be very challenging, especially if you play with three players instead of the usual two.

1 Start with any number of matches, toothpicks or coins and lay them down in any number of rows, with any number of objects per row.

2 Players take turns picking up objects. You can pick up as many as you like, as long as they are *side-by-side in the same row*. For example, if another player picks up the middle object from a row of seven, you can't pick up the other six objects left at once because there is a gap between the two groups of three.

3 The person who picks up the last match is the loser.
4 A good pattern to start the game with is four rows of objects with one in the first row, three in the second, five in the third, and seven in the fourth row.

98
BOOBY TRAP
two players

First of all, you need a piece of string about three feet long. Tie one end around a wad of paper or some other small object that is easy to tie a string to – ever tried to tie a string around a coin? Next you'll need a disposable cup, preferably an empty one.

One player gets the cup and the other gets the string and paper ball. They sit on opposite sides of the seat. Put the paper ball in the middle of the seat. The player with the cup holds it four or five inches above the paper ball, but no closer! The cup person tries to trap the paper ball under the cup before the string player can pull it to safety. When the ball has been trapped five times, players switch places and start a new round. No fair catching the string! The ball must be under the cup to be 'trapped.'

99
SNAKE EYES
two or more players

In the dice game of Craps, double sixes are known as 'boxcars,' and the elusive double one is known as the 'snake eyes.'

In the game of Snake Eyes, double ones are the only points that score. You'll need two dice for the game, of course, which can be very easily made from sugar cubes or paper. For complete instructions on making dice, see Number 70 in the last chapter, as well as Number 23.
1 Players take turns throwing the dice.
2 If any player throws any double number, he gets another throw.
3 Any player who rolls snake eyes (double ones) scores one point.
4 The first person to score ten points wins the game.

100
FIVE DICE

two or more players

Make five sugar cube or paper dice (see Number 70 and Number 23).

1 The object of the game is to get all five dice in number order, that is, in the sequence 1,2,3,4,5, or 2,3,4,5,6.

2 Throw all five dice. If there are no dice in numerical order, you lose your turn. If there are two or more dice in numerical order, leave them down and throw the rest of the dice again. If there are two groups in number order (for example 1 and 2 plus 4 and 5), you can only leave one group down.

3 If, on the second throw, there are some dice that can be added to the number sequence already down, leave them there and throw the rest of the dice. For example, if on the first throw you got 3 and 4, you must get a 2 and/or a 5 on the second throw in order to stay in the game, and if you get a 1 with the 2, or a 6 with the 5, you can leave them down too.

4 If on any throw there are no numbers that can be added to the sequence, you lose your turn and the next player throws.

5 Each player that gets a 'straight' (or sequence of five dice in order) scores one point and gets a free throw. The first player to score ten points wins the game.

A sample game might go like this: the first player throws all five dice and gets 1, 3, 5, 5, and 6. He leaves down one of the 5's and the 6 and throws the other three dice. On his second throw he gets 1, 2, and 4. He leaves the 4 down and throws the other two dice again. This time he gets a 2 and a 3, which means he has completed a straight, and so scores one point, and gets to throw again.

On his second round, he throws all five dice and gets 2, 3, 3, 5, and 6. He must now choose whether to leave down the 2 and 3 or the 5 and 6. He decides on the 5 and 6 because it was so lucky last time. On the second throw he gets 2, 2, and 4. He leaves the 4 and throws the other two dice. On his next throw he gets 1 and 2, which are not in sequence with 4, 5, and 6; so he loses his turn and the next player tries his luck.

Got the idea now? Okay, get shakin'!

101
CRAPS

two or more players

This has to be the most popular dice game in the world today. It goes back to about 1890 or so, and comes from somewhere in the New Orleans area in the U.S. From there it spread like wildfire and firewater across the continent. It was played on Mississippi riverboats and is still played in gambling casinos. It is played with two dice, and the rules are as easy as pie.

1 The first player throws the dice.
2 If the total of the two faces on the first throw is 7 or 11 (called a 'natural'), the first player wins that round, scores one point, and throws again. (You can also 'pass,' or not throw again, if you want.)
3 If the first player rolls 2, 3, or 12 (called 'craps') on the first throw, he loses and the next player throws.
4 If the first player throws 4, 5, 6, 8, 9, or 10 on the first throw, he has a

'point' to make. This means that he keeps throwing the dice, trying to get the same number again. If he does, he wins the round and scores one point. But if he rolls a 7 before he rolls his point, he loses and the next player throws.

For example, if you throw a 6, you must pick up the dice and throw again and keep throwing until you get either a 6 (which means you win) or a 7 (which means you lose). All other throws are meaningless; so if you throw a 2, 3, 11 or 12, just ignore it and keep trying to make your point. 2, 3 and 12 are losing rolls, and 7 and 11 winning rolls, on the *first throw only*.

FWAAP
RPM

DEALING WITH A CARD

Wild as the wind and dressed like a fool, the Joker nevertheless always appears in the best of company. He can be found rubbing shoulders with royalty – the kings and queens and jacks of the European card decks – but he is not above an occasional game of poker with the boys. They are always glad to see him when he shows up, because he is known as a wild card who can do wonderful impersonations of the high-powered personalities of the deck. He has been found as far away as China and Korea, where he puts in an appearance with the peculiar long narrow playing cards used there. He is even seen on the circular cards used in India. Master of many disguises, he appears in the Tarot deck (usually used for cartomancy, which is fortunetelling with cards) dressed like a gypsy vagabond and called the Fool, but he is still the same old Joker.

In all these decks, the Joker is the Zero card. He has no number and not even a suit! He is the mad, impetuous wanderer that no one can count on. For this reason, he is left out of most games, which certainly shows a lack of respect for someone as old as he is. He was first seen with a pack of Chinese cards about a thousand years ago. These early playing cards (who knows, maybe he invented them) were a kind of shorthand version of the games of Chess and Dominoes, and are still used in Oriental card games. Sometime in the late fourteenth century, the Joker got itchy feet and traveled with the rest of the pack to Europe, where card games caught on like the plague, which was also popular that century. Things got so bad that by the fifteenth century, no one would put down his hand long enough to plough the fields or do the dishes. In many countries, cards, also known as the Devil's Picture Book, were declared illegal. Old ladies caught sneaking a game of solitaire with a black market pack were fined and thrown in the stocks where they passed the time (usually a sentence of six hours) playing an innocent game of dice with their fellow prisoners.

In those days, as today, there were many different kinds of cards in use. Italians still play some games with the Tarot deck, and others with a deck that has money, swords, cups and batons as suits instead of the hearts, diamonds, clubs and spades that we know so well. In Switzerland, some decks

MAKE YOUR OWN

still have shield, acorn, bell and flower suits. The suits may have originally stood for the different levels of society – diamonds for merchants and the rich, hearts for priests and the church, spades (from the Spanish word for spear) for soldiers and the army, and clubs for serfs and peasants.

The Joker, or Fool, is the card that represents everyone, on every level of society. Wherever and whenever he appears, from the noisy gambling casinos on the Mississippi riverboats and in Las Vegas, to the smoky backroom poker games or the quiet game of Cheat with friends, wherever or whenever, the Joker is a card. We should deal with him!

If you didn't bring a pack of playing cards along with you on your journey, don't despair. There's no need to skip over this chapter. Before the development of woodblock printing in Europe, cards were always made by hand. They were sometimes very elaborate affairs with all kinds of detail and color. In India, they still manufacture their round cards by hand, and some of these are made of ivory with gold trim! There's no real need to get that fancy though – all that flash is just for show. It doesn't make the cards any luckier. If you are traveling and have at hand only a pencil and paper, you can do what shipwrecked castaways have been doing since there were ships and cards – namely, make your own!

In the modern deck there are 52 cards (not counting the Joker, of course). In some older European decks there were 56 cards, and as many as 78 in the Tarot pack. In India, decks usually have about 120 cards, but one type of deck contains 320! That's enough for over 40 people to play Old Maid with the same deck!

If you are making your own deck of cards, I recommend the modern deck – four different suits (hearts, clubs, diamonds and spades) with thirteen cards in each (one to ten, and jack, queen and king). This makes a total of 52 cards, which is also the number of weeks in a year. You don't have to use hearts, clubs, diamonds and spades for suits if you don't want to. You can make up your own symbols! Like apples, hotdogs, sneakers and dollars. Or squares, circles, triangles and stars. Or whatever.

One thing to remember when you make your own cards is that the backs of the cards all have to look the same, or you will be able to tell which card is which, after a while, by just looking at the back! The best way to avoid this is to fold and crease the sheet of paper into even rectangles before tearing along the creases. Fold an ordinary-sized sheet as shown in the picture. This should give you 16 even-sized cards, which means four sheets of paper will yield 64 cards, more than enough to cover for rips and mistakes.

When you have torn all your paper and decided on your suits, the rest is easy. For each suit of 13 cards, number ten of them from one to ten, and mark the other three as jack, queen and king. If you like, you can decorate these cards with designs, or just write on the numbers and suits.

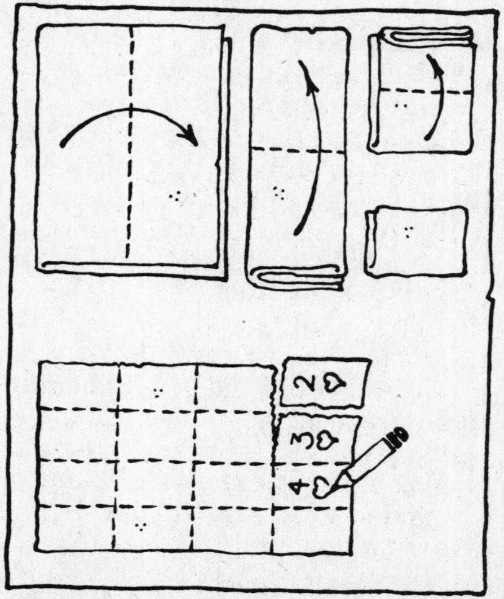
2♡
3♡
4♡

103

CHEAT

For those who do

two to thirteen players

Hats off to the genius who invented Cheat. It's a brilliant game that allows us all to get it out of our systems. You know, in some countries, cheating itself is not considered so bad. In fact, you are thought of as quite clever if you can get away with it, but heaven help the cheater who gets caught in the act! In these parts of the world, cheating is actually a time-honored custom, and is considered a natural part of playing any game. 'All's fair in love and war,' as the old saying goes. But if you are caught cheating, you risk being banned from the game, and if you are caught often enough, you are banned from playing any games whatsoever. So most game players just don't bother to cheat because the stakes are too high.

Perhaps the game of Cheat was invented by an incurable cheater

who had been banned from all other games. He or she liked the new game so much that two versions were made up and spread all over the world. One of the versions is now known as 'I Doubt It' and is not quite as exciting as the real game of Cheat.

One pack of cards is enough for up to seven players, but for any more than that you'd better shuffle two decks together.

1 The object of the game is to be the first player to get rid of all your cards.

2 The dealer deals the cards one at a time, face down to each player until one card is left. This card is turned face up in the middle of the table.

3 Players look at their hand. Try to sort your cards into the four suits, as it is the suit and not the number of the cards that's important in this game.

4 Players take turns laying one card at a time *face down* on top of the card on the table.

The cards you lay down are *supposed* to be the same as the one on the table, but in actual fact, you can lay down any kind of card you like. But keep a straight face!

5 If at any time a player suspects that another player has put down a card that is not the right suit, he says, 'Cheat!' The other player must then turn over the card he just played, and if it is *not* the right suit (if he 'cheated') he must pick up *all* the cards on the table and put them in his hand. If, on the other hand, the player who called 'Cheat' is wrong, *he* must pick up all the cards!

6 The player who picks up all the cards must place a new card of a *different* suit face up on the table, and play continues as before.

7 The first player to get rid of all the cards in his hand is the winner.

HEY! YOU DIDN'T CHEAT!

104
THIS MEANS WAR!!

two or three players

In some games, the Ace is the highest card, and in some games it is the lowest card. In the official rules for this game, the Ace is high!

1 The object of War is to win all the cards in the deck.

2 The dealer deals out the whole deck face down, one card at a time to each player, until all the cards are dealt.

3 Players must not look at their cards, but put them in one pile face down in front of them.

4 At the same time, all the players turn over the top card from their pile.

5 The highest card wins. The player with the highest card picks up the other players' turned-up cards and puts them face down on the bottom of his own stack.

6 If two or three of the cards on the table are the same rank (two kings, two 2's, whatever), the players with those cards cover their own card with three more cards *face down,* and then one more face up. The person with the highest card up wins all the other player's cards, and puts them on the bottom of his pile.

7 If the second face-up cards are the same again, the players put down three more face down, and one more face up, the winner taking all cards. If you have no more cards to put down, you are out.

8 The first person to get all the cards is the winner.

105
CRAZY EIGHTS

two to five players

In this card game, the eights are wild. Absolutely and utterly crazy. The jacks are kind of strange too!

1 The object of the game is to be the first player to get rid of all your cards.

2 The dealer deals eight cards face down to each player, turns one card over, and puts the rest of the deck face down beside it.

3 Players take turns putting one card face up on the face-up card. The cards played must be of the same suit as the first card.

4 If you can't play a card of the same suit as the cards on the face-up pile, you must pick up one from the other pile, and your turn passes to the next player.

5 You can change the suit by playing a card with the same value, or number, as the last card played. For

instance, if the last card played was a six of spades, you can play a six of another suit on top, and change the suit being played to the suit of the new six. All cards played after this must be of the new suit, until it is changed again.

6 Some of the cards are special. If you put down a jack, you can put down another card of the same suit on top, thus playing two cards on one turn. If you have two jacks, you can put the second jack on top of the first (if the first one is playable), and then a card of the same suit as the second jack, on top of it. (Sounds complicated doesn't it?) This means that you have changed the suit being played, as well as playing three cards at one turn!

7 Another way to change the suit being played is to play an eight. Since eights are wild, you can change the suit to anything you want.

8 There are still a few more special cards. If you play a two, the player next to you must pick up two cards, then play.

9 If you play the queen of spades, the player next to you must pick up *four* cards. This is known in the business as 'The Kiss of Death.'

10 If the pick-up pile runs out of cards, shuffle the face-up pile, turn it over, and use it for the pick-up pile.

11 The first player to run out of cards in his hand is the winner!

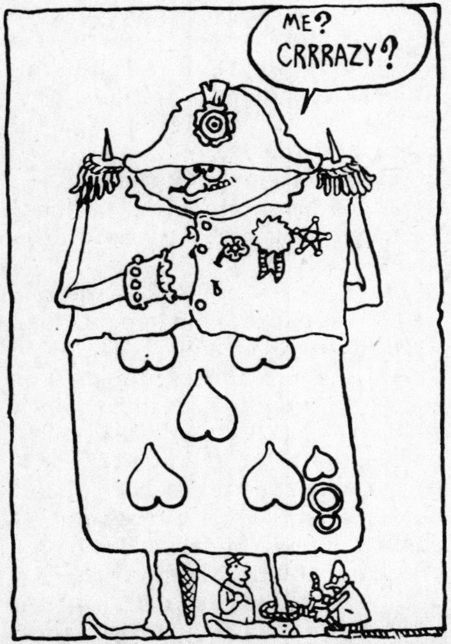
ME?
CRRRAZY?

106
THIRTY-ONE

two to ten players

31
31

1 The object of the game is to have three cards of the same suit that add up to 31, or to be the player with the highest hand. Ace counts as 11, face cards 10, all others as their face value.

2 The dealer deals three cards face down to each player, turns one card face up in the middle of the table, and puts the rest of the deck face down beside it.

3 Players take turns picking up the top card from either the large pile or the face-up pile, then discarding any one of their cards face up onto the face-up pile. The object is to collect high-ranking cards of one suit, trying to get three that add up to 31, or as close to it as possible.

4 Players at their turn *must* pick up a card and discard a card. You can only have three cards in your hand.

5 If a player has 31 (an Ace and two ten-value cards), he knocks on the table. This means that all the other players get one more turn, and then all the players turn up their cards.

6 If no one else gets 31, the player who knocked wins the round and scores a point. If, however, another player gets 31 in the last round after the knock, *that* player wins and the player who knocked loses.

7 If two players other than the one who knocked both get 31, the player who got it first wins.

8 At any time, a player can 'bluff' and knock without having 31. You can do this if you have three cards of the same suit and if you think your total will beat out everyone else's. If another player's score is the same, higher, or if somebody else gets 31, you lose.

107
RED DOG

two to eight players

In this game, each player starts off with 10 points, and there is a 'pot' in the center with 20 points. Players bet against the pot by saying 'I'll bet five' or whatever. No player can bet more than the amount in the pot. If the player who bets wins, he keeps his bet points, and takes the same number out of the pot. If he loses, his bet points go into the pot.

Players keep track of their points on paper, and the dealer keeps track of how many points are in the pot. Each player should have his own score sheet, and the score sheet for the pot should be left in plain view in the center of the table.

1 The object of Red Dog is to have one card in your hand that is the same suit as, and higher than, the top card of the pile.

2 The dealer deals five cards to each player, one at at time, face down.

3 The rest of the cards sit in one stack, face down in the center of the table. Players look at their hands.

4 The player to the dealer's left goes first. He or she bets any number of points against the pot.

5 The dealer then turns up the top card on the pile.

6 If the player has a card in his hand that is the same suit as the card turned up, and higher than it

DAD! HORACE ATE THE CARDS!

(Ace is the highest card), he wins, and collects his points back, plus the same number from the pot.

7 If the player doesn't have a card of the same suit as the one turned up, or if he has no higher card of the same suit, he loses and his bet points go into the pot.

8 After the first player has either won or lost, he lays his hand face up on the table and the next player plays.

9 After every player has played once, the cards are picked up and the player to the dealer's left shuffles and deals the next round.

10 If at any time the pot becomes empty, each player puts one of his own points into the middle to make a new pot.

11 When a player loses all his points, he is out of the game.

108

GO FISH

two to five players

'Got any sevens?'
'Go fish!'
For this kind of fishing you need neither hook, line nor sinker, just a plain old deck of 52. Go Fish is one of the all-time great card games. It's very easy to play, but fast moving, and exciting enough for card sharks of all ages.

1 The object of the game is to collect as many 'books' as you can. A book is two cards of the same kind, say two kings, or two jacks, or two threes.

2 The dealer deals out five cards one at a time, face down, to each player. The cards left over are placed face down in one stack in the center of the table. Players take any pairs from their hands and place them on the table.

3 Players take turns asking any one other player for a card they need to make up a book. It must be a card that you have one of already. For example, you might say to someone, 'Do you have any queens?' If the other player does, in fact, have some queens, he or she must hand them *all* over to you. If he doesn't, he says 'Go fish!' and you must pick up the top card from the middle stack.

GOT ANY SIXES?
GO FISH

4 If you get the card you asked for, from the other player or from the stack, you get another turn at asking. You can ask the same or any other player for the same or any other card. If you get your card again, either by asking or fishing, you can ask again.

5 If you don't get your card, the next player gets a try.

6 Whenever you form a complete book of two cards, place them face up on the table.

7 The game is over when all 26 books have been found by the players. The player with the most books wins.

8 If you suspect that a player is asking for a card that he has none of, challenge him to show you his card. If he doesn't have one, he misses that turn.

109
TRY PATIENCE
one player

Patience, besides being a virtue, is the name for a group of card games designed specially for one player. There are hundreds of different kinds of Patience (also known as Solitaire), and bored, lonely card sharks are probably thinking up new ones all the time.

This is a very simple version.

1 Go through the deck and take out all cards lower than seven, leaving in the Aces.

2 Shuffle the rest of the cards and deal them out one at a time face up, at the same time saying 'Seven, eight, nine, ten, jack, queen, king, Ace . . .' Say one word for each card you lay down. After you have laid down the first eight cards, go through the sequence again.

3 If the card you lay down is the same as the name you call out, remove that card from the pile.

4 The object of the game is to get rid of all the cards in your shortened deck in this way.

5 When you have gone through the deck once, shuffle the cards and start again, but start the sequence where you left off. For example, if you say 'jack' as you put down the last card, you shuffle the cards, put the first one down, and say 'queen.'

6 If at any time you go through the deck once without taking out at least one card, you lose and must start again with all the cards.

HA HA! I WIN AGAIN

110
ANOTHER KIND
one player

Don't let the fact that Patience or Solitaire games are often called 'Idiot's delight' fool you. Some of them take a lot of skill, luck, and (of course) patience to play. This next game is known as Accordian Patience, and you will need a lot of room to play it, so make sure you have a whole table or backseat to yourself.

1 The object of the game is to get all the cards into one stack.

2 Deal out thirteen cards face up in one long row.

3 If any card in the row is the same number *or* suit as the card on its left, or the *third* card on its left, it can be moved over onto that card. This is where the skill comes in handy. Think carefully about your moves. Sometimes it is better to move one card before you move another. For example, see the draw-

ing. It would be better to move the three of spades onto the six of spades first, and then move the ten of spades onto that. Otherwise, if you moved the ten over first, the three would not be able to move.
4 When your first row has shrunk down as far as it will go, deal out another row of thirteen cards alongside it, so that all the cards form one long row.
5 When this row has shrunk down as far as it will go, deal out another thirteen cards, and so on.
6 If you are able to get the entire row of cards to accordian down into one single pile, you win! If not, try again. Your skill improves greatly with each time you play the game, and you will soon find that it is easier than it sounds.

CHINA OR BUST

111
YET ANOTHER KIND
one player

If those first two kinds of Patience didn't try your patience to the breaking point, try this kind of Patience.
1 Take the four Aces out of the deck and put them down, side by side, face up.
2 The object of the game is to get the sequence of cards, two, three, four, five, six, seven, eight, nine, ten, jack, queen, king, on top of each Ace, ignoring suits.
3 Deal cards one at a time off the top of the deck. If they fit in with any sequence already started on the Aces, place them there. If they don't, place them face up on *any one* of four 'waste' piles at the bottom.
4 At any time, the top card of any waste pile can be played.
5 For example, the picture shows a game in progress. The first row is almost finished, and the player can

add the nine, ten, and jack from the top of the waste piles. If there are any cards just under these that fit in with any sequence, they can be used once they are exposed.

6 If you complete all four rows in order from Ace to king, you win!

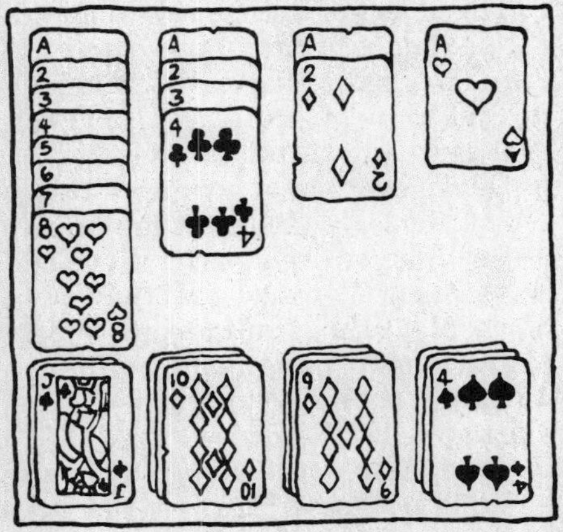

112

BEGGAR MY NEIGHBOR

two to eight players

Beggar My Neighbor is a fast-moving game that will keep you on the edge of your seat for the whole journey.

1 The object of the game, as in War, is to win all the cards.

2 The dealer deals out the cards, one at a time and face down, to each player until all the cards are dealt.

3 Players *do not* look at their cards, but hold them in one pile, face down.

4 Players take turns putting one card, face up, in the center of the table on one pile.

5 When one of the players turns up a jack, queen, king, or Ace, the next player has to pay one or more 'penalty' cards. The person who played the face card picks up all the cards in the center of the table, shuffles them, and puts them on the bottom of his pile.

6 These are the penalties: if a jack turns up, the next player must put down one card. If a queen turns up, the next player must put down two cards. If a king turns up, he must put down three cards, and if an Ace turns up, he must put down four cards!

7 If you turn up a face card when you are playing your penalty cards, you stop, and the player next to *you* must pay the penalty for it, and *you* get to pick up all the cards. But if this second player puts down a face card when he is paying his penalty, the third player must pay the penalty, and the second player wins the cards. Sometimes this can go on and on, until finally one player pays his full penalty without playing a face card. Then the last person who played a face card wins the pile of cards.

8 If a player runs out of cards to play in his turn, he may 'borrow' one card from the bottom of the center pile, and can continue to do so until he either wins or loses.
9 The last person left in the game wins.

113
OLD MAID
two to ten players

1 The object of Old Maid is to make pairs of cards, and not to be the player left with the last card, the 'Old Maid.'
2 The dealer discards one queen from the deck and deals out all the rest of the cards one at a time, face down, to each player until the whole deck is dealt.
3 Players look at their hands and take out any pairs of cards with the same numbers on them. If they have three cards with the same number, they can only take out two of them.
4 The dealer turns to the player on his or her left and holds out his cards, *face down*. The other player takes one card from it, discards any pair that might be formed, or puts the card in his hand and then offers his cards to the player on his left, and so on.
5 The game continues like this until there is only one card left that has not been made into a pair. This is the odd queen. The player who has this card is the Old Maid, and can't score. All the other players score one point for every pair they have collected.

EUREKA!
PHZZZTL
X-12
RPM

RADIO MANIA

This chapter is about that great dashboard traveling companion, the radio. Radio, as you know, is music and most people think of music as something to listen to. Not so with our good buddy, the caveperson. Whenever the mood struck him, he would burst into song with a swingin' rendition of Dyna-Soar Blues – a series of slaps, dull thuds, low moans, high-pitched whistles, and grunts, with a driving backbeat from the hollow log bongos. Music from the soul. This is known as the 'Rough Age' of musical history.

Later on, people developed more refined methods of making music, such as horns, flutes, rattles and stringed instruments – along with musical ideas like rhythm, melody and harmony – and music, as we know it, was born. Over the centuries, music and musical instruments have become more and more complicated, to the point where recording a record these days is like landing a man on the moon! But the beautifully simple music produced by ordinary people on ordinary instruments all over the world just goes to show that you don't need all that hardware to make great sounds.

Somewhere around the end of the last century, for heaven only knows what reasons, folks began to invent radio. Inventing something as great and as nebulous as radio takes time. It's not the kind of thing that happens overnight. People with names like Hughes, Hertz, Lodge and Marconi began fooling around with coils, tubes, and wires – sending noise, static, squawks, dull thuds and high-pitched whistles across their labs or down the street, by means of radio waves! Science triumphs again! But all this was mere child's play compared to what came next. In 1901, Marconi succeeded in sending a signal across the Atlantic – three short dots of static. Marconi is largely responsible for the installation of radio equipment on ships for sending messages to shore and to each other using Morse Code – a series of dots and dashes for each letter of the alphabet.

Imagine the ship radio operators' surprise when, in 1906, they heard actual voices and music in their headphones instead of the usual dots and dashes! The signal was generated from Massachusetts by a Canadian inventor named Fessenden, and it was *almost* the first time that the human voice and music had traveled the radio waves.

(What the world didn't know was that a New York inventor named Nikola Tesla and a Kentucky farmer named Nathan Stubblefield had both beat the whole bunch to the draw and sent voice and music over radio waves back before 1892!) The great Age of Radio had begun. From there, the technicians and businessmen took over, and it was only a matter of time before nearly every family in North America and Europe was listening to the Shadow, Jack Benny, music from the Crystal Ballroom and Radio City Music Hall, commercials, soap operas, commercials, news of war and disaster, and commercials, in the comfort of their own homes, and a little later on in cars.

But modern radio stations are nothing like the old ones, and, as a result, listening to AM radio these days can drive you totally and

THHZZT
THERE IS LIFE ON EARTH!

utterly insane in ten minutes flat. The solution? (If it's not too late already...) Make your own radio station! Imagine your vehicle as a rambling radio station on wheels, broadcasting signals into the ether as you roar along the road. Centuries from now, aliens in a far-off galaxy will receive your signals on their inter-space telecohearers and wonder what the hairy heck was going on down here on this back-water planet! Don't blame them if they get the idea that Earth folks are a little weird.

Singing and music are great traveling things to do when it's too dark to do anything else. Before you start, check with the driver to see if he minds your music. Okay, everyone ready? Step up to the microphone, set your wind, and wail! We're on the air!

114
MOCK OPERA
Sing 'n' tell

two or more players

One thing about the radio is that you hear the same songs over and over until you think you've memorized every note and word. Mock Opera is a good way to see if this is really true. The basic idea is that one person imitates a song, and the other players have to guess which song it is, and/or who sings it. There are three ways you can imitate the songs, and you should choose one of the three methods and stick to it through the game. The first method is to hum the song; the second method is to whistle the song; and the best method of all is to sing a few lines.

The player who correctly guesses which song you are warbling wins a point and sings a song for the next round. If no one guesses, you get to sing again. If you like, have the players guess the original singer.

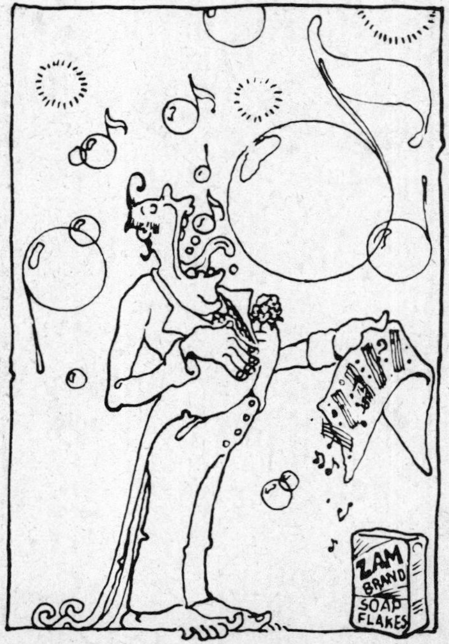
ZAM
BRAND
SOAP
FLAKES

115
HOMEMADE MUSIC
Away from home

Moving vehicles seem to attract things like paper cups, straws, pop bottles, bottle caps, candy wrappers and other litter. If you find some of these things kicking around in your sound-studio-on-wheels, don't throw them out just yet! Not only can they be used for all kinds of games (see the tenth chapter), but they can also be made into some of the finest musical instruments!

If you have a few people traveling with you, you could form a real live down-to-earth jug band.

Cup Banjo

If you are lucky enough to find a rubber band, you have the basic component for any kind of stringed instrument you want to make. Just strumming the elastic by itself doesn't make much of a noise. You need something to amplify the

sound. Wrap the elastic around a cup as shown in the drawing, and strum on the part that crosses the mouth of the cup. Now *that's* music! Put a pencil or your finger under the elastic on the side of the cup. As you pull it away from the side of the cup, the sound of the notes will change, and you'll find that you can play a whole range of sounds. A very versatile little instrument.

The Jug
What would a jug band be without an honest to goodness jug? Any old pop bottle makes a good jug. Put the top of the bottle against your bottom lip and blow across the opening. If you hold the bottle at the right angle, music will appear! This makes good background music for the banjo and the 'woodwinds.'

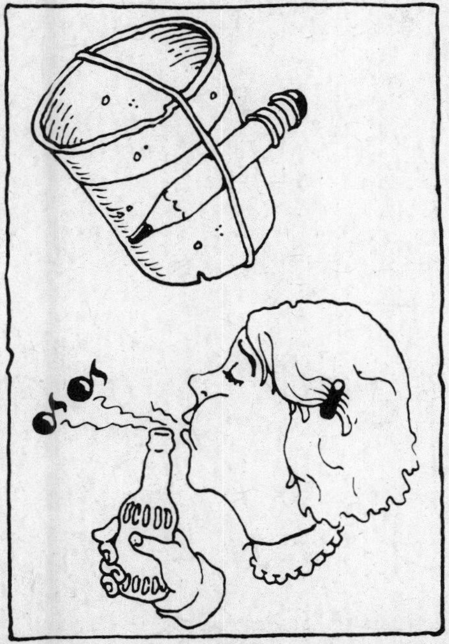

Tambourine
To play the tambourine, you have to have rhythm, you got to have beat, and you must have money! What? Why money you ask? Because money is what this tambourine is made of, that's why. Yep, nothing beats the sound of cold hard cash hitting more cold hard cash.

To make this tambourine, just reach into your pocket or purse, pull out a handful of any kind of coins, cup both hands together with the coins inside, and shake them for all your worth! The job of the tambourine is to lay down the beat that the other instruments play to. But remember, be careful with your new tambourine, it's a valuable instrument!

YOU ARE MY SUN - SHINE
RIP
BRAAP
BRAAAAP

Saxa-phony

This saxa-phony is as easy to make as it is to play, and that's easy! Its range of sound is limited (it only produces one note, but oh, what a note!), but it is good for filling in to give that 'Big Band' sound.

To make it, tear a strip of paper about six inches long and two or three wide. Fold it in half in the middle and fold up the two ends as shown in the picture. Tear out a small v in the middle fold, and your saxa-phony is finished. To play it, hold it in your hand as shown, and place the two folded-up flaps against your lips. Blow through, and the most beautiful sound will issue forth, not unlike the lonely evening call of the lovesick duckbilled platypus.

Percussion
All you need to make this instrument is one good hand, and one good mouth. It's easier if they are both your own. Open your mouth without showing your teeth, and lightly hit your mouth with the fingers of your hand, which are held together, straight out. This looks like you are performing an Apache war whoop without the whoop. This will make a sort of 'bip, bop' sound that changes as you open and close your mouth.

Marimbas
Aye Yi Yi! Having a good marimba player in your band can really snazz up your sound. The marimbas are a lot like the tambourine described earlier, but the sound is much louder and deeper. Take a disposable cup, with the lid if you have it (if you don't, you can cover the top with your hand). Put a few small coins or pebbles or bottle caps in the cup. Put the lid on or cover the cup. Shake well. The traditional sound is three short shakes, then pause, three short shakes, then pause, and so on, but let the music move you.

BIP
BOP
BUP
AREBA
AREBA
KA-KLUNK
KLUNK-A
KLUNK

Drums
Drums have been a big favorite for giving music 'punch' since the days of cave living. Almost anything can be used for a drum – a suitcase, a book, an upside down pot or box, or whatever. Things that are hard and hollow produce a lower, louder sound than anything else. One thing to watch out for – don't play the drums too loud or you will drown out the other players.

Kandy Kazoo
If you find one of those little candy boxes with a cellophane 'window' in the front, you've just found yourself a kandy kazoo! Open one end of the box, cover it with your mouth, and blow. Play it the same way you whistle, in short and long bursts of varying intensity. To vary the sound even more, try squeezing the sides of the box in and out.

Organically Grown Trumpet
Like the jug, the saxa-phony and the kandy kazoo, the o. g. trumpet is a wind instrument, because your wind is what makes the sound. It's called an organically grown trumpet because that's what it is! It's made from a single piece of crabgrass held between your two thumbs as shown in the drawings. The piece of grass should be flat,

PLAY YO' HARMONICA SON....
SUCH BE-YUTIFUL MUSIC

with the edge toward you, and held tightly between the top and base of your thumbs. When you blow just right in the opening between your thumbs, the most bee-yutiful high-pitched squawk comes forth. Blow harder and lighter to change the sound.

Vocalize
Of course, just instruments do not a jug band make. Every good jug band needs a little bit of the human voice to lend meaning to the music. You can write your own songs, make them up as you go along, or sing ones that you already know. When in doubt, hum or whistle.

Got your instruments all tuned up? Quiet on the set – 1,2,3,4!

116
POISON PENNY

four or more players

This game is the traveler's version of Musical Chairs. Obviously, when you are riding in a vehicle, you can't have the passengers leaping madly from seat to seat while the music plays. It tends to make the driver edgy. So instead, some thoughtful game-inventor said to himself, 'Why don't the people sit still instead of the chairs sitting still, and why don't they pass a chair around ...? No, no, that won't do. It'll have to be smaller than a chair. I've got it! An alarm clock! No, it might go off. An ice cream cone! Nope, no good. Hmmm ... What's this in my pocket ... a penny! I'll call it ... Painful Penny! No. How about Palm-the-Penny? Uh-uh. Pass-the-Penny? No. Palooka's Penny? Penny Palingenesis? Paradisiacal Penny? ...' Anyway, to make a long story short, the game was finally called – yep, you guessed it – Poison Penny!

IS IT A RIOT?
NO - THEY'RE PLAYING MUSICAL CHAIRS
BLANDVILLE HIGH FOOTBALL TEAM
13

If you have made some of the musical instruments described in the last game, Poison Penny is the perfect game to try them out on. Each person gets a chance to act as a soloist. The soloist closes his or her eyes and plays some music – any kind of music will do – while the other players pass a penny from hand to hand, around in a circle. When the music stops, the person left holding the Poison Penny becomes the soloist, and the former soloist takes his place in the circle.

If the penny is in between two players, being passed from hand to hand when the music stops, it doesn't count as 'poison.' Neither player has to leave the circle. Instead, the soloist starts again and tries to trap someone else.

117
TEN TONGUE-TANGLERS
For up-and-coming disc jockeys

'Howdy howdy howdy!! This is Carry LaRock for WHUH Radio, bringin' you some of the hits most of the time, most of the hits some of the time, and all of the hits none of the time!!'

Good D.J.'s have to be able to talk clearly and *fast,* without saying anything at all. If you want to be the disc jockey for your traveling radio show, you'd better loosen up your vocal cords so you can babble the small talk like a real D.J. without a single slip of the lip. Practice these tongue-tanglers faithfully, and before you know it, you'll have a voice like honey and a tongue like rubber.

Start out with a few of these 'simple' ones. Say each of these ten times:

- Unique New York
- Rubber baby buggy bumpers
- A proper copper coffee pot
- A stewed sow's snout
- Three gray geese in a green field grazing

Is your voice beginning to sound like that smooth baritone? Okay, finish off your warming-up session with these next twisters:

A woman to her son did utter
Go, my son, and shut the shutter.
The shutter's shut, the son did mutter,
I cannot shut it any shutter!

There's no need to light a night-light
On a light night like tonight
For a night-light's a slight light
On a light night like tonight.

A tutor who tooted the flute
Tried to tutor two tooters to toot,
Said the two to the tutor
Is it harder to toot
Or to tutor two tooters to toot?

Of all the felt I ever felt,
I never felt a piece of felt
That felt the same as that felt felt
When I first felt the felt of that felt hat.

How much wood could a woodchuck chuck
If a woodchuck could chuck wood?

B.I.N.G.O.

Bingo was his name, sir!

If you have a group of people in your vehicle, there is nothing quite like a good ol' singsong to make the miles fly by. Even the driver can join in on the singing part, but keep an eye on him to make sure he doesn't start slappin' his hands and stompin' his feet. Or closing his eyes in sheer delight!

Bingo looks like a simple ordinary song at first glance, but there is a trick to singing it. If one of your traveling companions knows how to read music, he should be the 'leader.' If no one knows how to read music, don't worry. It's not too hard to figure out. Just compare the words of the song with the notes of the music. Each syllable (farmer has two syllables, dog has one) has a note on the lines. The higher the note is on the lines, the higher you sing the word. You'd better sing the song through once or twice so that everyone is familiar with the tune.

Here are the words:

There was a farmer had a dog
And Bingo was his name, sir.
B.I.N.G.O. B.I.N.G.O. B.I.N.G.O.
Bingo was his name, sir!

That farmer's dog at our back door,
Begging for a bone, sir.
B.I.N.G.O. B.I.N.G.O. B.I.N.G.O.
Bingo was his name, sir!

1 Everybody sings the song right through once.
2 Sing the song through again, but this time, instead of singing the B when you are spelling out Bingo's name, clap your hands instead.
3 Sing the song again, but this time leave out the B and the I in the spelling, and clap your hands twice in rhythm instead.
4 Repeat the song again, but clap your hands three times in rhythm instead of singing B, I and N.
5 Keep singing the song through, leaving off another letter each time and clapping your hands instead, until on the last time, you will clap five times instead of singing B.I.N.G.O.

119
LONDON BRIDGE

Almost everyone must know how to sing London Bridge by now. The song is usually sung as part of a game. Two of the players hold their arms up to form an archway, while the other players run underneath. When the verse is over, the two players drop their arms and try to catch another player.

Most people know about this game, even if they haven't played it, but what most people don't know, is that London Bridge is actually a very long song that is great to sing with a group of people when you are traveling.

Here are all the words from one of many versions:

1 London Bridge is falling down, falling down, falling down.
London Bridge is falling down, my fair lady, oh!

2 Build it up with iron bars, iron bars, iron bars,
Build it up with iron bars, my fair lady, oh!

3 Iron bars will rust away, rust away, rust away,
Iron bars will rust away, my fair lady, oh!

4 Build it up with needles and pins, ...
(as you can see by now, the last bit is always the same).

5 Pins and needles will rust away ...

6 Build it up with penny loaves ...

7 Penny loaves will tumble down ...

8 Build it up with gold and silver ...

9 Gold and silver I have none ...

10 Here's a prisoner we have got ...

11 What's the prisoner done to you? ...

12 Stole my watch and broke my crown ...

13 What's it take to set him free? ...

14 A hundred pounds will set him free ...

15 A hundred pounds we have not got ...

16 Then off to prison he must go, he must go, he must go,
Off to prison he must go, my fair lady, oh!

SINGING IN ROUNDS

If you have never sung in rounds before, you have been missing out on one of the great things that life has to offer. The basic idea is this: one person starts singing the song. When he has finished singing the first line, he keeps going, but the next person starts singing the first line when the first person is starting on the second line. When the second person is starting on the second line, the third person starts singing the first line, and so on, until everyone is singing a different line.

You would think that this would sound like so much radio static, but in fact it sounds very beautiful. Round songs were incredibly popular in the Middle Ages, and Frère Jacques comes from this time.

Here are the words for three of the most popular round songs, with the English words for Frère Jacques. Somebody in your studio-on-wheels is bound to know the music for at least one of the songs.

Three blind mice, three blind mice.
See how they run, see how they run.
They all ran after the farmer's wife,
She cut off their tails with a butcher knife!
Did you ever see such a sight in your life,
As three blind mice?

Row, row, row your boat
Gently down the stream.
Merrily, merrily, merrily, merrily,
Life is but a dream.

Frère Jacques, Frère Jacques,
Dormez-vous? Dormez-vous?
Sonnez les matines, sonnez les matines,
Ding dang dong! Ding dang dong!

Are you sleeping? Are you sleeping?
Brother John? Brother John?
Morning bells are ringing, morning bells are ringing.
Ding dang dong! Ding dang dong!

If you are singing Frère Jacques, you could have every second singer singing the English version.

You may find singing like this very difficult at first, but after you get used to it, it's the most natural thing in the world.

121
THE POETRY HOUR

There's an old saying that goes, 'When I hear the word culture, I reach for my revolver' and let's face it friends, what's a radio station without a little culture? To some people, culture is something you do with bacteria, but to others it means things like opera, ballet, and poetry, among other things. Well, we've already covered opera with all the singing games, and even if you could find room in a moving car for ballet, it's not the kind of thing you usually find on a radio program! So that leaves poetry.

Put a little culture in your radio programming for your highbrow listeners and start a Poety Hour show! Give a chance to the budding bards in your midst to read their own verse out loud, or try out some of the examples below:

Mary's Song

Mary went down to Grandpa's farm,
The billy goat chased her around
the barn.
Chased her up the sycamore tree,
And this is the song she sang to me:
'I like coffee, I like tea,
I like the boys and the boys like me!'

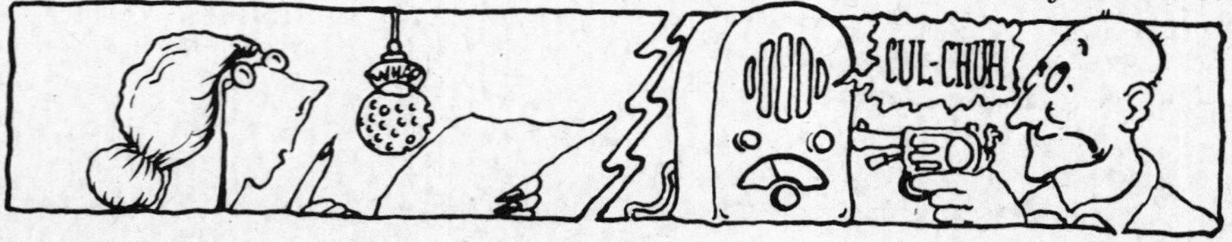
CUL-CHUH

'Tis Midnight

'Tis midnight, and the setting sun
Is slowly rising in the west;
The rapid rivers slowly run,
The frog is on his downy nest.
The pensive goat and sportive cow,
Hilarious, leap from bough to
bough.

The Ill-fated Promenade

Three young rats with black felt
hats,
Three young ducks with white
straw flats,
Three young dogs with curling
tails,
Three young cats with demi-veils,
Went out to walk with two young
pigs
In satin vests and sorrel wigs;
But suddenly it chanced to rain,
And so they all went home again.

AND NOW, HERE'S THE NEWS...

Dumb Boids
Toity poible boids,
Sittin on da coib
Choipin and a boipin
An eatin doity woims.

The Common Cormorant
The common cormorant, or shag
Lays eggs inside a paper bag.
The reason you will see no doubt –
It is to keep the lightning out!
But what these unobservant birds
Have failed to notice is that herds
Of wandering bears may come with buns
And steal the bags to hold the crumbs.

Picture this: the African grasslands at dusk. The setting sun turns the sky the color of old roses, while on the plain below a herd of gnus (pronounced *nooz*) peacefully grazes. Suddenly there is a furtive movement in the tall grass, and with an ear-splitting roar that shatters the evening silence, a huge lion leaps upon the gnus! The King of the Beasts is merciless! With powerful strokes of his razor claws he slashes left and right, and soon all the gnus lie slaughtered on the plain, and silence returns once more to the African dusk. A hyena walks slowly out from the edge of the forest, turns towards you, and says, 'Well, that's the end of the gnus, and now, here's the sports.'

If you've always wanted to be in the news, here's your big chance. As you know, every radio station has at least a few news programs every day, and some stations are nothing *but* news! Most of the time the news is pretty dull, but that's because the newsmen report only what *actually* happens! If you are going to have a news program on your radio station, you can report anything you like! Wouldn't it be a switch if the six o'clock news was nothing but *good* news? We'd hardly recognize it!

Because you are reporting only imaginary news, you can let your imagination run wild! Fill out your news program with interviews, expert opinions, stock market reports, weather reports, and sports. Have on-the-scene reports from disasters and great events.

Here we are at Yankee Stadium, where Mickey Mantlemouse has just kicked his 54,697th home run of the season. Do you have a few words for all your fans at home, Mickey?

'Shucks, yes. If I have to autograph another darn hockey puck I swear I'll be mad enough to spit.'

And, on the home front, we have an up-to-the-minute report from the driver of this vehicle. Excuse me, sir or ma'am. What up-to-the-minute news do you have for the ever-eager ears of our limp listeners?

'Well John, the vehicle in question seems to be moving in a direction that can only be described as forward at a fairly uniform speed, and other than that I guess I have nothing to report, unless you count the fact that we are rapidly running out of gas, and two of our fellow passengers have to go to the bathroom immediately if not sooner. So I would guess that a gas station is at the top of our list of things to keep an eye out for.'

Thank you. We'll be back with the weather after this message …

WELL, THAT'S THE END OF THE NEWS, AND NOW HERE'S THE SPORTS..
ON THE AIR
NEWS

X-13
23°
NO VACANCY
RPM

GAMES FOR ONE TEAM

The problem with winning is that someone has to lose. If you have been playing games for a while, you are probably getting tired of all the winning, losing, heckling and haggling that go with ordinary competition – and especially the losing! Let's face it, we all have a bit of the poor loser in us: otherwise, no one would ever try to win. One of the hardest things to break out of is a losing streak, because no matter how many times in a row you lose, you always think that the *next* game is the one that will put your score up to the top, and if not the next game, then the game after that, or the game after that, or . . .

Now don't get me wrong, I have nothing against a good honest game

WE WIN AGAIN!

played by the rules, but we all know that most games are just friendly wars, and sometimes everyone gets the feeling that they would rather just relax for a while and have fun, without having to worry about the score sheet.

How would you like to leave all this silly competition behind? How would you like to play games that have never heard of things like 'winning' or 'losing?' How would you like to play *with* your friends instead of *against* them? The games in this chapter are specially designed with this in mind. There are no winners, and so there are also no losers. There is only one team of friends with one object in mind: having fun!

123
SUDDENLY...

two or more players

This is a game where you can really let your imagination carry you away. The group works together to make up one long story about the adventures and misadventures of one central character. Each player adds a sentence or two at a time.

The first player describes our character as he or she is performing some action, and then puts the character in danger. The next player picks up at this point. He has to save the character, and then put him in a new dangerous situation. The next player saves our poor character again, and then puts him in *another* situation.

A sample story about the adventures of Wide Wally Wombat might go like this:

First player One day Wide Wally Wombat was out mountain-climbing. He was pulling himself up on a rope over an especially difficult stretch of rock, when suddenly the mountain turned into an active volcano, and Wide Wally's rope burnt up!

Next player Luckily, there was a lake full of soft water right under Wally, and it broke his fall and saved him from the flying lava and molten magma. Suddenly, from the bottom of the lake there appeared an unfriendly submarine, firing man-eating torpedos!

Next player Wally quickly inflated his inflatable Wide Wally Wombat decoy, and sent it swimming out into the middle of the lake to distract the torps, while he swam to shore. He crawled up on a rock to dry off, but he suddenly realized that the rock had become surrounded by red-hot lava, and it was rising quickly!

This story could go on forever, or at least as long as you don't run out of imagination.

124
A LIKELY STORY

two or more players

This game is a good test of your memory and imagination. One of the players makes a list of about six or eight objects, then reads it out loud, slowly. The list is then hidden.

The first player makes up one sentence, using the first object on the list. The second player repeats the first player's sentence, and then makes up a new sentence that carries on the story and also uses the second object on the list. The third player repeats the first two sentences, then adds a new one, using the third object on the list.

The story travels around the circle of players in this way, each player repeating all the previous sentences, then adding on a new one that uses the next object on the list. If one player makes a mistake, you have to start over again from the very beginning.

For instance, if your list of objects looked like this: cage, bird, tree, rabbit, bridge, telephone, train, city; your finished story might go something like this:

Once upon a time, there was a beautiful gold and silver cage covered in jewels.

In this cage lived a beautiful bird.

One day the bird escaped and flew to a nearby tree.

Under the tree sat a rabbit.

The rabbit saw the bird, and walked over a bridge.

He went to a telephone to phone the owners of the bird to tell them where it was hiding out.

'You rat fink!' screeched the bird, and hopped onto a passing freight train.

It was last seen heading east for the nearest city.

125
ACTION SHUFFLE

two or more players

This game is almost the reverse of the last one. This time, one of the players writes a short simple story, but keeps it secret from the others. In the meantime, all the other players make up a list of verbs. Verbs are action words like run, ran, eat, ate, jump, saw, see, look, move, draw, drew, guess, need, tell, etc.

The person who wrote the story goes through it and circles all the verbs in it, and then reads it out loud. Every time he comes to one of the circled verbs, instead of reading it he reads the next verb from the list. In this way, a simple ordinary story becomes a hilarious mish-mash of nonsense, especially if the verb-creators have thought up some weird and funny action words.

Here is a sample story with its new verbs added in:

One morning the wonderful Wide Wally Wombat *broke* up. He *slumped* downstairs, *crushed* breakfast, and *jumped* to work. At work he *screamed* hello to his boss. Suddenly his telephone *moaned* and he *chewed* it. It was Superthing, his super-powered buddy. Superthing was *burning* into his costume in a phone booth and his zipper *leaned* in the door. What's more, he *ate* his last dime to *drink* Wally. 'Wally, you've got to *see* me!' Superthing *flopped*. Wide Wally *gurgled* as he *fell* out the door to Superthing's rescue.

Can you figure out what the original verbs were?

P.S. You can add -ed or -ing on the end of a verb, or change its tense (change eat to ate, see to saw, or vice versa) to make it fit better.

126
BEEP

two or more players

This game is also sometimes known as Buzz, but if you are traveling in a car, it seems better to call it Beep, because, after all, that's the sound the car's horn makes.

The players count in a circle. The first player says 'one,' the second player says 'two,' the third player says 'three,' and so on. Sounds pretty easy so far. But whenever any player comes to the number seven, or any multiple of seven (14, 21, 28, 35, 42, 49, etc.) or even a number with seven in it (17, 27, 37, 77 ...), instead of saying one of those dirty 'seven' numbers, he or she must say 'BEEP!' instead.

If you forget to say Beep, everyone must go right back to the beginning and start counting over again. (Groan!) The object of the game is to try to count up to 100 without anyone making a single mistake.

Remember your seven times table!

Here's how the first part of the counting should go: 1, 2, 3, 4, 5, 6, beep, 8, 9, 10, 11, 12, 13, beep, 15, 16, beep, and so on.

BEEP!

127
TOM, DICK & HARRY

two or more players

Tom, Dick and Harry is a game named after its inventors, Tom, Dick, and last but not least, Harry. It's a lot like the last game, Beep, but it's much more complicated. Like Beep, the players count in a circle, each one saying one number at a time. In this game you can say seven as often as you want, but instead of saying one, you must say Tom, instead of saying two, you must say Dick, and instead of saying three you say Harry. When you come to ten you say Tom-zero, for eleven you say Tom-Tom, and the number thirty one is Harry-Tom.

The first bit of counting goes like this: Tom, Dick, Harry, 4, 5, 6, 7, 8, 9, Tom-zero, Tom-Tom, Tom-Dick, Tom-Harry, Tom-4, etc.

128
EXQUISITE CORPSES

two or more players

Exquisite Corpses sounds like the name for some kind of weird horror movie, but in actual fact it is the name of a hilarious game that a few of you are probably familiar with.

It can be played in many different ways, but the most common one goes like this:

1 The first player takes a piece of paper, and at the top draws the head of a figure, keeping the drawing hidden from the other players. He or she folds the paper over so that just a little part of the neck can be seen, and passes the paper to the next player.

2 The next player draws the top half of the mystery figure's body, without looking to see what the head looks like. He then folds the paper over, so that none of the other players can see what has been drawn, and passes the folded paper to the next player, who does the legs, and so on.

4 When the last player has finished drawing the feet, open the paper and have a look at the strange creature your imaginations have hatched.

The weird name Exquisite Corpses comes from a game invented by the Surrealists (a group of artists and poets) in France around 1925 or so. When this game was first played, words were used instead of pictures, the object being to have several people construct a sentence, each one adding a word or two, not knowing what the other players had written. The first sentence written in this way was 'Le cadavre exquis boira le vin nouveau,' which in English means 'The exquisite corpse drinks the new wine,' hence the name!

129
WORD ASSOCIATION

two or more players

This is a game that's usually played by a psychiatrist (otherwise known as a head shrinker) and a patient, for the purpose of finding out what is on the patient's mind.

You don't have to be suffering from any kind of psychosis or brain fever to have fun playing Word Association, though. It's very relaxing to play with other people, and can also be incredibly funny!

The basic idea is this: the first player starts off the game by saying the first word that comes into his head. The second player then says the first word that comes into *his* (or her) head, and so on. If you like, you can have each player take turns, one after the other, or you can just have the whole group saying the first words that spring up onto the tips of their tongues at any time.

Either way, you'll be amazed at some of the things that you find yourself and others saying. If you follow the only rule of this game and say the very first word that you think of, without actually 'thinking' about it, the things you say will be a real reflection of what is going on in the depths of your subconscious. Don't be surprised if you get a surprise!

oh?
OH!
OH?
oh.
OH.
OOH!
OH!

130
QUIET PLEASE
Silence is golden

two or more players

You may think that it's the simplest thing in the world to keep quiet and just not say anything, but sometimes, especially when you are with a bunch of other people, it can seem like the *hardest* thing in the whole universe!

Make a rule that everyone has to keep their traps shut until you drive past the next town, or the next gas station, or whatever. You can point, write notes, and use sign language, but if any person makes even the tiniest sound, you *all* lose!

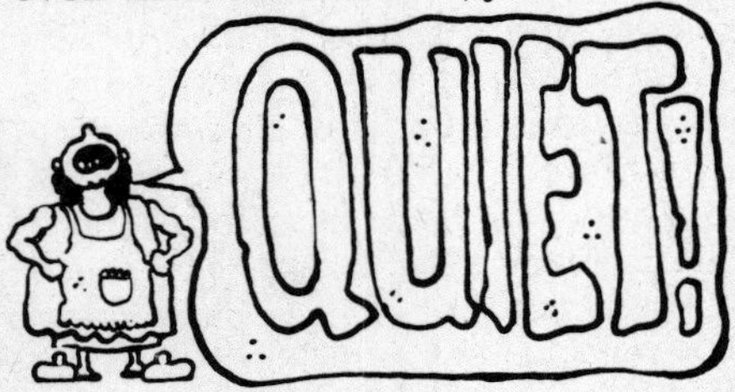
QUIET!

131

ONE LINERS

An exquisite corpse story

two or more players

Working with other people on the job of making up stories can be an incredible experience. You see the story start moving in one direction, and next thing you know, it has taken off in every direction at once, and things start happening that you would never have thought possible.

The first player starts the story by saying one sentence – any sentence that comes to mind. Each player then takes turns adding one more sentence at a time. By the time the third player has added a sentence, a general story line should begin to show up.

If you have the time and inclination, the story could go on forever, but if you want to make the game more difficult, make a rule that each player can only say a total of three sentences, and that the last three sentences of the story must tie it up somehow, and end the story, leaving no loose ends.

THEN WHAT HAPPENED?
YOU TELL ME

132
SOUND EFFECTS

three or more players

Each player should think of what kind of animal he would like to be, if he could, and what kind of noise that animal makes. Have one of the players who is good at storytelling make up a story that tells the adventures of all the animals that the other players have chosen to imitate. You could all take turns at this part if you like, or work together as a group to make the story, and have one person read it.

Whenever the storyteller mentions the name of one of the animals, the person who is that animal must make the right animal noise. So whenever the storyteller mentions a horse, the 'horse' should whinny, and whenever a dog is mentioned, the 'dog' should bark and growl, and so on.

The storyteller can make all the other sound effects for the story, such as stampeding gophers, rocket blast-offs, giant's footsteps, toasters popping, train whistles, gunshots, screams, crowds cheering, and that sort of thing.

...SO DEN DIS BIG DOG SEZ TO HIS BUDDY, "HEY RALPH! GET A LOAD O' DAT! A TALKIN' HORSE!"
ARF! ARF!
NEIGH!

133

EXCUSES, EXCUSES!

two or more players

A master excuse-maker can come up with a good excuse for every occasion, at the drop of a hat. 'My alarm clock is on the blink.' 'I left my homework on the bus.' 'I forgot.' '*They* said I could do it.' 'The sun was in my eyes.' 'Oops, I slipped!' 'I'm no good at that kind of thing.' 'Honest, judge, I was in Antarctica at the time, playing golf with a nun!' These are some of the classic excuses, used time and again.

Making excuses for everything that goes wrong is a poor substitute for finding and correcting the real cause of the trouble. Still, it can be a useful talent, if used wisely.

How good are you at coming up with original excuses? This game will give you a chance to sharpen up your excuse-making abilities in preparation for real life.

.... WELL, NO SOONER DID I FINISH TAPING UP ALL SEVEN MILLION OR SO CHARRED FRAGMENTS OF MY HOMEWORK, WHEN WHAT SHOULD HAPPEN BUT BLABLABLA

1 The first player says a very simple sentence, describing an event in the shortest possible way. For example, 'I flunked my math test.'
2 The next player then thinks up a good reason, and begins his sentence with 'Because ...' For example, 'Because the night before the test a meteor from beyond the farthest star crashed through the roof of my house and smashed all my math books to atoms!'
3 The next player (or the first player again) then adds what the effect of the first player's statement was, for example, 'And so my teacher gave me three weeks of math homework.'
4 The next player then starts with a new sentence.

Try to think up the wildest excuses you can, as fast as you can, to add excitement to the game.

PORE PORE LONE-SOME ME...
BEEP
BEEP
12
RPM

GAMES FOR A TEAM OF ONE

Traveling alone? Castaway by yourself on a desolate desert isle? Drifting between galaxies in a one-man spacebuggy without so much as a rough-hewn robot cometscrubber to keep you company?

These are the times when your imagination and inventiveness are put to the true test. It's easy enough to have a good time when you are playing games with other people, but when you are alone, a whole new set of rules comes into play. For one thing, a game of Battleships or Ghosts is definitely out of the question. But there are many other games and activities in this book which need only one willing participant, or which can be changed slightly so that one person can play.

Most of the string figures and games in the fourth chapter, Why Knot, can be done by one person, as well as a lot of the paper activities in the chapter called Rip and Wrinkle. In the chapter after that, For Fingers, you will find a couple of good tricks you can practice, plus a couple of puppets you can make for company, and some other things to make. The seventh chapter, Mind-games, has many games and

tests of mental skill and stamina that can be played by any number of people, including zero, and, of course, one! And in the chapter called Count Me In, the eighth chapter, most of the abraca-algebra and some other numbertricks can be enjoyed by lone wolves. The ninth chapter is all board games like Checkers, and if you like, you can play against yourself, which is much harder than playing against another player, because you want both sides to win! Chapter ten, What To Do With the Loot shows lots of things you can make and do with stuff you might find on your trip. Most of these games are for two people, but a versatile loner should be able to figure some way around that. In the eleventh chapter, Dealing With a Card, there are three kinds of Solitaire, or Patience,

BALANCE BOOK

which are card games for one person. Chapter twelve, Radio Mania, describes some musical instruments you can make, plus a few tongue-tanglers that are always good for a laugh. There aren't many games in Chapter thirteen that can be played by one person, but you could practice the magic in the fifteenth chapter, Miscellaneous Magic, or try some of the looking-out games in the last chapter.

That leaves Chapter fourteen, Games for a Team of One, which is the chapter you are reading right now! You are the team of one!

If all the games and activities in the other chapters aren't enough to keep a lone wolf busy for a month of lonesome Sundays, here are a few more games, stunts and feats to add to the list of things to do when you are traveling all, all alone.

If you are traveling alone, you have probably been sitting in one place looking out the window for a long time, and anyone who does this is bound to get a stiff neck or back because of the infamous 'Bad Posture' (shudder). Bad posture, no matter what the car salesmen tell you, is

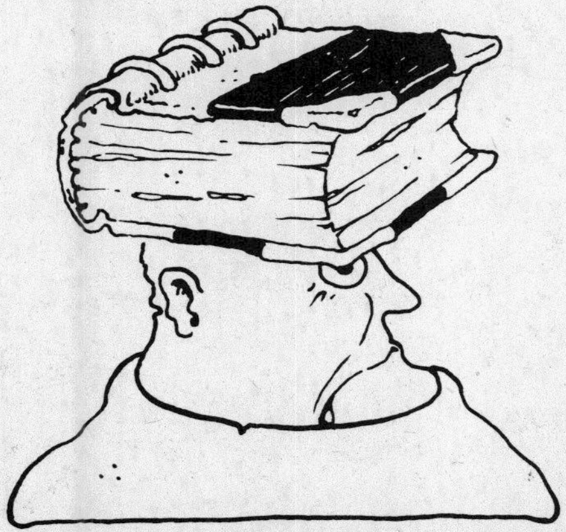

mostly caused by poorly designed seats and chairs. Many of them are too soft, or lean back too far, and most of them are not made with kids in mind, but instead are designed for that legendary creature that everyone has heard about but never seen, the Average Human.

Anyway, so much for the cause of bad posture. It's the effect that you are mainly worried about – the stiff neck and back. Putting something hard on the seat to sit on, like a board or hardbound book, helps you to sit up straighter, and when you sit straighter, you see more!

And of course, there's always that age-old trick for developing good posture, balancing a book on your head. A stiff or hardbound book works best, or anything flat and not too heavy. See how long you can keep the book balanced!

LOOSEN UP

One of the dangers of modern traveling is the stiffness caused by too much sitting in one spot. You know the spot I'm talking about. There is nothing worse than getting out of a car at a gas station and stumbling around stiff-legged like some kind of store-window dummy. If you feel like you need some oil in your joints and some life in your deadened nerves, try some of these exercises.

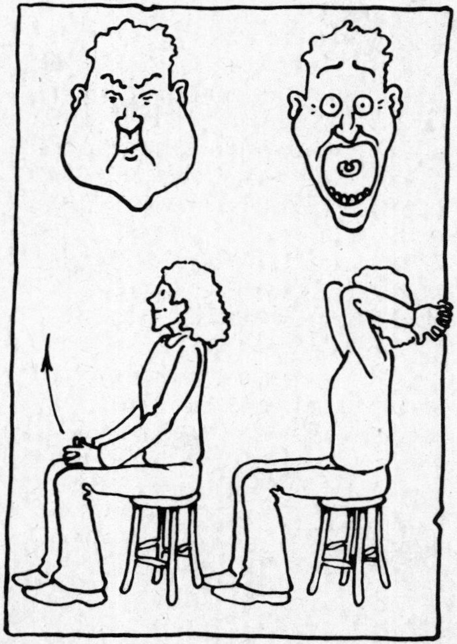

1 Facelift

If you have been sitting gaping out the window, gaping at the scenery, or gaping at this book, chances are that your face muscles are in need of a little loosening up. Start out by making the ugliest face you can think of. Feeling better? Okay, now puff out your cheeks with air, and squinch your eyes closed as tight as you can. Then open your eyes wide and open your mouth as far as it will go, as if you are in the grips of a monster yawn. Stick your tongue out and wiggle it around, just for good measure. Do these a few times, closing your eyes and puffing out your cheeks, then opening your mouth and opening your eyes. Soon the juices will start flowing in your face, and you'll feel almost human again, although if anyone has been watching you, they will start to wonder!

2 Push!

This one is great for the muscles in your arms, shoulders, neck and chest. Start out by sitting up straight in your seat and letting out your breath. Hold your hands together in your lap. Slowly bring them up in front of you and over

your head, at the same time taking a slow, deep breath. Keep moving your hands back until they touch the back of your neck. Hold your breath for a few seconds, then slowly let it out, at the same time bringing your hands back over your head, down in front of you, and into your lap.

Do this a few times until you get used to the motion (up and breathe in, down and breathe out). Then, as you move your hands up, press them against each other, as if you are trying to squeeze something between them. Relax them as you lower them again. Each time you raise your arms, press harder until, on the last time, you are pressing as hard as you can. Don't forget to breathe in slowly as you raise your arms, and out slowly as you lower them.

3 Stre-e-etch

If you have the whole seat to yourself, put your legs up on it with your feet about a foot apart. Keep your legs as straight and stiff as boards, and lean forward and take hold of one of your feet with both hands. Lean forward even more and try to touch your nose to your knee, without bending it (your nose *or* your knee). Don't worry if you can't do it on the first try, it's just a sign that you are rusty. Sit up again, and then lean forward and grab your other foot with both hands, and try to touch *that* knee with your nose. Do this about three times with each leg, and then try the next one . . .

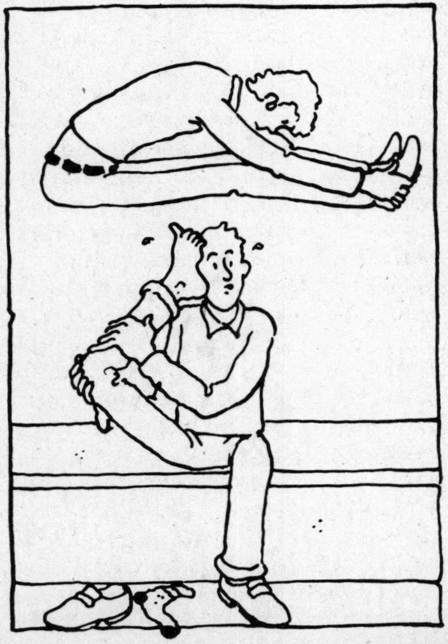

136
BACKSEAT BASKETBALL FEATS

4 Foot to Forehead
The title says it all. Sit tall in your seat with your back straight, looking straight ahead. Bring your left foot up into your lap, take hold of it with both hands, and without bending your back or leaning forward, try to raise your foot to your forehead. If you have been sitting still for some time, your foot probably won't go all the way up on the first try, but don't worry about it. Put your left foot down again, and try to lift your right foot up to your forehead. Do this three times with each leg.

Well, if that hasn't loosened you up, try going through the exercises one more time. Also, try the finger exercises at the beginning of the sixth chapter, For Fingers.

To play basketball, you need a court, a ball, baskets and two teams. For this backseat version of the popular sport, the seat is your court, a wad of paper is the ball, a cup is the basket, and you are the team!

Stretch out on the seat with your feet up, and hold the cup between your feet, with the top pointing toward you. Lean back as far as you can, and hold your throwing arm near the elbow with the other hand. The trick is to try to toss the paper basketball into the basket without moving any part of your throwing arm, except your hand. Holding your throwing arm near the elbow helps you keep it from moving.

Make several paper basketballs, by wadding up pieces of paper, so that you don't have to move around as much. Two points for every basket!

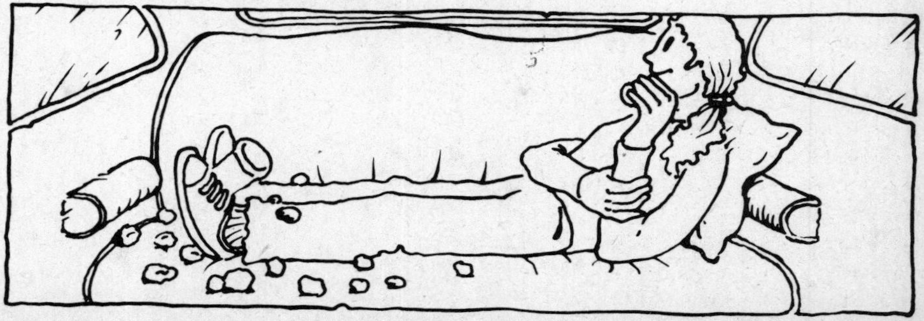

YES, YES... MARVELOUS TRICK... NOW, CAN I HAVE MY CAR BACK?
RPM

MISCELLANEOUS MAGIC

With string, cards, coins, dice, handkerchiefs, and numbers

Everyone knows that magic isn't *really* Magic. Magic with a capital M is a different thing altogether. Everybody knows that all a magician does is take perfectly ordinary objects and do things with them that look absolutely and totally impossible, which is exactly what a juggler, fire-eater, or sword-swallower does. Or even a carpenter for that matter. So don't try to fool your audience into thinking that you have some kind of Magical Powers, because they know as well as you do that it's just not true. What appears to be magical mind-over-matter is merely a matter of the hand being quicker than the eye.

What any audience wants is to be entertained. They are amazed and amused by the performances of clowns, jugglers, acrobats, fire-eaters, comedians and actors, not because they think the performer is Magic, but because of the performer's skill. The audience doesn't enjoy an act less even when they know exactly how it's done.

The magician and the audience must come to some kind of an agreement. If the performer doesn't try to act superior to the audience, as if he were trying to fool them, the audience in turn will be willing to sit back and enjoy the show for what it is – a display of skill.

Even though they know that every incredible miracle and impossible trick has some kind of perfectly good explanation, they will still be excited, amused, mystified, bewildered, perplexed and downright baffled!

'Well,' they will say, 'I'm sure glad all that has a perfectly good explanation, otherwise I would have to believe that impossible miracles can really happen! I wonder how the Great Wund-O did it?' They, the audience, will be impressed with your skill and knowledge of things uncanny and illusionary. And we all know that these things come with practice, and plenty of practice is what you'll need to perform some of these tricks.

But sometimes it's not possible to practice. For instance, what if you are just reading about a trick in this book for the first time, and your audience is waiting patiently, no more than a foot away, for you to perform the trick? Well, luckily some of the tricks need little or no practice (Feat of Strength,

Double Handcuff Escape, Triple Dice Guess, The Loop Escapes, The Two Robbers, Triple Flip, and more). All that is needed is a basic understanding of the rules and principles of the trick, and maybe this book to check for the tough bits.

Some of the other tricks, however, definitely need practice; there is no way around it. So you have two choices; you can perform the trick without practice and hope the audience will be as amused watching you totally flub it as they would be if you did it right, or you can practice the trick right there in front of the audience, and let them learn it at the same time you do. That way, you can all spend the time that you would normally spend gaping out the window, learning a new trick to spring on your friends and relatives

..FOR MY NEXT... OOPS!
OH
UGH!

when you get back home or to your destination. And as I said earlier, the audience really doesn't mind knowing how a trick is done.

There are some basic rules that you should know before performing magic. If you are doing something secret with your left hand, look intently at your right hand. If you are doing something tricky with *both* hands, look your audience right in the eye, so that some of their attention will be distracted. Also, keep talking! Keep up a pleasant patter, try to look calm and innocent at all times and, above all, keep a straight face when you are slipping cards out of your sleeves, performing a phony shuffle, or palming a coin!

137
FEAT OF STRENGTH

This is another trick that works itself; all you have to do is follow instructions.

Tell the spectators that due to your intimate knowledge of the human anatomy, you have discovered certain positions from which it is impossible for someone else to remove you. 'For instance,' you say, 'what would you think if I told you that you could not move my arm, no matter how hard you tried?' They're bound to think you're a little bit nuts, especially if they are bigger than you, but that won't help them!

The Secret
Put the palm of either hand on the top of your head and ask a volunteer to try to lift your hand off your head by *pushing* up on your arm from below. Chances are he will find it a downright impossible!

200
LB

138
INTO THIN AIR!

For this trick, all you need is a coin, or some other small object. You may need to practice this a bit before you get it just right, but once you know how to do it, you will never forget.

The audience sees you holding a coin in your left hand. You then seem to pick up the coin with your right hand. But when you open your right hand, the coin just isn't there – it apparently has disappeared into thin air! Just when the audience has given up hope of ever seeing it again, you reach up and pull the coin out from behind someone's ear!

The Secret
Sounds spectacular, doesn't it? If you do it quickly and well, it *is* spectacular.

Hold the coin between the tips of your left index finger and thumb.

Then, quickly and with a smooth motion, pass your right thumb under the coin as if you are going to pick it up. But in actual fact, what you really do is drop the coin into the palm of your left hand! Without stopping, your right hand closes as if it has just grabbed the coin. All the tricky action is hidden by the fingers of your left hand. Look at the drawings and this will be clear – just remember the picture is seen from *your* point of view.

Remember not to look at your hands during all this, but to look into the eyes of the audience. Otherwise, they will suspect that something tricky is going on.

Draw all attention at this point to your right hand, which is actually empty. Hold it up and let your left hand drop to your side. Blow on your right hand, and then quickly open it up. The coin's gone! While your audience is goggling, quickly reach up with your left hand, and touch someone behind his ear.

When you open your left hand revealing the coin, it will seem as if it came from his ear!

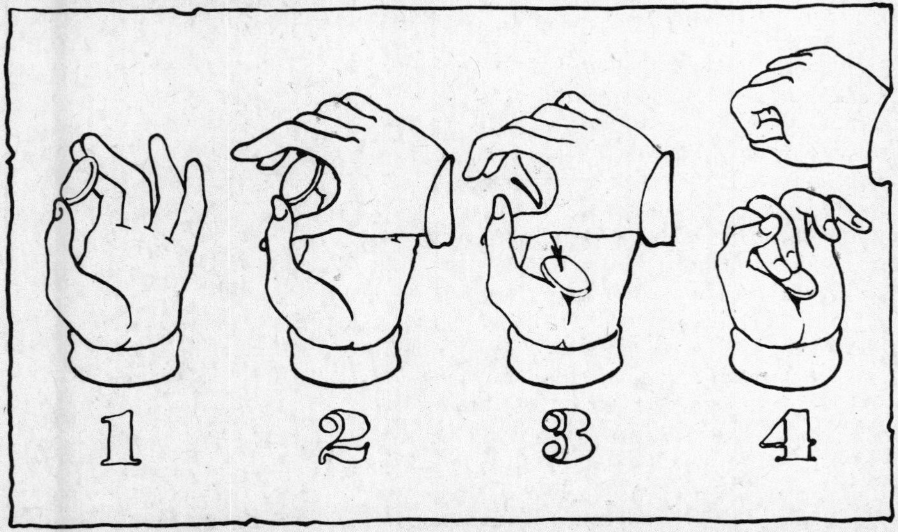
1
2
3
4

139

DOUBLE HANDCUFF ESCAPE

For this trick you need two pieces of string about two feet long, one volunteer, and no practice whatsoever – as long as you follow instructions carefully!

Tie each end of the string loosely around the wrists of a volunteer, so that he is wearing a pair of string handcuffs. Tie one end of the other string to your right wrist. Pass the free end *under* the string crossing between the volunteer's wrists, and tie it to your left wrist. To the audience, it looks as if two people are each wearing a pair of string handcuffs, linked permanently together.

Suddenly, with a flash of your hands, you free the pairs of handcuffs from each other! It looks as if the strings have passed right through each other!

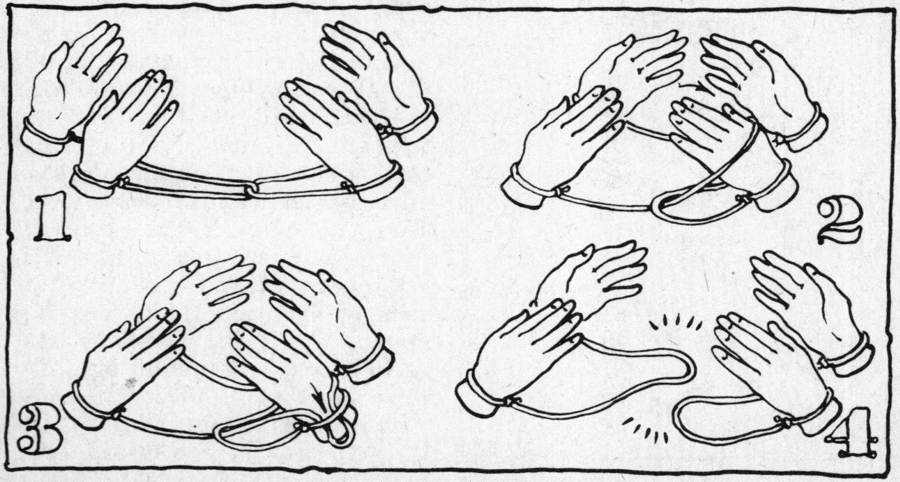
1
2
3
4

The Secret

This trick uses a principle that is used in many other tricks, like the 'Loop Escapes' in this chapter.

Take the center of the string tied to your wrists and pass it over the volunteer's left hand. Push a bit of it under the loop around his wrist, and pull the rest of it through. When you lift your string over his hand again, the handcuffs are no longer linked together!

SHUFFLE SORCERY

Ah, yes! The never-ending wonders of our old pal, the humble deck of 52! If you brought some cards along, you are ready to go. If not, don't despair. In the beginning of the eleventh chapter, Dealing With A Card, there is a description of how to make your own. The next tricks work better with a real deck of cards, but anything's worth a try.

What you are about to learn is the basis for many card tricks. It is called the Trick Shuffle, and if you can perform it well, you are well on your way to becoming a bona fide Card Sorcerer.

The Trick Shuffle can be done as a trick by itself as well. You tell a spectator to pick a card, any card. You cut the deck, and he puts his card back on top of the bottom pile. You put the two piles together again, shuffle the cards well, and then proceed to pull his card from the top of the deck!

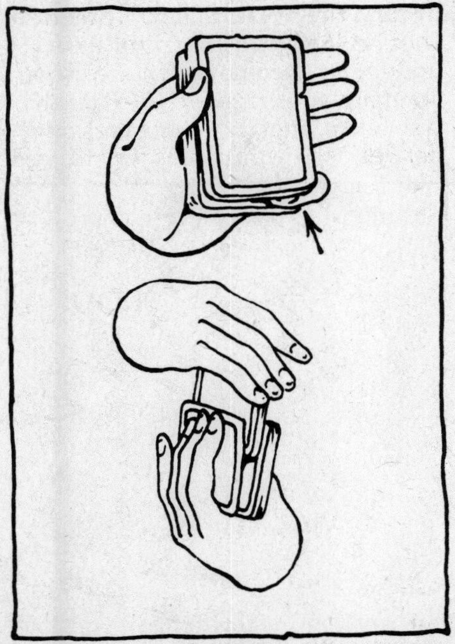

The Secret

'Cutting' the deck means splitting it into two piles. The spectator put his card *face down* on top of the pile in your left hand, and you put the pile in your right hand down on top of that. But just before the top pile hits the bottom pile, curl the tip of your left little finger over the top of the bottom pile. If you do this quickly enough, and hold the deck tightly, the spectator will not suspect a thing; he will think that his card is lost somewhere in the middle of the deck, while in actual fact your little finger marks exactly where it is!

Now, as you start shuffling, lift the whole top pile off from above your little finger, and shuffle it to the bottom of the pile. Shuffle as

shown in the drawing, with the bottom card showing. The chosen card should now be on the top of the deck. This is where the actual Trick Shuffle comes into play. Pull on the top part of the deck as if you were going to perform a normal shuffle, but keep your fingers pressed lightly against the top card. As you pull out the top half of the deck, the top card will slip off, held in place by the pressure of your fingers, and will stay in place. This 'slipping' action is why this is also known as 'slipping a card.' You can continue to perform what looks like a perfectly normal shuffle, while in reality, the top card is always the same one! After you have 'shuffled' for a few minutes, quickly flip over the top card, and, lo and behold! It's the very one! 'Recognize this card?' you innocently ask, and the audience is astounded. Put it back down again, shuffle for a few more minutes, and there it is again! The Trick Shuffle is so easy to do that the spectators will never suspect a thing!

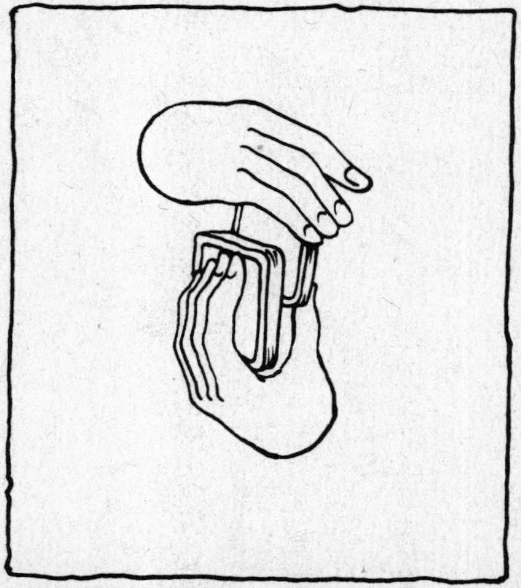

141 TRIPLE FLIP

This trick is so incredibly easy to perform that it is hard to believe that people are always amazed by it!

What happens is this: you shuffle the deck, lay it on the table or seat, and ask someone to cut it into three piles without further shuffling. Suddenly, you call out the names of the three top cards, just *before* you pick each of them up. And when you lay them down on the table, sure enough, they are the ones you called out!

The Secret

You won't need the Trick Shuffle (the last trick) to do this one, but you do need to get a look at the top card on the deck. This is fairly easy to do if you are the one to shuffle. Pretend that you are straightening the edges of the deck, and let the top

card fall back slightly so you can get a look at it. Do this quickly and without pausing. Put the deck on the table and ask someone to cut it into three piles without shuffling. Keep track of which pile has the top card on it. Call out the name of the card that you secretly know about, but lift up a card from a *different pile*. Don't show this to the audience just yet. Now call out the name of the card you just picked up, and lift up the other unknown top card from the second pile. Call out the name of this card, and lift up the final top card, the one that you know about. Get the idea?

The last card you picked up was actually the first one you called out, but don't let the audience know this! If you lay the cards down one at a time in the order you called them, no one will suspect a thing. If you

KING OF SPADES
K♠
ACE OF DIAMONDS
A♦

are practiced at it, you can show this trick a second or third time, but it is usually not a good idea, because after the first time, everyone will be watching your every move very closely.

TWO OF CLUBS
2♣
K♠
!

142
POCKET PICK

No, this is not a lesson on the age-old art of picking pockets. It's a spectacular magic trick that uses a pocket, though, as well as a deck of cards. Both these things are the ordinary variety, of course, just as long as one fits inside the other. (It's best if the cards fit inside the pocket, in fact, and not the other way around!)

You ask a member of the audience to pick a card, any card; to look at it; and to memorize it without letting you catch sight of it. Pretty standard so far. He puts his card back in the deck, and you 'shuffle' it. Now you need to ask for another volunteer, who comes complete with an easy-to-reach pocket. A shirt or coat pocket works best. You put the deck of cards safely away in the pocket and have the first volunteer blindfold you (or just close your eyes tightly). Have one of the volunteers direct your hand to the pocket in question, and then, with one lightening-fast swoop, you pull out a card! When the dust has cleared, the audience sees that it is no ordinary card, but none other than the card chosen by the first volunteer!

The Secret
This is really nothing other than a fancy way to show off the Trick Shuffle that you learned one or two tricks ago. Using the Trick Shuffle, you make sure that the chosen card is on top of the deck. When you put the deck into the pocket, make sure that you know which way it is facing. (The deck, not the pocket.) When you reach in, it will be an easy matter, blindfold and all, to find the top of the deck and to pull out the chosen card. To the audience, it seems as if you have just reached in and pulled out the first card that came to hand, especially if you tell them that this is what you are going to do. A first class trick, but really very simple.

143
MEET THE COUNT

The standard card trick opening – a member of the audience picks a card, looks at it, and puts it back in the deck. You shuffle the cards calmly, not saying a word. Then you start counting cards one at a time off the top of the deck, asking the volunteer to tell you when to stop counting. When he tells you to stop, you put the pile of cards back on top of the deck, hand it to him, and ask him to count off the same number of cards in the same way. He does so. 'What was your card?' you ask innocently. He tells you, and when you turn over the last card that he counted out, there it is! Amid the thunderous applause, you hear murmurs of 'How did the Great Wund-O do it?'

The Secret
Like the last trick, this is really only a fancy way of doing the simple Trick Shuffle described earlier in Shuffle Sorcery. It is known in the business as a card 'force.' Using this shuffle, you bring the chosen card to the top of the deck. Then you start dealing the cards one at a time face down, into one pile on the table, at the same time counting them out loud. Ask the spectator to tell you when to stop, as long as it's somewhere before 52! Let's say he tells you to stop at the number 15 (although it doesn't matter when he tells you to stop). The top card (which is the chosen card, don't forget!) is on the bottom of this pile, so when you put it on top of the deck again, the chosen card is now the fifteenth card. So when the spectator takes the deck and counts out the same number in the same way, the chosen card comes out to the top again, and when you turn it over the audience gets the shock of its life!

144
HANKY PANKY

This is a simple trick, but very spectacular if done right. You might need a bit of practice until you get familiar with the movements. You need a small hanky or silk scarf, and you must be wearing some kind of jacket or sweater that is open at the front.

You roll up the handkerchief into a tiny ball, hold it in your right hand, and after a few passes through the air, throw it as hard as you can. But then when it comes time to find the hanky again, it is nowhere to be found. No one saw it land, in fact, no one even saw it leave your hand! It has truly disappeared!

The Secret
The secret to this trick is merely a matter of directing the audience's attention away from what's really happening. It's also the old 'hand is quicker than the eye' theory, in action. Hold the balled-up hanky in your right hand, and focus your eyes on it as if you are watching for something special. At the same time, have your left hand holding the edge of your jacket as if it were the most natural thing in the world for a left hand to be doing.

Swing your right hand down in front of you and then up again, as if getting ready to throw the hanky over the horizon. Keep your eyes fixed on the direction the hanky will travel – off to the right. Make a couple of practice swings like this, and then as you bring your hand down again, secretly toss the hanky under the edge of your jacket, which your left hand is so nicely holding slightly open for you. Don't stop the swing of your right hand, but bring it up again as if it still held the hanky, and then open your hand at the top of your swing, as if you were tossing the hanky away. Of course, the hanky has long since disappeared under the edge of your jacket, where it is being held against your body by your left arm. It will take a moment or two for the audience to realize that the hanky has, in fact, disappeared! If you keep your eyes looking off at the distance at your right, they will think that all the action is going on over there, and will not notice when your hand lightly tosses the hanky under your jacket.

145
STRING FROM AIR

The last trick was a disappearing trick. This one is an appearing trick. Show the audience your hands, roll up your sleeves to show that there's nothing up there, make a fist with your right hand, and then proceed to pull from it an almost endless piece of string!!

The Secret

Before you start, check to make sure that you have some sleeves to roll up, because they are very important to the trick. Roll your piece of string around your finger so it forms a tight little ball. Take it off your finger and tuck it under a fold of your left sleeve at the elbow. If you hold your arms slightly bent, the string will stay in place, hidden from view.

STRING
HIDDEN
IN FOLDS
GRAB
STRING
&
SLEEVE

Now you are ready to face your audience. Show them your hands, roll up your right sleeve with your left hand, then, as you roll up your left sleeve, take the ball of string into your right hand. Hold your right hand (still empty as far as the audience knows, but actually holding the string) in a fist. Make a couple of showy passes over it with your left hand, then slowly reach into it and begin to edge out the end of the string. Your string doesn't really have to be endless, or even very long, but if you pull it out slo-o-owly, it sure will seem endless!

146
THE STRANGLER

Here is a trick to perform with the string you produced out of thin air in the last trick. The string should be about five feet long or so. Tie the ends together so you have one big loop. The audience sees you put the loop over your head, wrapping it around once so that your neck is in a noose. Then with the free end of the loop, you do some fancy fingerwork, throw yet another loop around your neck, and then, just when it seems you're thoroughly tied up, you pull one string, and the whole twisted noose seems to pass through your neck as if it were made of butter, and you are free!

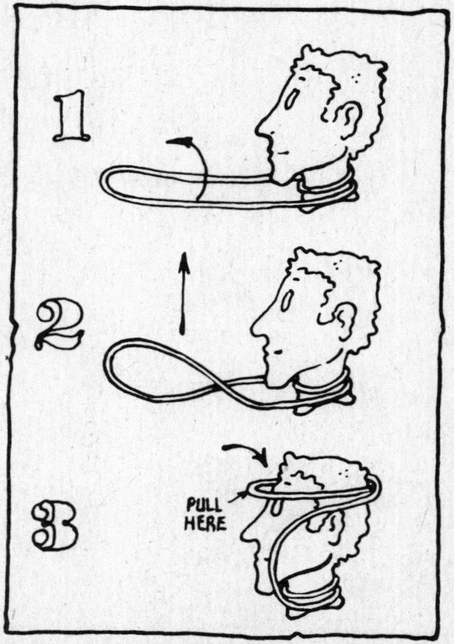
1
2
3
PULL HERE

The Secret

This trick needs a bit of practice to get it right. Put the loop over your head. Take the *right* hand string and pass it once more around your head so that your neck is in a noose like the one in the first picture. Then with the rest of the string that is in front of you, form another noose by twisting the whole loop over a half-turn. This is hard to describe, but look at the next picture and you will see what the string is supposed to look like when you are finished. Make sure that the string on your left side is on top of the string on your right side. Pick up this whole noose and put it over your head so that the part where the two strings cross over is at the *back* of your neck. When you pull on the front part of the loop, the whole string slides off your neck as if it had never been twisted around it in a strangler's noose. Warning! Don't pull too hard in case you goofed, or it really *will* be a strangler's noose!

147
THE LOOP ESCAPES!

For this amazing trick all you need is a rubber band, a piece of string about two or three feet long, and a gullible audience. A member of the audience ties each end of the string around one of your wrists, so that you are wearing a pair of string handcuffs like the ones shown in the picture. You then take the rubber band, turn your back for a second, and when you turn to face the audience again, the rubber band is hanging from the middle of the string. Turn around again, and the loop escapes from the string again! The knots on your wrists have not been touched, and anyway, you didn't have time. How did you do it?

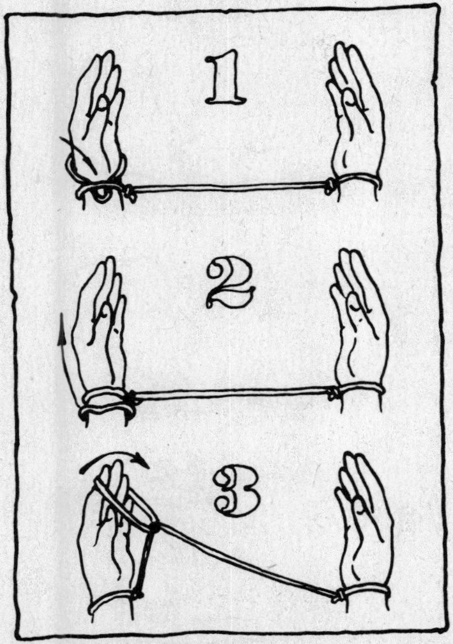
1
2
3

The Secret
Well, it's really very simple. It involves the same principle used in the Double Handcuff Escape described earlier. When your back is turned, slip the rubber band over your left hand (if you don't have a rubber band, you can use a loop made of string or ribbon, with one big impossible-to-untie knot). Slip a bit of the rubber band under the string around your wrist, and then pull the rest of it through so that the band is now below the string. Pass the rubber band back over your hand, and it will be trapped in the middle of the string, much to your audience's surprise. Turn around again and take the loop off by doing the whole thing backward.

Before you take the string handcuffs off your wrists, have a look at the next trick . . .

148
MAKING THINGS WORSE

This is an old trick and, if done well, a good trick. A member of the audience ties your hands in a pair of string handcuffs like the ones used in the last trick. (If you still have them on from the last trick, use those!) Tell the audience you are going to escape from these 'chains.' You turn your back on them for no more than a few seconds, certainly not enough time to untie your handcuffs, and when you turn back to face them again, there is a series of knots in the middle of the string! You have not escaped. You have only made things worse!

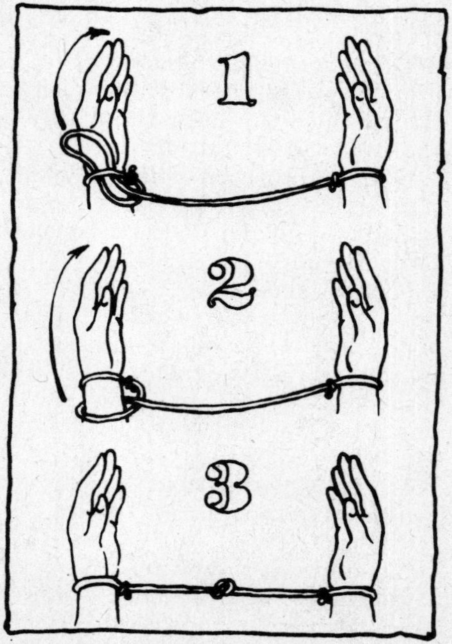
1
2
3

The Secret
It might take everyone a while to realize that it's impossible for those knots to be there, right in the middle of the string like that. Or at least it *seems* impossible. It's actually the same principle that's used in the last trick that makes this trick go. When you turn your back, take the center of the string and push it under the loop around your wrist from below, as shown in the first drawing. Pass the new loop over your left hand, and then pull it from under the loop around your wrist, so that it now looks like the second drawing. If you pull this loop off your left hand it will form an overhand knot in the center of the string. Once you have the technique mastered, you can do as many of these as you want in a few seconds, and the entire audience will be at a loss as to how you did it. Pretend that you don't know either, and ask for some help to get free!

149
NOW YOU SEE IT...

And now you don't! This trick is a little complicated to learn, but it's actually quite simple once you get the hang of it, and very spectacular. You can do it with string or rope, but it is most impressive if you use a long silk scarf. It is similar to the last trick, and it's not a good idea to perform them both at the same sitting.

Ask a member of the audience to try to tie a knot in the scarf without letting go of the ends. After they have tried and failed, take hold of the ends of the silk scarf, and, without letting go once, you tie a big knot in the center – much to the scarf owner's dismay! Blow on the knot, and it disappears!

The Secret
Before you can do this trick well, you'll need to practice.

1 Hold the scarf in both hands as shown in the first drawing.
2 Bring your right hand over and around your left hand so that a loop is formed on your left wrist, as shown in the second drawing.
3 Still holding both ends, put your right hand into the loop from above, under the part marked **x**, and over the part marked **z**.
4 When you move your hands apart, you will have a twisted mass of silk scarf wrapped around them which looks a little like the fourth picture.
5 Let the loop slip off the left hand (don't let go of the end!) and pull the left end slowly until the loop bunches up into a knot.
6 Then slip the loop off the right hand, and pull slowly until the right-hand loop joins the left-hand loop in the center as a big, nasty-looking knot.
7 Don't pull too hard, because this isn't a real knot, it's an imposter! If you blow on it, and pull sharply on both ends of the scarf, it will disappear! (The knot, that is ...)

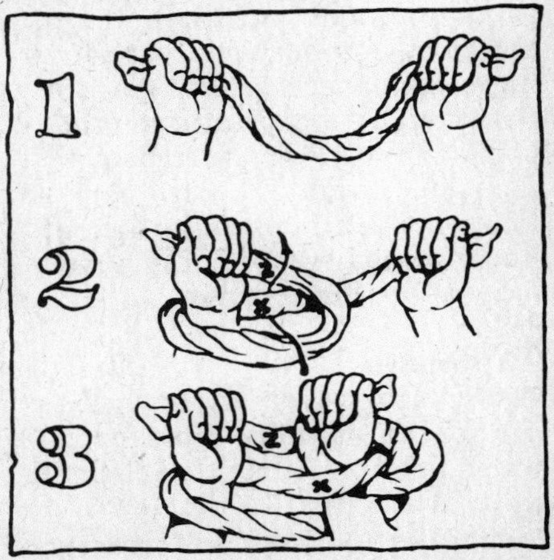
1
2
z
x
3
z
x

150
A USEFUL KNOT

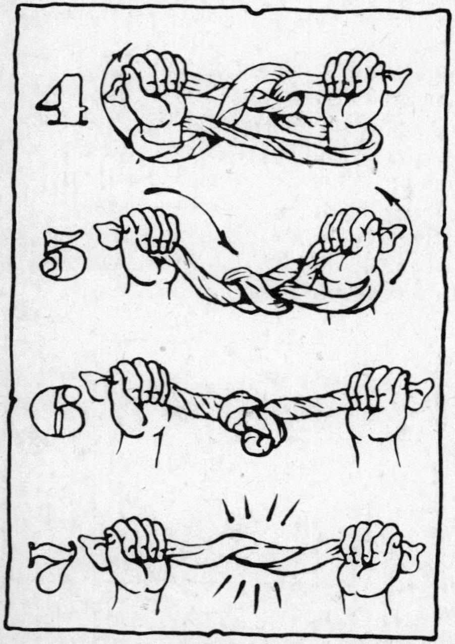
4
5
6
7

This is the kind of knot that is nice to have around. Not only is it very easy to tie, but it knows how to untie itself!

The Secret

You can use string, rope, or a handkerchief for this trick, but a silk scarf works best.

1 Hold one end of the scarf, or whatever, in each hand.

2 Twist the ends around each other once, then hold them in the same hands again. See the first drawing.

3 Next, tie one knot above this twist, and pull on the ends and sides of the scarf at once, tightening the knot.

4 This knot will hold together well enough, but if you take hold of one end of the scarf and shake it hard once or twice, the knot will seem to dissolve!

151
TRIPLE DICE GUESS

If you pull this trick off, your friends will be totally dumbfounded. It's one of those things that looks absolutely impossible, but if you know the basic principle, it is as easy as throwing the dice. The trick itself is very old – it is first found in a book written in the year 1612! – but chances are that nobody in the audience has heard of it, or seen it.

You need three dice. For complete instructions on making dice, see number 70 in the ninth chapter, Bored Games. It is very important that the opposite faces add up to seven!

1 You turn your back, and someone from the audience rolls the three dice, and adds up the numbers on their faces. Tell him not to move or touch the dice unless you say to.

2 Then, following your instructions, he picks any two dice, and adds their *bottom* faces to the total.

3 He then throws the two dice and adds the top two faces to the total.

4 Then he takes any *one* of the two dice and adds its bottom face to the total.

5 He then throws it, and adds its top face.

When he is finished this complicated and devious dice trickery, you turn around, look at the dice on the table for a second, and tell him the total that he so carefully worked out!

The Secret

Your audience may be in a state of shock after you show them the trick, but can you blame them? After all, you must admit that it's a pretty amazing trick. And it's so simple too. The total is always equal to the sum of the top faces on the dice plus 21. So you merely turn around, add up the top faces on the dice, add 21, and announce the total!

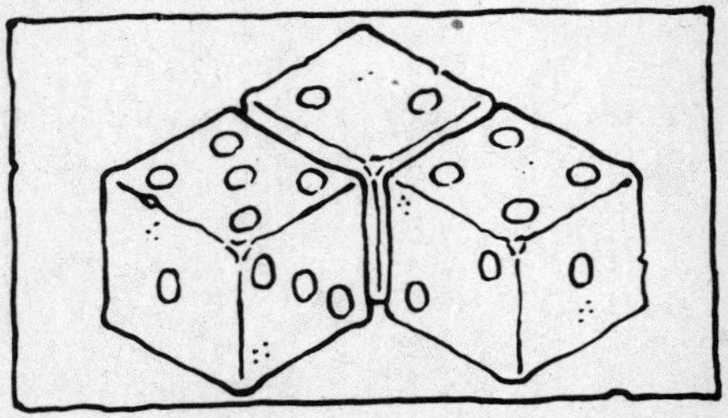

152
MATHEMENTICS

You don't need any practice for this trick, but it is so stupendous that your friends will be stupefied.

You write a number down on a piece of paper, and hand it to someone from the audience, who tucks it safely away in a pocket. Ask this person to write down any number between 50 and 100 on another sheet of paper. Ask him to subtract a number from his number, do a couple of other simple mathematical calculations, and then look at the piece of paper you gave him at the beginning of the trick. The number on it is the same as his final result!

The Secret

This trick involves simple mathematical principles.

1 You write down any number between 1 and 50 on a scrap of paper, fold the paper, and give it to your friend to put in his pocket. Let's say you pick 18.

2 Ask your friend to choose a number between 50 and 100, and to write it down on another piece of paper without letting you see it. Let's say he picks 75.

3 In your head, subtract the number *you* wrote down from 99, and ask your friend to add the result to his number.

99 - 18 = 81   75 + 81 = 156

4 Now ask your friend to cross off the first digit of his new number (in this case, the 1 of 156), and then to add that digit to the result, still keeping his calculations hidden from you.

$$\begin{array}{r} \not{1}56 \\ +\ 1 \\ \hline 57 \end{array}$$

5 Tell your friend to subtract this new number from his original number and then to open the piece of paper you gave him in the beginning of the trick. The numbers are the same!

75 - 57 = 18

If you want to learn more number tricks, look up Abraca-algebra in the eighth chapter.

..WHICH MAY BE EXPRESSED AS
$C\int \frac{(\pi dz)(x+9)}{\sqrt{z(z-1)(z-f)}}$

153
THE HYPNOTIZED CIGARETTE

'Your slightest wish, Master, is my command.'

'Actually,' you tell your audience, 'there is no hypnotism involved in this trick, it's merely an effect of static electricity. The funny thing is, I seem to be the only one who can do it.'

This is a good trick to play in a restaurant, or anywhere with a hard surface. The audience sees you lay a borrowed cigarette down on the table, and then start rubbing your finger around it in a circle.

'Building up a static electrical charge around the cigarette . . .' you say. Your finger circles the cigarette a few more times, and then you slide your finger away from the cigarette. Suddenly, to your audience's surprise, the cigarette rolls away, following your finger along the table top!

1

The Secret

It is dangerous to do this trick more than once. You may need to practice a bit, but basically it's very simple.

You lay the cigarette on the table, and begin rubbing your finger in a circle around it. Rub harder and harder, focusing all your attention on the cigarette. Finally, after everyone else is looking intently at the cigarette, waiting for something to happen, rub your finger away from you along the table. At the same time, blow slightly on the cigarette, and it will roll along the table top, seeming to follow your finger. The others will be looking so hard at the table that they will not see you blowing. Of course, if they don't know the secret, the trick won't work when your friends try it.

2
3
4